My Words *will* *not* Pass Away

**Reflections on the weekday readings for
the liturgical year 2021~2022**

D1343075

FR MARTIN HOGAN

Designed by Messenger Publications Design Department
Typeset in Times New Roman & DIN Condensed
Cover image: solarseven / Shutterstock
Printed by Hussar Books

Messenger Publications,
37 Leeson Place, Dublin D02 E5V0
www.messenger.ie

INTRODUCTION

This book is the sixth publication of reflections on the weekday readings for the liturgical year that begins on the First Sunday of Advent 2021. I have been encouraged to publish a further collection of reflections because various people have told me that they have found previous publications helpful. These short reflections on the weekday gospel readings for the coming liturgical year may prove helpful to priests who like to give a brief homily at the weekday Mass and to all people of faith who base their daily prayer on the gospel reading for the following day. Many people have told me that they find the reflections helpful for their daily prayer. I am also told that in parishes where Mass is not celebrated every day, the Minister of the Word who leads a Service of the Word in place of Mass often reads aloud the reflection that corresponds to the gospel reading of the day.

For each of the six volumes I have tried to find a Scripture quotation that relates to the value of prayerfully reflecting on God's Word. The quotation for this volume is taken from a verse towards the end of Luke's account of Jesus' announcement of the dark and traumatic times that lie ahead in advance of the glorious coming of the Son of Man, 'Heaven and earth will pass away, but my words will not pass away' (Luke 21:33). Jesus had announced that the Temple in Jerusalem, considered one of the Seven Wonders of the World at the time, would pass away, 'not one stone will be left upon another' (21:6). The city of Jerusalem itself, the city where it was believed God had chosen to dwell, would pass away, 'Jerusalem will be trampled on by the Gentiles' (21:24). Even nature as it is commonly experienced will pass away, 'the powers of the heavens will be shaken' (21:26).

The recent pandemic has shown us how much that we have taken for granted can so easily pass away. It was such a cataclysmic event that we have begun to think of time in relation to it, speaking of the pre-Covid and the post-Covid era. Many people's employment has passed away because of the pandemic. Sadly, many more have experienced the passing away of loved ones from the pandemic. For months on end the opportunity for people of faith to gather to celebrate the Eucharist passed away. There has been a litany of loss. At such a time of major and traumatic loss and change we long for some stability, for something of value that will remain and endure. Our faith assures us that when all else passes away the Lord endures. He is 'the Alpha and the Omega, the first and the last, the beginning and the end' (Revelation 21:13).

The Lord's enduring presence when all else changes finds expression in his enduring word. Even though all else passes away, his words will never pass away. The Lord continues to speak to us in good times and in bad, on the glorious mountain top and in the dark valley. As we walk along struggling to come to terms with devastating loss, like the two disciples on the road to Emmaus, the risen Lord walks with us and opens the Scriptures for us. Because the Lord is a living Lord, his word is 'living and active' (Hebrews 4:12). The Lord is never silent. He is always seeking to communicate with us. In every era we hear the invitation, 'Let anyone who has ears listen to what the Spirit is saying to the churches' (Revelation 2:17). Each day we can pray with the young Samuel, 'Speak, Lord, your servant is listening'. The Lord's word will always be a word that brings life where there is death, hope where there is despondency and light where there is darkness. It is my hope that these reflections on the word of God in the daily readings for this coming liturgical year will help people to become more attuned to the living word of the Lord that never passes away.

29 November, Monday, First Week of Advent

Matthew 8:5–11

I have always thought it striking that the words of a Roman centurion, a pagan, have come to make their way into our text of the Mass: 'Lord, I am not worthy to have you under my roof ...'. According to our gospel reading, Jesus was astonished at those words of the centurion. Clearly, the Church has shared Jesus' astonishment because the centurion's words became part of the text of the Eucharist. Jesus said of the centurion, 'Nowhere in Israel have I found faith like this.' Those words of Jesus remind us that faith can often be found in unexpected places. People we might not suspect of having much faith may have a very deep faith, even if it is not expressed in the conventional manner. The centurion did not worship or serve God in the conventional way Jesus the Jew and other Jews did. Yet, Jesus acknowledges his exceptional faith, stronger than any faith he had encountered among his fellow Jews. Many of Jesus' Jewish contemporaries would not have recognised the centurion as a man of faith, because he didn't express faith in the usual way. We can easily get it wrong when it comes to assessing the quality of someone else's faith. A person's relationship with the Lord is very personal to them, and we don't always have easy access to it. The gospel reading invites us to be as ready as Jesus was to be astonished at the faith of others, even when it does not find expression in the traditional ways. Sometimes those we think may have little faith can have a very deep faith.

30 November, Tuesday, Feast of Saint Andrew

Matthew 4:18–22

According to Paul in today's first reading, 'faith comes from what is preached'. We could extend that to say that faith comes through the preaching and teaching of those who believe. Who were the preachers and teachers in our lives through whom we came to believe? We can include among those preachers and teachers all those who spoke to us as children about the life of faith, about God, Jesus, Mary and the saints, about the Church and the sacraments. The primary preachers and teachers were our parents; they spoke to us about the faith from our earliest years. We may have encountered preachers in church and teachers in school who helped to open up the riches of the faith to us. Books or articles written by people of faith may have touched us deeply. The preachers and teachers in our lives took many forms. We owe our faith to them. We don't come to believe on our own. We need people of faith to lead us to faith. Today we celebrate one of the earliest preachers and teachers of the faith, Saint Andrew. He can easily end up in the shadow of his more famous brother, Saint Peter. Yet, according to John's Gospel, it was Andrew who brought Peter to Jesus. In other words, Andrew was the first preacher of the faith in the life of Peter. Andrew reminds us that we all have a role in bringing others to faith. None of us goes to the Lord on our own. We need companions in faith who help to bring us to the Lord, as Andrew brought Simon to the Lord. We are all called to be preachers and teachers in that sense, people of faith who witness to our faith in ways that help others to meet the Lord for themselves.

1 December, Wednesday, First Week of Advent
Matthew 15:29–37

The disciples' question in today's gospel reading sounds somewhat despairing: 'Where could we get enough bread in this deserted place to feed such a crowd?' Jesus wanted to feed the hungry crowd and didn't want to send them away. The disciples could see no way of doing this. Their question is a very human one. It is the kind of question we all ask when we find ourselves faced with a situation that seems beyond us. We often encounter situations in life that make us very aware of our limitations. We can easily shrink before such situations and we can be tempted to lose heart and throw in the towel. Yet, where we see problems, the Lord often sees possibilities, provided we do whatever we can do, little as it may seem to us. In today's gospel reading, Jesus took the few resources the disciples had, seven loaves and a few small fish, and then, with their help, he fed the whole crowd with those resources. It wasn't a case of everyone getting barely enough. No, 'they all ate as much as they wanted'. The evangelist, Matthew, is suggesting that we must never underestimate what the Lord can do through our human resources, small as they may seem in our eyes, provided we give generously of them. As Saint Paul knew from his experience, the Lord can work powerfully through our weakness. Indeed, sometimes it is our very weakness, our vulnerability, our inadequacy, that can give the Lord the greatest scope to work through us, provided we trust in him to do so.

2 December, Thursday, First Week of Advent
Matthew 7:21, 24–27
In the gospel reading, Jesus makes a distinction between two kinds of listening, the listening that leads to action, to doing, and the listening that has no impact on behaviour. He calls on us not only to listen to his words, but to act on them. Jesus wants his word not just to impact on our ears but to impact on our lives. Every minute of every day we are hearing something, if we are fortunate to have reasonably good hearing. However, we are not always listening to what we hear. Much of what we hear doesn't require attentive listening. There are other times when we really do listen to what

we are hearing. When someone we love, someone who matters greatly to us, has something important to say to us, we listen very carefully. What they say may enter deeply into us and impact on what we do. Attentive listening to what we consider significant can really shape our whole life. This is the kind of listening that Jesus calls for. He loves us so much that he laid down his life for us; he calls us to love him as he loves us. When he speaks to us, he has something very significant to say, because his words reveal God and God's purpose for our lives. Here is a speaking that calls for the most attentive listening possible. Such deep listening will impact on us deeply and will shape our way of life. When that happens, Jesus says, we are like the builder who built on rock. Our lives will be solidly grounded and deeply rooted. In the words of today's first reading, 'the Lord will be our everlasting Rock'. In the words of Saint Paul, we will be 'rooted and grounded in love', in the Lord who is love.

3 December, Friday, First Week of Advent
Matthew 9:27–31

The opening of today's gospel reading says that two blind men followed Jesus, shouting, 'Take pity on us, Son of David'; they followed him until he reached the house to which he was going. It is tempting to ask, if they were both blind, how did they manage to follow Jesus? They couldn't see Jesus, yet they were able to follow him for some time. They are a little bit like ourselves. We cannot see Jesus with our physical eyes, yet we follow him, or at least try to follow him. Even though the blind men couldn't see Jesus physically, they believed in his power to heal them. In a sense, they saw him with the eyes of faith and it was their faith that allowed them to follow Jesus even in their blindness. Like those men, we too see the Lord with the eyes of faith. At the Eucharist, we recognise him in the breaking of bread. Hopefully, we see him, we are aware of his presence, in the circumstances of our day-to-day lives. With the eyes of faith, we see him in the people who cross our path in life. Yet we are aware that, while following the Lord, while seeing him with the eyes of faith, there is also some blindness in us. In that sense too, we are like the two blind men. When life is difficult, we can be so absorbed by the struggle that we become blind to the Lord walking ahead of us or alongside us. We behave as if we were on our own, which is why we often need to make our own the prayer of the two blind men, 'Take pity on us, Son of David', 'Heal our blindness'. In response to that prayer, if the Lord were to ask us, 'Do you believe that I can do this?' we could do no better than make our own the response of the blind men, 'Lord, we do'. The Lord is always at work in our lives, healing whatever blindness may be within us, assuring us in the words of the first reading, 'after shadow and darkness, the eyes of the blind will see'.

4 December, Saturday, First Week of Advent
Matthew 9:35–10:1, 5a, 6–8
The opening verse of the gospel reading gives us a sense of all the work Jesus did during his public ministry. He made a tour of all the towns and villages, teaching in the synagogues, proclaiming the good news of the kingdom and curing all kinds of diseases and sickness. He clearly did not spare himself in doing the work God had given him to do. Yet he knew that even he could not do God's work alone. When he saw crowds that were harassed and dejected, even after all the work he did, he didn't respond by saying he had to work harder. He responded by asking his disciples to ask God to send labourers into God's harvest. The harvest was so rich, the work to be done was so great, that Jesus alone could not do it.

Many labourers were needed, through whom Jesus would work. That is why he went on to send out his twelve closest disciples to do the same work he had been doing, proclaiming the good news of the kingdom and curing all kinds of diseases and sickness. Yet Jesus knew that even these twelve could not do all God's work that needed doing. Many more labourers would be needed. The Lord needs each one of us to be a labourer in God's harvest. Each of us has a combination of gifts and experiences which the Lord needs to continue God's work in the world today. Each of us has a unique role to play in helping the risen Lord to bring more of the kingdom of God to earth. There is a corner of God's harvest that needs our labour. The Lord wants to work through each of us to bring his healing and life-giving presence to bear more fully on the world. None of us, no matter where we are on our life's journey, is surplus to his requirements.

6 December, Monday, Second Week of Advent
Luke 5:17–26
Very often in the gospels we find people of faith making their way to Jesus. Many of those people are in need of healing of some sort, whether it is physical healing, like the two blind men, or spiritual healing, like Zacchaeus. In today's gospel reading, a person of faith cannot make his way to Jesus because of his physical condition of paralysis. He needed other people of faith to bring him to Jesus. He was fortunate enough to have such people of faith around him. These men would stop at nothing to bring the paralytic to Jesus, even going as far as removing the tiles of the roof of the house where Jesus was at the time. When Jesus saw the paralysed man on a stretcher coming down towards him from a hole in the roof, he didn't get annoyed, rather, according to the gospel reading, he saw their faith; he recognised the faith of this little community around

the paralytic. This man was fortunate to belong to a community of faith. This community created an opening, not just in the roof, but in the life of this paralytic to receive from Jesus a wonderful healing that was both spiritual and physical. Just as the paralytic needed a little community of faith to bring him to Jesus, we need the community of faith to come to Jesus. We don't come to the Lord on our own. As people of faith, we bring each other to the Lord. That is one of the reasons we gather as a community of faith, whether physically in the church or virtually through the parish webcam. As people of faith, we feel the need to be together in some way. We need each other's faith to find the Lord. I need other people of faith for me to meet the Lord and others need my faith to come to the Lord.

7 December, Tuesday, Second Week of Advent
Matthew 18:12–14
In the parable of the lost sheep Jesus is giving us an image of God. A shepherd will go looking for one of his flock of a hundred sheep who rambles off and gets lost. Similarly, God is always seeking out those who have grown distant from him and from his community of believers. It was this searching God that Jesus came to reveal and make present. He spoke of himself as the Son of Man who came to seek out and save the lost. Jesus was the fullest revelation possible of the God that Isaiah sings about at the end of today's first reading, the God who is like a shepherd feeding his flock, gathering lambs in his arms and holding them against his breast. It is a very tender image of God, far removed from the warrior God of other passages of the Jewish Scriptures. It is this tender side of God that Jesus reveals above all. Jesus sought out those who had been written off by the religious establishment. Rather than judging them to be sinners, breakers of God's Law,

he shared table with them and showed them very graphically that God wanted to be in communion with them. Because Jesus was revealing a seeking God, he was looking for people who allowed themselves to be found by God. This is the attitude that Jesus continues to look for from us today. He is looking for a receptive, open heart that allows us to be found by the God who is always seeking us through his Son.

8 December, Wednesday, Solemnity of the Immaculate Conception
Luke 1:26–38

The annunciation of the angel Gabriel to Mary is one of those gospel scenes that has inspired stained-glass artists, painters and sculptors down the centuries. They sensed the significance of this event in God's dealings with humanity. This was the moment when God needed Mary's consent to become the mother of his Son. God had chosen Mary for this hugely significant role. A great deal would depend on whether or not Mary consented to the choice that God was presenting to her. Out of all the women in history, God chose this teenaged woman from a small village in Galilee during the reign of the Roman Emperor Augustus. God's choice of this young woman was a wonderful privilege for her but would also make great demands on her. At that moment, the whole human race desperately needed her to say 'yes' to God's choice and God's call. The gospel reading speaks of Mary being 'deeply disturbed' by this visitation from God and full of questions, and, yet, in the end, she lived up to humanity's expectations. She surrendered wholeheartedly to God's choice of her, God's call on her. 'I am the handmaid of the Lord, let what you have said be done to me.' She said 'yes' to God, on behalf of us all, for all our sakes. It was because of her 'yes' that we would receive the gift of Jesus from God.

The story in our gospel reading expresses the meaning of today's feast of Mary's 'Immaculate Conception'. Today we are celebrating Mary's total responsiveness to God's call, her complete openness to God's will. To say that Mary was immaculately conceived is to say that there was no sin in her life from the first moment of her existence. Her life was one constant 'yes' to God's choice and call, from her conception to her final breath. She allowed herself to be touched by God's grace in a very complete way. She was 'full of grace', full of God. God's will was done in her, as it is in heaven. She was, truly, a woman of God, and this made her a woman for others. According to Luke's Gospel, after the annunciation, Mary immediately gives herself in love to her older cousin Elizabeth, staying with her for several months. She went on to give herself to Jesus, her son, and then to let go of her precious Son so as to give him to us all. After her Son's death and resurrection, she gave herself in love to the disciples. She was present with them at Pentecost when the Spirit of the risen Lord came down upon them. As a woman of God for others, we see in her the human person we are all called to become. In our second reading, Paul declares that God 'chose us in Christ to be holy and spotless, and to live through love in his presence'. Mary is the person God desires us all to be.

The story of Adam and Eve tells a very different story from the one Luke tells in the gospel reading. Adam had said 'no' to God's call, eating of the tree that was out of bounds. The break in his relationship with God led him to hide from God, and God had to call out after him, 'Where are you?' In hiding from God, he also hid from himself. Refusing to take responsibility for his actions, he blamed his wife Eve – 'It was the woman' – who then blamed the serpent – 'The serpent tempted me'. For the author of the Book of Genesis, the story of Adam and Eve is the story of us all. We are all prone to going our own way, turning away from God's call and then hiding from God, and, as a result, losing touch with our true selves and damaging our relationship with others. Yet, when that happens, the Lord continues to ask us, 'Where are you?' The Lord asks this question not in an accusing way but in a loving way. Jesus, Mary's Son, came to seek out and save the lost, which is all of us. Adam hid from God out of fear, but the Lord in the gospels constantly says to people, 'Do not be afraid'. As Saint John says in his first letter, perfect love casts out fear.

Today's feast reminds us that we have someone we can look to and be inspired by in our efforts to respond to the Lord's searching love. Mary, the mother of Jesus, is also our mother. She knows the power of sin and what it can do to human lives; she saw what it did to her Son. She surrounds us with her intercession and prayer so that we too can become the human person God desires us to be. That is why we can ask her with confidence to pray for us sinners now and at the hour of our death.

9 December, Thursday, Second Week of Advent
Matthew 11:11–15

We all appreciate a little bit of praise from time to time. We appreciate praise for who we are as a person even more than praise for what we have done. In today's gospel reading, Jesus praises John for who he is in glowing terms: 'Of all the children born of women, a greater than John the Baptist has never been seen.' Jesus praises John the Baptist as greater than any other human being. It is an extraordinary compliment. What is so great about John, in the eyes of Jesus? Towards the end of the gospel reading, Jesus identifies John as the Elijah who was to return. There had been an expectation among the Jewish people that a prophet like Elijah would come to prepare God's people for the coming of the Messiah. Jesus identifies John the Baptist as that Elijah figure. He had a unique role and he fulfilled it to perfection. Yet Jesus then goes on to make the even more extraordinary statement, 'the least in the kingdom of heaven is greater than' John is. All who, through their close ties to Jesus, experience the coming of God's kingdom have a higher status than John the Baptist. Jesus is referring there to all of us. He is reminding us that God has privileged us in a way that John was not privileged. John was executed shortly into the public ministry of Jesus. He was not graced through the death, resurrection and ascension of Jesus and the coming of the Holy Spirit as we have been. He did not live to see the formation of the Church, the community of the risen Lord's disciples. We are being reminded that we have received a great deal from God, through his Son, without any merit on our part. Our calling is to live out of what we have received. As Jesus says elsewhere in the gospels, 'You received without payment, give without payment'.

10 December, Friday, Second Week of Advent
Matthew 11:16–19

There was a time, perhaps less so today, when children liked to play by imitating the behaviour of adults. They might play at being a doctor or a nurse or an airline pilot or whatever. In today's gospel reading Jesus imagines a group of children playing at being the musicians at a wedding and the singers at a funeral. However, this group of children find no response at all from another group of children. When the first group pretend to play the pipes as at a wedding, the other group of children won't dance. When they pretend to sing dirges as at a funeral, the other group of children won't mourn. Jesus applies this image to his own ministry and the ministry of John the Baptist, contrasting his own joyful, celebratory ministry with the more austere and mournful ministry of John the Baptist. Jesus observes that like the second group of children his own contemporaries failed to be moved either by his own ministry or the ministry of John. They were behaving like God's frozen people. The gospel reading invites us to ask how we are responding to the joyful, celebratory ministry of the risen Lord today. Does the Lord's presence and ministry among us keep placing a new song in our hearts? Do we allow our lives to move to the rhythm of the Lord's joyful tune, the joyful music of the Holy Spirit? In times when we are tempted to get despondent, do we allow the Lord to keep us hopeful? The Lord's daily coming in love to us is always good news to be grateful for and to rejoice in, even when times are difficult.

11 December, Saturday, Second Week of Advent
Matthew 17:10–13
There was a tradition among the Jewish people that the prophet Elijah would return to earth just before the coming of God's anointed one, the Messiah, to prepare people for his coming. That is why, at the end of today's first reading which was written less than two hundred years before Jesus, the author says, 'Happy shall they be who see you', in other words, 'Happy shall they be who see Elijah when he returns', because they can be assured that the coming of the Messiah is imminent. In the gospel reading, Jesus identifies John the Baptist as the prophet Elijah who had been promised. He had worked to prepare people for the coming of Jesus. Yet, by the time Jesus spoke in today's gospel reading, John the Baptist had been executed. As Jesus says, 'they did not recognise him but treated him shamefully'. People should have been happy to have seen Elijah present in John the Baptist: 'Happy shall they be who see you.' Instead, many wanted rid of him. Jesus goes on to say, 'the Son of Man will suffer similarly at their hands'. People should have been even happier to see Jesus, God's anointed

one, yet some wanted Jesus dead. We don't always respond well to the gifts and graces that God sends us. We fail to recognise the ways that God is blessing us. We reject God's gifts to us, or carry on as if they are not there. Today's gospel reading encourages us to grow in our appreciation of all that God is doing for us, all that God is giving to us, all that God is holding out to us in his love. Advent is a season when we are invited to learn to receive all that comes to us from God. The Advent prayer 'Come, Lord Jesus' is one expression of our desire, our openness, to receive the coming of the Lord and all the blessings he brings with him.

13 December, Monday, Third Week of Advent
Matthew 21:23–27

As we draw nearer to the feast of Christmas, cribs will start appearing in our homes and in our churches. At the centre of the crib is a vulnerable baby, the son of Mary and Joseph. We recognise this baby as also the Son of God. He would come to realise at an early age that his heavenly Father was a greater authority in his life than his earthly father, Joseph. Jesus was always about God his Father's business. He was always doing God's work and, as a result, people recognised that he acted and spoke with great authority, the authority of God. In the gospel reading, the chief priests who worked in the Temple asked Jesus, 'What authority have you for acting like this?' He had just driven out from the Temple all who were selling and buying, overturning the tables of the money changers and the seats of those who sold doves. The answer to their question was, 'Jesus' authority comes from God'. It was God who empowered him, authorised him, to do what he did in the Temple. The religious leaders were unsettled and disturbed by the authoritative way in which Jesus spoke and acted. However, those who had little power or status welcomed Jesus' authoritative presence. They found it liberating. They were amazed at it and glorified God because of it. On one occasion, when the religious leaders questioned Jesus' authority, the people of Capernaum exclaimed, 'We have never seen anything like this!' This is how we are to respond to the authoritative presence of Jesus among us today. God continues to work powerfully and authoritatively through Jesus in a life-giving, healing, liberating way. We readily submit to the authority of Jesus in our lives, to his Lordship, because we recognise that his authority over us is a loving authority that we can trust. It is the kind of wholesome, life-giving authority that can leave us saying, 'We have never seen anything like this.'

14 December, Tuesday, Third Week of Advent
Matthew 21:28–32

We are familiar with the parable of the father and his two sons that is found in Luke's Gospel, often called the parable of the prodigal son. The parable of a father and his two sons in Matthew's Gospel, which is our gospel reading today, is less familiar. Yet, both parables have something in common. In both there is a son who starts off badly but then comes right in the end by reversing his original decision. The younger son who left home to indulge himself came to realise his error and began the journey home. In today's parable, the son who originally said 'no' to his father's request to work in his vineyard thought better of it and eventually went into the vineyard to work. In the two parables the other son who started off being dutiful towards his father ended up going against his father. What seems to matter to Jesus is not so much where we begin but where we end up. We can turn away from the Lord in various ways, but the Lord never turns away from us. He is always prepared to wait for us to come right, to 'think better of it', in the words of today's parable. The first reading states that the Lord desires a 'humble and lowly people'. Thinking better of what we have said or done and then taking the necessary change of direction requires humility on our part. It seems that such humility is a quality that the Lord is always delighted to respond to.

15 December, Wednesday, Third Week of Advent
Luke 7:19–23

In the gospels, John the Baptist comes across as a person of very strong faith. He knows his own identity as the messenger who announces the coming of someone more powerful than himself. He calls on people to repent, to turn more fully towards God, in preparation for the coming of Jesus who will baptise with the Holy Spirit. John seems very sure of his God-given identity as the one sent to prepare a way for the Lord. Yet, in today's gospel reading, we find a somewhat different John the Baptist. From his prison cell, he sends some of his followers to ask Jesus if he really is the one who was to come. Is he the one whom John identified as God's special messenger? It seems that John was beginning to have doubts about his whole life's work. He may have wondered if he had been pointing people in the right direction. Even people of strong faith can have moments of great religious doubt. No matter how strong our faith is, uncomfortable questions come along that can make us doubt our faith convictions. Faith is no stranger to doubt and doubt can help to keep faith honest and pure. Our faith in the Lord can be especially undermined by the darker experiences of life. John was a man of the open wilderness; he must have found his prison cell a very dark place indeed. In response to John's doubting question, Jesus in effect says to him, 'Look at all God is doing through my ministry. Open your eyes and see.' In moments of doubt, we often need to look again at the many ways the Lord is actually working in our own lives and the lives of others.

16 December, Thursday, Third Week of Advent
Luke 7:24–30

Jesus is very fulsome in his praise of John the Baptist in today's gospel reading. He acknowledges John as that unique prophet announced in the Jewish Scriptures who would come to prepare the way for the Lord. Jesus goes so far as to say that no one born of woman is greater than John the Baptist. He does not speak in such terms of any other contemporary figure. Yet he immediately goes on to make an even more striking statement, declaring that the least in the kingdom of God is greater than John the Baptist. John came before Jesus; he was put to death before Jesus had completed his own ministry. He was not part of the community of God's kingdom that Jesus gathered about himself. He did not live to experience the death and resurrection of Jesus and all that flowed from this pivotal event, the sending of the Holy Spirit, the formation of the Church, the preaching of the Gospel, the celebration of the sacraments. In that sense, we are all more privileged than John the Baptist. We have come to see and to hear what he did not see or hear. The birth of Jesus, which we are soon to celebrate, has graced us in a much fuller way than John the Baptist was graced. In acknowledging with gratitude to God this privilege, this grace, we are also aware of the call that goes with it. We are to live our lives out of that fullness we have received. We are to allow the many ways we have been graced by the birth of Jesus to flow through us and to bless and grace the lives of others.

17 December, Friday, Third Week of Advent
Matthew 1:1–17

Today we begin the Octave of Christmas. The readings during the octave, especially the gospel readings, relate much more to the birth and childhood of Jesus. The alleluia verses are a series of beautiful Advent prayers, each of which is worth making our own this Advent season. The genealogy of Jesus with its list of strange names may strike us as an unusual gospel reading. Why include it in the lectionary at all? Yet it reminds us very forcibly of the humanity of Jesus. Yes, we believe that Jesus is the Son of God, but he was also a son of Abraham and a son of David. He belonged to the people of Abraham's God, the people of Israel. Through Joseph, his father, he was a descendant of King David. Jesus was deeply rooted in the Jewish world and tradition. His family tree was a Jewish family tree. His Scriptures were the Jewish Scriptures. When God became human, he did so among a particular people, in a particular place, at a particular time in history. Yet God sent his Son into the world for all peoples, for every place and for all future time. Jesus, now risen Lord, is to be found among us, in this place, in this time. When God sent his Son into the world it was for everyone, in every time and place. The child Jesus was born not just to Mary and Joseph of Nazareth two thousand years ago, but to each one of us today. That is why we celebrate the birth of this child as good news for us, for me personally. Christmas is the time when we give thanks to God for the greatest gift he could have given us, the gift of his very self, the gift of his Son, who is light from light. Having given such a wonderful gift, God will never take it back. Because of the birth of Jesus to Mary and Joseph, we have all been eternally graced and we are called to live out of that grace.

18 December, Saturday, Third Week of Advent
Matthew 1:18–24

A year ago, Pope Francis issued an Apostolic Letter called *With a Father's Heart*, in which he recalls the 150th anniversary of the declaration of Saint Joseph as Patron of the Universal Church. In his Apostolic Letter, the Pope describes Saint Joseph as a beloved father, a tender and loving father, an obedient father, an accepting father; a father who is creatively courageous, a working father, a father in the shadows. He wrote the letter against the backdrop of the Covid-19 pandemic, which, he says, has helped us see more clearly the importance of 'ordinary' people who, although far from the limelight, exercise patience and offer hope every day. In this, the Pope says, they resemble Saint Joseph, whom he describes as 'the man who goes unnoticed, a daily, discreet and hidden presence', yet played 'an incomparable role in the history of salvation'. In today's gospel reading, Joseph consents to become the father of the child of his betrothed, Mary, a child conceived through the power of the Holy Spirit. The gospel reading suggests that when he first heard the news of Mary's pregnancy he decided to divorce her informally. He didn't understand initially what God was asking of him. When he realised that what he had planned to do was not what God was asking him to do, he submitted completely to God's will for his life, which was to take Mary home immediately as his wife. Like Joseph, we can all struggle to know and to do what God is asking of us. We can begin to go down a path which is not God's desire for us, just as Joseph did. However, Joseph shows us that if we keep on seeking after what God is asking of us, God will somehow reveal his will to us. Joseph had to discern over time what God was asking of him, and that can be true of us all. In our efforts to discern God's will, God's desire, for our lives, Saint Joseph can be a good companion, someone we can turn to in prayer, for help with our discernment.

20 December, Monday, Fourth Week of Advent
Luke 1:26–38
There is a pattern in today's gospel reading that is often found in the Jewish Scriptures. God calls someone to take on some role,

the person called feels either unworthy or incapable of doing what God is asking, God promises to give them his empowering help for their role and task and, finally, the person says 'Yes' to God's call. In the gospel reading God, through the angel Gabriel, greeted Mary as 'highly favoured' because he called her to a unique role. She was to conceive and bear a child who would be called 'Son of the Most High'. Initially, Mary was deeply disturbed and asked, 'How can this come about?' When Gabriel assured her that the Holy Spirit would come upon her and the power of the Most High would overshadow her, she gave an unreserved 'yes' to what God was asking of her: 'I am the handmaid of the Lord, let what you have said be done to me.' The role that God was asking Mary to take on was completely new. There was nothing comparable to this in the Jewish Scriptures. No one had ever been asked to become the mother of God's Son. If anyone had reason to hesitate before God's call, it was Mary. Yet, once assured that 'nothing is impossible to God', she did not hesitate to respond fully to God's call. God's call comes to each one of us. It will not have the same dramatic form it had for Mary, yet each of us is called to play a role in God's purpose for the world. Today's reading assures us that the God who calls us also empowers us to answer his call. Saint Paul expresses this conviction very simply, 'The one who calls you is faithful and he will do this'. We go forth in response to God's call, our baptismal call, not relying on ourselves, but, like Mary, relying on God who gives us his Spirit, and trusting, like her, that 'nothing is impossible to God'.

21 December, Tuesday, Fourth Week of Advent
Luke 1:39–45
Today's gospel scene depicts the meeting between two pregnant Jewish women, Mary and Elizabeth. As Luke describes the

encounter, it is Elizabeth who does all the talking. When Mary speaks it will be to give praise to God in her Magnificat. Yet it is Mary's initial greeting of Elizabeth that moves Elizabeth to speak. In response to Mary's greeting, the child in Elizabeth's womb leapt for joy, recognising who Mary was and who the child was that she was carrying. It was this movement of her child within her that moved Elizabeth to speak. Because of this movement of her unborn child, she now recognises Mary's identity as 'the mother of my Lord'. Elizabeth declares Mary blessed as a woman, firstly as a mother of a special child, 'blessed is the fruit of your womb', and secondly as a woman of faith, 'blessed is she who believed that the promise made her by the Lord would be fulfilled'. It was because she believed the word of God spoken by Gabriel that she became the mother of the Lord. In that sense, her faith was even more fundamental that her motherhood. In the writings of Luke, Mary is a model believer. Luke wrote a gospel and the Acts of the Apostles, and the last appearance of Mary in this two-volume work is of her gathered with other believers in prayer in an upper room, just before the coming of the Holy Spirit upon them at Pentecost. Mary, the mother of Jesus, was becoming the mother of believers. As a woman of trusting, prayerful faith, she can help us to become people of trusting, prayerful faith. Just as her faithful response to God's word, spoken by Gabriel, allowed her to become the one through whom God's Son came into the world, so if we can respond as faithfully to God's word as she did, God's Son will continue to come into our world through us.

22 December, Wednesday, Fourth Week of Advent
Luke 1:46–56
Mary's prayer in today's gospel reading has become the prayer of the Church. It is prayed every evening by those who pray the

Evening Prayer of the Church. Although it is Mary's prayer, it can be prayed by anyone who wishes to celebrate God's loving deeds on behalf of all God's people, especially those in greatest need. Mary's song is about the loving power of God working for the ultimate well-being of all. She celebrates God as one who does great things for us, whose mercy reaches from age to age to those who know their need of it. She sings of a God who comes to the defence of the lowly and the hungry and who opposes those who oppress them, the proud and wealthy princes of this world. She proclaims a God who is faithful to his ancient promises of providing help for his people in their need. Luke would have us believe that this is the God in whom Mary believed. This was also the God that Jesus her Son fully revealed. In his opening sermon in Nazareth he announced that the Spirit of God was upon him to bring good news to the poor, to proclaim release to the captives, to let the oppressed go free. The God of whom Mary sang is the God who became flesh in Jesus who was born of Mary. This is the God in whom we are all asked to believe. Our calling as believers is to allow the loving and liberating power of God of which Mary sings to become flesh in our own lives, so that through us the Lord can continue his work of raising up the weak and vulnerable.

23 December, Thursday, Fourth Week of Advent
Luke 1:57–66
Names in Hebrew often have significant meanings. The name 'John' means 'the Lord is gracious'. This was the name that God wanted Zechariah and Elizabeth to give to their newborn child. The birth of this child was a sign that God's gracious favour was about to touch the world in a significant way. The child of Zechariah and Elizabeth would, as an adult, point people towards the son of Mary and Joseph who would proclaim the year of the Lord's favour.

What's in a name? Well, for Zechariah and Elizabeth, there was a great deal in the name 'John'. The neighbours objected to this name: 'But no one in your family has that name.' This was a break with tradition that could not be tolerated. Yet, the God of Israel could not be bound by tradition. God was about to do something new, and this new name within the tradition of this family was a sign of God's exciting new initiative towards humanity. On this occasion, the children's parents stood up against the naysayers. 'He is to be called John.' There can be much in the traditional way of doing things that is worthy of respect. Yet, when it comes to the ways of God, we cannot allow ourselves to become prisoners of tradition. There was a newness to the coming of Jesus. He would go on to speak of his ministry as new wine that needed new wineskins. The Spirit of the risen Jesus is always at work in creative new ways among us. God's gracious initiative towards us in Jesus is always prompting us to open new doors. The Spirit blows where it wills, where God wills, and we are asked to have the freedom to go where the Spirit is leading us. When John was born, people asked, 'What will this child turn out to be?' They were asking, 'What is God doing in the life of this child?' It is a question we can all ask, 'What is God doing in our lives?' 'Where is God leading us?' 'What new direction is God asking us to take?'

24 December, Friday, Fourth Week of Advent
Luke 1:67–79
Today's gospel reading is the prayer of Zechariah, the father of John the Baptist. His prayer has become part of the Church's prayer. It is prayed every morning as part of the Church's Morning Prayer. Zechariah prayed his prayer in response to the birth of his son, John the Baptist. He had come to recognise that his son would have a special role in God's purpose. His son would go before

Jesus to prepare the way for him. Jesus is spoken of in this prayer as the rising Sun who comes from on high to visit us, to give light to those who live in darkness and the shadow of death. It is a lovely image of Jesus and one that is very appropriate for this time of year when the sun begins to make a return and the days start to get longer. As we look upon the rising sun we thing of Jesus who has come to visit us from on high and who remains with us until the end of time. Towards the end of his *Confession* Saint Patrick declares, 'we believe in and worship Christ the true sun who will never perish, nor will anyone who does his will'. Zechariah celebrates this rising sun as the manifestation of the tender mercy of our God. At Christmas we call on Jesus, the rising Sun, to shed the light of God's loving mercy into the dark areas of our lives. We position ourselves beneath the rays of the light of God's mercy and love that shine upon us through Jesus, Emmanuel. In gratitude for that rising Sun from on high, like Zechariah, we praise and bless God who has visited all people in this life-giving way.

27 December, Monday, Feast of Saint John the Apostle
John 20:2–8

Today's gospel reading is also the gospel reading for Easter Sunday morning. I have often been struck by the repeated reference in that reading to people running. When Mary Magdalene discovered that the tomb of Jesus was empty on that Sunday morning, she ran to Simon Peter and the other disciple, the one Jesus loved. These two disciples then ran together to see for themselves what Mary told them, with the other disciple running faster than Peter and reaching the tomb first. The running of these three disciples captures something of the initial distress and confusion of that first Easter morning. The body of Jesus had been placed in the tomb two days previously. Where was it now? Mary Magdalene was of the opinion that the body of Jesus had been taken away or stolen. We are not told the opinion of Simon Peter. However, it is said of the other disciple, the one Jesus loved, that when he saw the empty tomb he believed. He understood the true significance of the empty tomb. Jesus had risen from the dead. This 'beloved disciple', as he is often referred to, has been identified with the disciple John, whose feast we celebrate today, and who stands behind the gospel that bears his name. This disciple is portrayed as seeing more deeply than either Mary Magdalene or Simon Peter. He recognised the presence of the risen Lord in the emptiness of the tomb. We need something of this disciple's way of seeing today. We sometimes fail to recognise the presence of the risen Lord in the various distressing experiences of emptiness in our lives. At such confusing and troubling moments, we can feel that the Lord is absent. Yet Christmas is the feast of Emmanuel, God with us, and today's gospel reading reminds us that the risen Lord is always with us, even in those times when we are tempted to feel he has abandoned us.

28 December, Tuesday, Feast of the Holy Innocents
Matthew 2:13–18

In today's first reading, we find that very striking statement about God, 'God is light; there is no darkness in him at all.' Elsewhere, in this same letter, the author says that 'God is love'. We are being told that God is the light of love. In God there is none of the darkness associated with the absence of love. God sent his Son into the world to reveal God as light, as the light of love. Christmas, which celebrates the birth of Jesus, is very much the feast of light, the feast of the light of God's love as expressed in a human life, the life of Jesus. It is very appropriate that on this feast of Christmas we light candles and we place lights on

Christmas trees. If the first reading proclaims that God is light, the gospel reading is full of darkness. It would be tempting to say of King Herod the opposite of what is said of God, 'He is darkness; there is no light in him at all.' When he realised that the Magi had not returned to tell him where the infant king of the Jews was born, he reacted furiously. Determining to kill this pretender to his throne, he ordered all male children up to the age of two to be killed in Bethlehem and its surrounding district. We celebrate the feast of these holy innocents today as Christian martyrs. The killing of innocent children by Herod points ahead to the killing of the innocent Jesus by Pilate. Herod symbolises the brutal use of political and military power throughout history, which has often resulted in the suffering and death of children, even to this day. Jesus, the light of God, was born into a dark world, marked by brutal violence. It is the world we continue to live in. Yet God shone a great light into that world, through the birth of Jesus, and God continues to shine a great light into our dark world today through the risen Lord alive in the Church and in our individual lives. Jesus continues to say to us what he said to his first disciples: 'You are the light of the world.' The Lord works in our lives so that the light of God's love continues to shine in our world through us. We are all called not only to light a candle in the darkness but to be a light in the darkness, to be the light of the Lord's love in our sometimes dark world.

29 December, Wednesday, Fifth Day in the Octave of Christmas
Luke 2:22–35
Whenever a relative of ours gives birth to a child and family members stand around all agog at the child, people invariably want to hold the child. There is something about holding this bundle of new life which is very special. Babies are endlessly fascinating;

they engage us at so many levels. We focus on them and find it hard to take our eyes off them. In today's gospel reading we hear of Mary and Joseph coming into the Temple of Jerusalem with their recently born baby, Jesus. There they came upon Simeon, on whom the Holy Spirit rested, an upright and devout man. He took the child in his own arms and blessed God. If every child is endlessly fascinating, how much more would that have been true of the child Jesus? Having held this child in his arms and having set his eyes upon him, Simeon was ready to leave this world for the next, 'Now, Master, you can let your servant go in peace.' His short but beautiful prayer has become part of the official Night Prayer of the Church. We have not had the privilege of holding the child Jesus in our arms, like Simeon, but we do behold the risen Lord with the eyes of faith. We recognise him in the breaking of bread in the Eucharist, we hear his voice when the gospels are proclaimed, and, if we are alert, we see him in each other. We also look forward to that day beyond this life when, like Simeon in the Temple, we will see him face to face.

30 December, Thursday, Sixth Day in the Octave of Christmas
Luke 2:36–40

In yesterday's gospel reading, Simeon was prompted by the Holy Spirit to go to the Temple just as Mary and Joseph were bringing their child there. In today's gospel reading, it is said of Anna that she never left the Temple. She lived in the Temple, serving God night and day with fasting and prayer. We could speak of her as a contemplative. When she saw the child Jesus, she broke into the prayer of praise, and spoke about the child to all who were waiting for God's deliverance. It is striking that Luke says of her that she served God night and day with fasting and prayer. Normally when we hear the term 'serving God' we think instinctively of various forms of good works. Today's gospel reading suggests that prayer and fasting are also forms of service to God. We may not always think of prayer as an act of serving God, but to pray is to serve God. Anna spent her time in the Temple praying, and yet she was as much a servant of God as those who served God by doing all kinds of good works. Mary who sat at Jesus' feet and listened to his word was serving him as much as her sister Martha, who was busy preparing a meal for her guest. To pray is to serve the Lord, because when we pray we give the Lord our time, our focus, our attention; we give him ourselves. We allow him to serve us and are empowered to continue serving him in others.

31 December, Friday, Seventh Day in the Octave of Christmas
John 1:1–18
New Year's Eve is often a time when we look back on the past year. For many, the past twelve months will have been a difficult period of time. The Covid-19 pandemic left many without a job. More painfully, many will have lost loved ones to the pandemic. Many are struggling to come to terms with a loss that was rendered all the more difficult by the restrictions that existed around visiting nursing homes and attending funerals. As well as looking back on the struggles and pains of the year, New Year's Eve can also be a time to look back in thanksgiving, a time to name the graces and gifts that have come our way and have enhanced our lives. No matter what we have been through, we all have something to give thanks for; we have all been graced in one way or another. It is that graced dimension of our lives that today's gospel reading draws attention to. The greatest grace and the source of all other graces is the Lord's presence to us. That grace is memorably expressed in the gospel reading: 'The Word was made flesh and he lived among us, and we saw his glory.' Jesus who was God became flesh as we

are flesh, and as risen Lord remains with us until the end of time. The gospel reading also declares that 'from his fullness we have, all of us, received – yes, grace upon grace'. We are invited to keep drawing grace upon grace from the fullness of the Lord's loving presence. That realisation keeps us thankful for the past and gives us confidence as we face into the future.

1 January, Saturday, Solemnity of Mary, Mother of God
Luke 2:16–21

In today's first reading we find that lovely prayer of blessing, 'May the Lord bless you and keep you, May the Lord let his face shine on you and be gracious to you. May the Lord uncover his face to you and bring you peace.' I have always been drawn to that prayer of blessing and I often pray it for others. It was above all through the birth of Jesus, Mary's child, that the Lord blessed us and kept us, made his face to shine upon us and was gracious to us. Today we celebrate Mary as mother, mother of Jesus, mother of God's Son, mother of God. It was because of her 'yes' to God's call that God blessed us so abundantly through Jesus, her son, and revealed the light of his face to us, displaying his gracious love. In the words of Saint Paul in today's second reading, it was because God sent his Son, born of a woman, born of Mary, that the Spirit of God's Son has been poured into all our hearts, drawing us into a share in Jesus' own relationship with God, enabling us to cry out, 'Abba, Father', alongside Jesus. There is much to treasure and ponder here, and that is what we find Mary doing in today's gospel reading. When the shepherds share their night-time experience of the visit of an angel announcing the birth of a Saviour, who is Christ, the Lord, we are told that 'Mary treasured all these things and pondered them in her heart'. As mother of God's Son, mother of God, she contemplates the wonder, the mystery, of it all, and she encourages us to do the same. On this New Year's Day, because of the way God has blessed us through Mary's son, we all have much to treasure and much to ponder, in a spirit of wonder and gratitude.

3 January, Monday before Epiphany
John 1:29–34

There are many ways of speaking about eternal life in the New Testament. In the gospels we find the image of the many-roomed house of God the Father and of the banquet at which people from north, south, east and west gather, to mention just two. Today's first reading speaks of eternal life as that eternal moment when we shall be like God because we shall see God as God is. Elsewhere in this letter, Saint John writes that 'God is Love'. In eternity, we will see God as God is, as Love, and we shall become as loving as God is loving. It is a wonderful way of speaking about eternal life. In the gospel reading, John the Baptist identifies Jesus as the Lamb of God who takes away the sin of the world. Jesus is the full expression of God's love working to reconcile all of humanity to God. Jesus is the fullest revelation possible of God's love for the world. The closest we can come to see God as Love in this life is to look upon Jesus as he comes to us in all of the gospels. In eternity we will become as loving as God is loving but each day we are called to grow more fully into Jesus, God's love in human form. Something of our eternal destiny can become a present reality when we grow up into Christ and allow him to live in and through us. According to the gospel reading, Jesus came to baptise with the Holy Spirit, the Spirit of God's love. Jesus gives us his own Spirit to empower us to become as loving as he is and so, to anticipate in the here and now our glorious destiny to be as loving as God is loving.

4 January, Tuesday before Epiphany
John 1:35–42

It is always worth reflecting on the questions that Jesus asks in the gospels. In John's Gospel, Jesus' opening words take the form of a question, the question we find in today's gospel reading addressed to two disciples of John the Baptist, 'What do you want?' A more literal translation would be 'What do you seek?' The question asks the disciples regarding their deepest desires, 'What are you really looking for?' By means of that question, Jesus invites us to bring our deepest desires and wants to him. Later in the gospel he will present himself as someone who can satisfy the deepest hungers and thirsts in our lives: 'Whoever comes to me will never be hungry and whoever believes in me will never be thirsty.' If Jesus' question invites us to get in touch with our deepest desires, his subsequent invitation to the two disciples of John the Baptist invites us to come to him as the one who can satisfy our deepest longings, 'Come and see'. Both the question and the invitation of Jesus are worth holding on to and pondering. We will hear the question and the invitation in different ways at different times in our lives. Jesus' question and invitation never go out of date. They are for all seasons and times of life. The disciples of John the Baptist had a question of their own for Jesus: 'Where do you live?' or, more literally, 'Where are you staying?' Their question expressed their desire to stay with Jesus, to spend time in his company. It is a question we can all make our own in response to Jesus' question to us. It is a question that helps us to enter more fully into our desire to spend time with Jesus, to get to know him better, with our heart as well as our head. This is a desire that the Lord will always respond to.

5 January, Wednesday before Epiphany
John 1:43–51

Have you ever found yourself responding negatively to a suggestion or a sharing from someone, and then thinking further about it and having a change of mind and heart? I certainly have. Someone makes a suggestion to me about the parish and initially I respond with little enthusiasm. I can only see the downsides, the problems, the complications, the demands it might make. Then, over time, I begin to see the suggestion in a different light. I come around to seeing that maybe there is something worthwhile here after all. In that regard, Nathanael reminds me of myself. Philip came up to him to share his enthusiasm for Jesus of Nazareth, declaring that he and others had finally found the Messiah that the Jewish Scriptures had foretold. Nathanael's initial response was a dismissive, 'From Nazareth? Can anything good come from there?' In the next chapter of John's Gospel we learn that Nathanael was from Cana, not too far from Nazareth. The people of Nazareth may have asked the same question about Cana! We can all be prone to dismissing people on the basis of where they are from or where they were brought up or the colour of their skin or whatever. However, thanks to the gentle persistence of Philip's 'Come and see', Nathanael came to see Jesus in a much different light, declaring, 'You are the Son of God, you are the King of Israel'. Something wonderful could come out of Nazareth after all. Jesus assures Nathanael that he has only begun to see: 'You will see greater things than that.' What a wonderful promise Jesus makes there to us all. The next time we meet Nathanael in this gospel, he is to be among the group of disciples who went back fishing after the crucifixion of Jesus, to whom the risen Lord appeared. Nathanael did indeed see greater things. When it comes to our relationship with the Lord, where we begin is not so important, because the Lord can always move us on, if we are open to being led by him. In the course of our earthly lives, the Lord is always inviting us to see greater things, to see him with new eyes, until that eternal day beyond this earthly life when we will finally see him face to face.

6 January, Thursday, The Epiphany of the Lord
Matthew 2:1–12

I came across a sentence in a book recently that caught my attention, 'We belong to an age when it is easier to see the darkness of the night than the bright spots that shine in the midst of the darkness.' As followers of a risen Lord who declared himself to be the light of the world, we are always looking for the bright spots that shine in the midst of the darkness. They are there to be seen for those who are searching for them. In his parables Jesus suggested that the kingdom of God, the powerful presence of God, is often a hidden presence among us. It is like the seed growing secretly underneath the earth. It does not come with dramatic flashes of lightning. Its presence is so subtle at times that we can be tempted to think that darkness is prevailing over the light of God's kingdom. Yet the small bright spots of God's benevolent presence are shining in the darkness if we have eyes to see.

On this feast of the Epiphany, the Magi enter the Christmas story and appear in our cribs. They were probably professional astrologers from Persia who were used to searching the night sky. They were pagans. They had no access to the Word of God in the Jewish Scriptures. Yet they had the infinity of the night sky, which fascinated them, and they had searching spirits and enquiring minds. They were open to the ways that God was drawing them to himself. They were attuned to God's light in the darkness. When they saw the small light of a new star in the midst of a dark night sky, it spoke to their searching spirits and their enquiring minds. As the star moved, they followed it. They left their familiar surroundings and set out on a journey of hope. They sensed that this star would lead them towards a special manifestation of God's presence, the infant King of the Jews.

The Magi are patrons of those who see signposts to God that others very often do not see. They encourage us to be alert to the signs of the Lord's presence in the darkness, to the ways that the Lord is drawing us towards himself. Today's feast invites each of us to ask, 'Where is the star that is guiding me towards Bethlehem, through which I am being called to set out on a journey towards Emmanuel, God-with-us?' Moving towards Emmanuel, the Light of the World, is the journey of a lifetime; it is never over. Even when the Magi reached Bethlehem, their journey wasn't over. We are told that having worshipped Emmanuel, they returned to their own country by a different way. Having given their precious gifts to the child, they set out on a new journey to share the treasure they had received.

If we are attentive to the star that the Lord sends us, if we are open to the ways he is drawing us, we will have our own Bethlehem moments too, times when we will have a special sense of the Lord's presence to us, a wonderful awareness of the Lord's love for us, a grateful experience of the Lord's light in the darkness. Such moments might inspire us to offer him what is most precious to us, the gift of our lives. Such Bethlehem moments are never the end of our journey, just as Bethlehem wasn't the end of the Magi's journey. They launch us on a new journey. In those moments when the Lord touches our lives in a special way, we often sense the call to share what we have received. Graced by the Lord's light at such times, we go forward carrying his light to others. Like the Magi, once we have encountered the light of the Lord, we will often see a different and better route for our lives.

The Lord will often lead us to himself by a variety of stars. Then, having drawn us to himself, he sends us out on another journey, to shine as his stars to others, to become ourselves that bright spot shining in the midst of the darkness. The magi's journey to Bethlehem and their different journey away from Bethlehem reflects the twofold pattern of our own lives as the Lord's disciples. The Lord keeps calling us to Bethlehem, to an ever deeper encounter with Emmanuel, the Light of the World, and he then sends us out as his light-bearers to others, especially to those who find themselves in darkness.

The ominous presence of Herod in the gospel reading reminds us that there are always dark forces in our world working to eliminate the presence of the Lord's light. Those forces will often seek to undermine our efforts to journey towards the light of Bethlehem and to journey away from Bethlehem as light-bearers. Yet Herod could not stop God's epiphany. God's light shone in Bethlehem and Herod's darkness could not overcome it. That remains true today. The Herods of this world can never stop God's continuing epiphany among us. The bright spots of the Lord's presence are stronger than the darkness and will, eventually, overcome it.

7 January, Friday after Epiphany
Matthew 4:12–17, 23–25

We have been celebrating the birth of Jesus, culminating yesterday in our celebration of the visit of the Magi to pay homage to the infant king of the Jews. In today's gospel reading we jump to Matthew's version of the beginning of the public ministry of the adult Jesus. Matthew interprets the beginning of Jesus' public ministry against the backdrop of a text from Isaiah that is read at the Christmas night Mass, 'the people that lived in darkness have seen a great light'. That image of light was central to our celebration of the feast of Christmas. According to John in his gospel, the Word who became flesh was the true light coming into the world to enlighten everyone. If God's light was associated with the birth of Jesus, it is just as powerfully associated with the beginning of his public ministry, according to Matthew. Most of us prefer light to darkness. We look forward to the days getting longer. We appreciate it when somebody throws some light on a mystery we have been struggling with. The gospel reading assures us that the ultimate source of all true light, the light that comes from God, is Jesus. We begin our year acknowledging whatever darkness we may find ourselves in and, at the same time, looking with confident and hopeful faith towards Jesus whose light, the light of life, shines abundantly on us all.

8 January, Saturday after Epiphany
Mark 6:34–44

Today's first reading expresses very succinctly the deeper meaning of the feast of Christmas which we have been celebrating: 'God sent into the world his only Son so that we could have life through him.' According to that reading, God sending his Son into the world so that we could have life reveals the wonderful truth that 'God is love'. It is the simplest and, yet, most profound statement about God in all of the Scriptures. Everything else that could be said about God is a commentary on that simple, profound statement. Out of love, God sent his Son into the world so that we could have life through him. 'Life' refers to eternal life, the life of God, which is a life of love, a life over which death has no power, a fullness of life without any of the suffering and sorrow of this earthly life. Although this 'life' is our destiny beyond death, God sent his Son into the world so that we could have a foretaste of this eternal life here and now, in the midst of our earthly life. God's

Son, now risen Lord, is a life-giving presence for us all here and now. In today's gospel reading, Jesus was a life-giving presence for the large crowd. He was like a shepherd to them, feeding their spirits with his teaching and their bodies with bread and fish. The risen Lord is present in our world today in the same life-giving way. He works to feed the various hungers in our lives, especially our hunger for a love that is unconditional and enduring. He not only wants to feed our various hungers but he also wants to work through us to feed the hunger of others, as he worked through his disciples to feed the hunger of the crowd. The disciples had very few resources, five loaves and two fish, but the Lord worked powerfully through them for the well-being of the large crowd. If we place our resources at the Lord's disposal, few as they may seem to us, he will work through them in ways that will surprise us.

10 January, Monday, First Week in Ordinary Time
Mark 1:14–20

Many people make their living from the sea, especially on an island such as ours. In today's gospel reading, we hear reference to the Sea of Galilee. It was really an inland lake, but it was so large it could be referred to as a sea. Fishing was a major occupation for people who lived along the shores of the Sea of Galilee, such as for the two sets of brothers in today's gospel reading who lived in Capernaum, a town on the seashore. In calling these two sets of brothers to follow him in a very complete and dedicated way, Jesus was asking a lot of them. He was asking them to leave behind their lucrative fishing business. The gospel reading tells us that the fishing business of Zebedee, the father of James and John, was sufficiently large for him to employ men from outside the family. These two sets of brothers, Simon and Andrew and

James and John, would go on to become the core of the group of twelve who formed the inner circle around Jesus. Not everyone in the gospel story whom Jesus addressed with his message was asked to leave their occupation to follow Jesus. However, the opening message of Jesus in today's gospel reading was addressed to everyone: 'The time has come and the kingdom of God is close at hand. Repent, and believe the Good News'. That message has two elements, an announcement of the good news of God's reign, God's powerful and loving presence through Jesus, and then a call to believe that good news, to turn towards the loving God present in Jesus. The same message is addressed to all of us today. The risen Lord continues to make present the loving power of God among us and keeps calling us to turn to that loving power of God ever more fully and to open ourselves ever more completely to God's loving presence, so that we can reflect his loving presence to others.

11 January, Tuesday, First Week in Ordinary Time
Mark 1:21–28

It strikes me that there is a very good description of prayer in today's first reading. Hannah tells the priest Eli in the temple that 'I was pouring out my soul before the Lord'. Her description of prayer is not too far from the definition of prayer I learnt from the green catechism in primary school, according to which prayer is the lifting up of the mind and heart to God. However, 'pouring out one's soul' seems a more visceral description of prayer. Hannah goes on to tell Eli, who supposed she was drunk, that 'all this time I have been speaking from the depth of my grief and my resentment'. For Hannah, pouring out her soul before the Lord amounted to speaking to the Lord from the depth of her grief and resentment. That was the state of her soul, so that was the way of her prayer. In prayer, we can come before God as we are, in our grief and even in our resentment. In the gospel reading, Jesus is confronted by a person who is described as possessed. He cries out to Jesus, 'What do you want with us, Jesus of Nazareth? Have you come to destroy us? I know who you are.' This was, in its own way, a cry from the depths, a pouring out of the soul before Jesus. Behind the aggressive questioning was a cry for help. Far from being put off by the man's aggressive tone, Jesus uses his authority to calm his spirit and heal his brokenness. We are being reminded that the Lord always hears our prayer, whatever form it takes, even if not in the way we expected.

12 January, Wednesday, First Week in Ordinary Time
Mark 1:29–39
We relate to people in a whole variety of ways and, likewise, we relate to God in a whole variety of ways, which is why our prayer can take a great variety of forms. Prayer links both of today's readings. The prayer of listening comes to the fore in today's first reading. God was trying to speak to young Samuel but Samuel had not yet come to recognise the voice of God. He needed the elderly priest Eli to help him become attuned to God's voice more fully. Eli was a kind of spiritual companion to Samuel, helping him to articulate a prayer of listening: 'Speak, Lord, your servant is listening.' Eli's suggested prayer to Samuel is a prayer we could all make our own today. It is a very good way of beginning a time of silent prayer during which we try to open ourselves to what the Lord may be saying to us through his word. The gospel reading describes a day in the life of Jesus. Having spoken in the local synagogue of Capernaum, he goes to the house of Simon Peter a short distance away to heal his mother-in-law, and the house then becomes a focal point for a healing ministry that extends into the

evening. Hopefully after some rest, Jesus then goes off on his own to a lonely place just before dawn to pray. We are not told how he prayed, but it is likely that the prayer of listening was central to his prayer time. When Simon Peter and his companions went looking for him to bring him back to Capernaum, Jesus was very clear that this was not what God was asking him to do. Rather, having listened to God in prayer, he knew that he had to go to the neighbouring towns to preach the gospel there too. Prayer helped Jesus to discern what God was asking of him, which often clashed with what others wanted him to do. Our prayer of listening will help to give us the clarity and the conviction to take the path the Lord is asking us to take today.

13 January, Thursday, First Week in Ordinary Time
Mark 1:40–45

The question 'Why?' is often asked by people in the Jewish Scriptures. It often arises from a situation of desolation, of abandonment by God. Sometimes the question is asked by individuals, and at other times by the people as a whole. In today's first reading, the whole people ask the question 'Why?' This was a moment of national defeat and humiliation at the hands of the Philistines. The people ask, 'Why has the Lord allowed us to be defeated today?' An even greater defeat and humiliation followed immediately, when the Ark of the Covenant, the very sign of God's presence to his people, was captured by the Philistines. That sense of the people's abandonment by God is picked up in today's responsorial psalm, giving rise to the same 'Why?' 'Why do you hide your face and forget our oppression and misery?' There were times when God's people wondered whether or not God really cared about them. In the gospel reading, the leper's request of Jesus suggests that he is not certain whether or not Jesus really cares about him. 'If you want to, you can cure me.' The leper did not doubt Jesus' power to heal him but he did wonder if Jesus cared enough to want to cure him. Jesus' immediate response dispelled the leper's doubt: 'Of course I want to'. Then he did the unthinkable, indeed, what was forbidden, physically touching the leper so as to heal him. Jesus is God's answer to our question 'Why?' Jesus reveals God to be God-with-us, especially in our times of desolation and abandonment. As God was with Jesus on the cross, suffering with him, even as he cried out, 'Why have you abandoned me?', God suffers with us in our own sufferings, while working to bring us through suffering to new life, as he did for Jesus.

14 January, Friday, First Week in Ordinary Time
Mark 2:1–12

We are familiar with the saying, 'Be careful what you wish for'. It reflects the experience of people who, on getting what they have always wished for, discover that it is not actually what they wanted or needed. In the first reading, the people of Israel wish for a king, like all the other nations around them. Up until then, they had spirit-inspired judges as their leaders. Samuel, prompted by the Lord, tries to show them that the institution of monarchy, for which they long so ardently, will create a whole set of problems and demands that they certainly wouldn't have wished for. Yet, the people insist, 'We want a king', and eventually, moved by the Lord, Samuel grants their wish. The people would learn from bitter experience that Samuel's warnings were well grounded. What we wish for isn't always what is best for us. Our wishes for ourselves and for others don't always correspond to the Lord's wishes for us. We have to keep shaping our wishes, our desires, so that they come to correspond more and more fully to what the

Lord desires for us. In the gospel reading, the wishes of a group of people for their paralysed friend corresponded perfectly with Jesus' wish for their friend. They wanted their friend to be healed of his paralysis, and so did Jesus. Their wish for their friend's well-being was so strong that it led to a section of roof over Jesus being removed, so that their friend could get as close to Jesus as possible. Such faith, such passionate desire for life, could not but elicit a healing response from Jesus: 'Your sins are forgiven ... pick up your stretcher and go off home.' The gospel reading shows us the good that can happen when our desires are brought into line with the Lord's desire that all people should have life and have it to the full.

15 January, Saturday, First Week in Ordinary Time
Mark 2:13–17

When I read the gospels I am often struck by the questions that people ask. Jesus himself asks many questions in the pages of the gospels, as do many of the other characters who appear in them. In today's gospel reading, the scribes and the Pharisees ask the question, 'Why does Jesus eat with tax collectors and sinners?' As far as they were concerned, to eat with tax collectors and sinners was to risk being contaminated by them. They would have argued that it was better to keep yourself separate from such people in order to preserve your moral health. However, Jesus did not share this concern. Rather than fearing that the sin of others might morally infect him, he knew that his goodness, God's goodness in him, would transform others. The Lord is never diminished by our failings; rather, we are always ennobled by his holiness and goodness. That is why the Lord does not separate himself from us, even when we might be tempted to separate ourselves from him because of what we have done or failed to do. The Lord is always ready to sit with us, to share table with us, to enter into communion with us, in order that in our weakness we might draw from his strength and in our many failings we might draw from his goodness and love.

17 January, Monday, Second Week in Ordinary Time
Mark 2:18–22

You have often heard the saying, 'you can't teach an old dog new tricks'. It is a saying that recognises that there comes a time in life when people find it hard to change. Habits of a lifetime don't change easily. I was reminded of that saying by the words of Jesus in today's gospel reading, 'nobody puts new wine into old wineskins'. We can all become like old wineskins, incapable of receiving new wine. Jesus was responding to people's criticism of his disciples for their failure to follow the stricter fasting practices of the Pharisees and the disciples of John the Baptist. However, for Jesus, these stricter fasting practices were like old wineskins that were ill suited to the new wine of his ministry. Jesus was proclaiming the good news of the presence of God's kingdom, God's loving rule. This was a joyful moment. It was more like a wedding feast than a funeral. Jesus was the bridegroom, calling people to become friends of the bridegroom, to join in the joyful celebration of the presence of God's liberating, redeeming power. It was time for the critics of Jesus and his disciples to join the party. We are reminded of the father in the parable of the prodigal son pleading with his older son to come and join the celebration to welcome his younger brother home. Throughout the history of the Church, there have been movements that wanted to make the following of Jesus a much dourer and gloomier affair than Jesus ever intended. There was often an over-emphasis on penance and mortification. However, Jesus did not come to burden further an already burdened people. He came to give people a foretaste in the present of the joy of the kingdom of God. The Lord wants us to taste here and now something of the eternal joy of the heavenly banquet, by opening ourselves to his liberating and life-giving love and by giving expression to his love in our dealings with others.

18 January, Tuesday, Second Week in Ordinary Time
Mark 2:23–28

The two readings today invite us to ask the question, 'What do we see when we look?' In the first reading, the Lord sends Samuel to find a king to replace Saul from among the sons of Jesse of Bethlehem. All the likely candidates among his sons were presented to Samuel, but he knew that the Lord had not chosen any of them. Finally, and reluctantly, the youngest son, David, was brought to Samuel. When the members of his family looked on him, they saw only an inexperienced youth whose age-appropriate task was to mind sheep. However, when Samuel looked upon him with the eyes of God, he saw a future king. As Samuel said to Jesse, 'God does not see as man sees; man looks at appearances, but God looks at the heart.' There is often more to people than meets the eye. People can look at someone without really seeing them. In the gospel reading, one Sabbath day the Pharisees looked upon Jesus' disciples picking ears of corn as they walked along, and chewing the corn, and what the Pharisees saw were law-breakers, people who disrespected the law of the Sabbath. When Jesus looked upon his disciples' action, he saw the hungry feeding themselves in a perfectly legitimate way. Jesus had to remind the Pharisees that the Sabbath was God's gift to his people, not God's burden. 'The Sabbath was made for people, not people for the Sabbath.' What do we see when we look? Both readings invite us to look beyond appearances to the heart of a person, where we can find something of the Lord, sometimes in spite of appearances.

19 January, Wednesday, Second Week in Ordinary Time
Mark 3:1–6

At the beginning of today's first reading, Saul says to David, 'You cannot go and fight the Philistine; you are only a boy and he has been a warrior from his youth.' The Philistine had everything on his side from a human point of view – size, experience, weaponry, reputation. David had nothing going for him. He was young and inexperienced, and had no weaponry of significance. Yet he had a deep trust in the Lord's ability to rescue him from the power of the Philistine. As a result, in this unequal contest, it was David who emerged the victor. There is a pattern in the Scriptures of people finding themselves before impossible odds, yet winning through because they place their trust in the Lord rather than in their own meagre resources. In the course of his ministry, Jesus often found himself up against opponents who, from a human point of view, seemed stronger, more resourceful and better equipped. At the end of his life, Jesus found himself up against the might of the Roman Empire and its supporting allies, the chief priest and elders of the people. As he hung from the cross, Jesus' opponents seemed to have won, but Jesus' trust in God at this moment of extreme vulnerability was vindicated when he was raised from the dead and the rejected stone became the cornerstone of a new spiritual temple. That deadly conflict at the end of his life is already anticipated in today's gospel reading, shortly into his public ministry. The same combination of religious and political leadership conspires to trap him and, at the end of the gospel reading, plot to destroy him. Yet Jesus is not intimidated by his enemies. He is determined 'to do good', on the Sabbath as much as on any other day. He would heal the man with the withered hand, although it would fan the flames of opposition to him. His trust in God left him free to do the good thing, even in the face of a formidable foe. Both readings encourage us to persevere in standing up to forces of death, trusting that the Lord will provide for us if we keep seeking to do what is right and good in God's eyes.

20 January, Thursday, Second Week in Ordinary Time
Mark 3:7–12

The beginning of today's gospel reading says that Jesus withdrew with his disciples to the lakeside. Elsewhere in the gospels, when Jesus withdraws it is usually to spend time in prayer. The demands on him were great, but he needed to withdraw from people from time to time so that he could be with God in prayer. On this occasion, according to the gospel reading, when Jesus withdrew, large crowds followed him, not only from Galilee, but from a wide area. They wanted to touch him so as to be healed. Whereas Jesus wanted to touch God his Father in prayer, the needy crowds wanted to touch Jesus for healing. Jesus did not spare himself when it came to serving the needy, but he also needed to withdraw to pray. His ministry to others flowed from his prayer. Prayer is as central to Jesus' life as risen Lord as it was during his public ministry on earth. He lives for ever to intercede for us. As well as praying for us, the risen Lord continues his active ministry among us that we find portrayed in the gospels. He remains close to us in our suffering to strengthen and heal us, inviting us to touch him. He also works through us for the strengthening and healing of others. Jesus continues to do as risen Lord what we find him doing in today's gospel reading, withdrawing to pray and serving the needy and broken. That same twofold movement is to shape our lives as his followers. We withdraw to pray and we come from prayer to bring God's healing love to those whom we meet.

21 January, Friday, Second Week in Ordinary Time
Mark 3:13–19

When I was in school we had to learn the names of the twelve apostles off by heart. I don't think that is a feature of today's teaching of religion. The twelve seemed to have been a significant group for Jesus. They symbolised the leaders of the twelve tribes of Israel. Their presence suggested that Jesus had come to renew the people of Israel and through them to renew all nations. The disciples in the gospels are a much larger group than the twelve. They include men and women. Indeed, by the end of Mark's Gospel, the twelve are nowhere to be found and it is the women disciples who stand by the cross, who make the discovery of the empty tomb and to whom the risen Lord first appears. The twelve were a mixed bunch and they left a lot to be desired. James and John asked Jesus for the best seats in his kingdom, in a rather self-serving way, Peter denied Jesus publicly three times and Judas betrayed Jesus to his enemies. Given the way some of the twelve are portrayed in the gospels, we might be tempted to say that Jesus' interviewing skills were not great. Yet the gospel reading says that 'he summoned those he wanted' and 'he appointed twelve' from among them. These were the people he wanted to form this symbolically important group, even though they had great flaws and failings. The Lord wants each one of us to be his companions and to share in his work in some way, in spite of our failings and imperfections. Sometimes it is our weaknesses that creates a space for the Lord to enter our lives more fully and to enter our world more fully through us. The Lord is faithful to us, having called us. All he asks is that we keep turning towards him and relying upon him in our weakness.

22 January, Saturday, Second Week in Ordinary Time
Mark 3:20–21

We don't hear a great deal about Jesus' family in the gospels once Jesus begins his public ministry after his baptism. There is an interesting reference to Jesus' family in today's very short gospel reading. Jesus is so involved in his work with the crowd that he and his disciples have no time even to eat. Such frenzied behaviour is understood by his family as a sign that Jesus has lost his mind. As a result, they set out on the thirty-mile journey from Nazareth to Capernaum to restrain him, to take charge of him. It seems that they had yet to learn to let Jesus go to do God his Father's work. They behave as if they know what is best for him. They set themselves on a collision course with Jesus. As we read on in the gospel story, Jesus refuses to step back from his ministry to the crowds and return to Nazareth with his family. In the course of the gospels, various individuals and groups wanted Jesus to take a path other than the one God was calling him to take. They wanted a Jesus in their own image, rather than receiving Jesus as he was. It seems his family were no different in that regard. They wanted Jesus to be more like themselves. We can all be tempted to imagine Jesus as we want him to be, yet we have to allow him to be himself in our lives. He is, after all, Lord of our lives. We cannot shape him to our liking or use him to serve our own purposes. We spend our lives surrendering ourselves to him, allowing him to take his own initiative towards us. We may not always understand what the Lord is doing in our world, our Church, within ourselves, but we seek to give ourselves over to his purpose humbly. We continually allow ourselves to be led by his word, and to be shaped by his Spirit.

24 January, Monday, Third Week in Ordinary Time
Mark 3:22–30

In Matthew's Gospel Jesus speaks of himself as gentle and humble in heart. In today's gospel reading from Mark, he speaks of himself in a rather different way. Jesus uses the image of a burglar who enters a strong man's house and ties up the strong man before burgling his property. Jesus is referring to himself, even though it may seem a strange image for Jesus to use for his ministry. His work consists in entering the property of the strong man, Satan, and binding him up. Jesus is the stronger one who has come to launch an assault on the domain of Satan. The gentle one is also the strong one who is ready to wage a spiritual warfare against the powers that enslave and dehumanise people. Although Jesus' opponents claim that the power at work in his ministry is the power of Satan, in reality the power that moves Jesus' ministry is the power of the Holy Spirit. Those who identify this power of the Spirit as the power of Satan are sinning against the Holy Spirit, in the words of Jesus. It will be almost impossible for God's forgiving and healing love to penetrate hearts that are so blind and prejudiced. They will never be forgiven because they are completely closed to the gift of Jesus' forgiving love. The same Holy Spirit that shaped the ministry of Jesus has been given to us all. One of the signs or fruits of the Spirit in our lives is that strong gentleness or gentle strength that characterised the life and ministry of Jesus. This will often involve for us, as it did for Jesus, standing up against all the forces and powers that enslave and dehumanise people and that prevent them living the fully human life that the Lord desires for them.

25 January, Tuesday, Feast of the Conversion of Saint Paul
Mark 16:15–18

In today's first reading, Paul says that before Christ appeared to him he was 'full of duty towards God'. Yet this duty towards

God expressed itself in a very destructive way. He persecuted a new movement within Judaism that had come to be called the 'Way' and, eventually, came to be known as Christianity. It was the appearance of the risen Lord to Paul and the Lord's question, 'Why do you persecute me?' that stopped Paul in his tracks. From that moment on, he remained full of duty towards the God of Israel, but it found expression in a very different way. Rather than persecuting those whose beliefs were different from his, he proclaimed the good news of God's unconditional love for all humanity, revealed in the life, death and resurrection of Jesus. In the words of today's gospel reading, he went on to proclaim this good news to all creation. As he would write in his letter to the church in Rome, the heart of this good news is that nothing 'in all creation will be able to separate us from the love of God in Christ Jesus our Lord'. Paul speaks in the first reading of this encounter with the risen Lord on the road to Damascus as an experience of light: 'A bright light from heaven suddenly shone round me.' He came to see God in a new way. His eyes were opened to the good news that the love in God's heart was boundless, and in the light of that love he came to see that the love in his own heart had been very narrowly focused, restricted to those who thought and lived like himself. Paul's relationship with God deepened as a result of what happened near Damascus and, as a result, he began to relate to others in the way God relates to them, in the way Jesus related to others during his public ministry and continues to relate to us as risen Lord. Paul's experience teaches us that the more we grow in our relationship with God the Father and his Son Jesus, the more expansive our hearts will become and the broader our horizon will be. As we open ourselves more fully to God as God really is, to God as Love, then we will relate to others in ways that bring people together in all their diversity. We will no longer feel threatened by those who are different from us but we will open ourselves to what God can teach us through them, while sharing with them the treasure of the Gospel that brings joy to our lives.

26 January, Wednesday, Memorial of Saints Timothy and Titus
Luke 10:1–9
Whenever I celebrate Mass in this church or come to pray here, I am always very conscious that this is the church where my maternal grandparents worshipped for over thirty years, and, where my parents worshipped for over ten years. When it comes to our faith, we always stand on the shoulders of others. Paul's first letter to Timothy was written towards the end of the first century. It is clear from today's first reading, that Timothy is a third-generation Christian. Paul makes reference to Timothy's sincere faith, which first came to live in his grandmother, Lois, and then in his mother, Eunice. Paul had the highest regard for Timothy as a co-worker; he refers to him in that reading as a 'dear child of mine'. He had the same warm regard for Titus. Yet, Paul knew that the faith of these co-workers was nurtured by the faith of others, especially the faith of their parents and grandparents. The ultimate source of this gift of faith was the Lord, but Timothy and Titus received this gift from the Lord through others, including Paul. In that reading, Paul calls on Timothy to 'fan into a flame the gift that God gave you when I laid hands on you'. The gift of the Spirit of power, love and self-control came from God through Paul and their families. The Lord draws us to himself through others. In the gospels, Jesus is not portrayed as drawing people to himself on his own. He works through others. In today's gospel reading, he sends out seventy-two as labourers in God's harvest, while calling on them to ask God in prayer to send out still more labourers. We each have a vital role to play in the Lord's work of

drawing others to faith in himself. Paul needed co-workers, men like Timothy and Titus, and women like Phoebe and Priscilla. The Lord needs us all to be his co-workers, because the harvest remains plentiful.

27 January, Thursday, Third Week in Ordinary Time
Mark 4:21–25

Today's gospel reading from Mark follows immediately after yesterday's gospel reading of the parable of the sower and its interpretation, which was a reflection on Jesus' proclamation of God's word and how it was being responded to. Today's gospel reading suggests that God's word is like a light that needs to be let shine. No one puts a lamp under a bed but on a lamp stand where it can give light to all. God's word proclaimed by Jesus is a lamp for our way and a light for our steps. It needs constant proclamation. We are aware of various forms of darkness in our world; we are always on the lookout for some light. The words of Jesus allow God's light to shine upon us. That is why, according to our gospel reading, we need to listen carefully to the Lord's word. 'Take notice of what you are hearing.' Jesus declares that the more attentively we listen to God's word, the more we will receive. 'The amount you measure out is the amount you will be given – and more besides, for the one who has will be given more.' The contrary is also true. If we fail to listen to the Lord's word, if we turn away from it, we can easily lose what we may have gained from listening to it in the past. 'The one who has not, even what he has will be taken away.' The Lord's word is a wonderful light in our lives; it has the power to bring us life. However, it needs our response. The Lord who speaks needs us to listen, and if we give ourselves over to really listening to his word then we will receive more than we ever anticipated. In the words of Jesus from another of the gospels, 'A good measure, pressed down, shaken together, running over, will be put into your lap.'

28 January, Friday, Third Week in Ordinary Time
Mark 4:26–34

The first of the two parables in today's gospel reading suggests that when a farmer has sown seed in the ground, he has to step back and allow nature to bring the seed to fruition. It is only when the seed is fully grown that the farmer swings into action again, harvesting the crop. Between sowing and harvesting, he has to leave the seed alone. If he were to start poking around in the soil to see how the seed is doing, he would greatly inhibit its growth. When Jesus says the kingdom of God is like that, what does he mean? He may be saying that the coming of God's kingdom into our lives and into our world isn't all down to us. We have our work to do, as the farmer has to sow and harvest. However, the real work of spiritual growth within ourselves and in our world is God's doing. As Saint Paul says in his first letter to the Corinthians, 'I planted, Apollos watered, but God gave the growth.' Having done what we can, we have to step back and allow God to do what only God can do. Sometimes, God's good work can be happening all around us, even when we are doing very little. God can be working powerfully in and through our lives in those times when we seem to have little to give, perhaps because of advancing years or illness. The good work we have done in the past can be bearing fruit in ways that we might never suspect. God's good work continues, even when we seem to have little to show for our efforts. What the Lord asks of us is perseverance, not to lose heart.

We are to keep faithful, especially when times are lean and difficult.

29 January, Saturday, Third Week in Ordinary Time
Mark 4:35–41

I have always been drawn to Mark's depiction of the demeanour of Jesus in the boat as it battled with a raging storm. While the disciples were panicking, it is said of Jesus that 'he was in the stern, his head on the cushion, asleep'. The disciples were overcome with fear, saying to Jesus, 'Master, do you not care? We are going down!' Jesus somehow knew that all was well and all would be well. He trusted in God's providential care in the midst of the storm and that gave him an inner peace and calm. He rebuked his disciples for not having something of his trusting faith in God's loving care: 'Why are you so frightened? How is it that you have no faith?' He spoke those words to his disciples, having first calmed the wind and the sea. His inner calm becalmed the raging elements. In the gospels, the boat with the disciples in it is often a symbol of the Church, the community of faith. The evangelist wants all of us to know that the risen Lord is with us in the storms of life. We are in stormy times at present; we sense that in these times we are battling with a strong headwind and heavy seas. In such times, the Lord is present to us as a centre of calm. He calls out to us to enter into his own trusting faith in God our Father, so that we are not overcome by fear and anxiety. If we can imbibe some of his inner calm, then we can be a centre of calm for others who may be struggling in the storms.

31 January, Monday, Fourth Week in Ordinary Time
Mark 5:1–20

When David was cursed by one of his opponents in today's first reading, he did not do what one of his soldiers suggested to him, namely to have this man's head cut off. Instead, David absorbed the man's curse and went on his way. In the gospel reading, Jesus is related to in a similarly threatening way by a very disturbed person: 'What do you want with me, Jesus, son of the Most High God?' Like David, Jesus did not return aggression for aggression. However, Jesus went beyond what David did. He did not simply continue on his way, like David, but, rather, he addressed his opponent in a very personal and respectful manner: 'What is your name?' and then went on to heal him of his demons, restoring him to himself and to his community. At the end, the disturbed man was so touched by Jesus that he wanted to stay with him and join him on his journeys. David, and to a greater extent, Jesus, reveal to us something of God's way of relating to us. God is not put off by our resistance to him, or even by our hostility towards him. Rather, regardless of how we relate to God, God continues to relate to us out of the goodness in his own heart. He keeps asking us, 'what is your name?' inviting us to reveal ourselves to him, to open our hearts to him, even when darkness lurks there. As Jesus shows in the gospel reading, God works in our lives to rid us of our demons, to restore us to harmony with ourselves and with others. What the Lord needs from us in response is some openness of mind, heart and spirit to his healing and life-giving presence, the kind of openness shown by the man in the gospel reading after his healing, when he begged to be allowed to stay with Jesus.

1 February, Tuesday, Feast of Saint Brigid
Luke 6:32–38
Saint Brigid is the secondary patron of Ireland, after Saint Patrick. She was born around 454. When she was young her father wished to make a suitable marriage for her but she insisted that she wanted to consecrate herself to God. She received the veil and spiritual formation probably from Saint Mel and she stayed for a while under

his direction in Ardagh. Others followed her example and this led to her founding a double monastery in Kildare, with a section for men and a section for women. Through Brigid's reputation as a spiritual teacher, the monastery became a centre of pilgrimage. She died in 524 and she is venerated not only throughout Ireland but in several European lands. She was renowned for her hospitality, almsgiving and care of the sick. Saint Brigid's cross remains a popular sign of God's protection. In legend it was used by Brigid to explain the Christian faith. The first reading that is often chosen for Saint Brigid's feast day is that wonderful prayer of Saint Paul from his letter to the Ephesians, one of my favourite passages in the New Testament. Paul is praying in intercession for his church, praying for their 'hidden self to grow strong', which he equates with Christ living in their hearts through faith. Our hidden self grows strong when Christ lives there. The more Christ lives within us, the stronger our hidden self will be. Brigid clearly had a strong hidden self in that sense. Christ lived in and through her. That is the baptismal calling of each one of us, to allow Christ to live in us, so that our deepest self is spiritually strong. Paul also equates Christ living in us with knowing the love of Christ, not just with our head but with our heart. When the love of Christ dwells in us, then, says Paul, we will be filled with the utter fullness of God. This is the goal of all our lives. It is a goal that will never be fully attained in this earthly life, but we can journey ever closer to it in this life, with the help of the Holy Spirit. When our inner self is strong, it will show itself in the kind of life that Jesus lived and that is portrayed in the gospel reading, a loving, compassionate, non-judgemental life, marked by a willingness to forgive. From all we know of her, this was Brigid's way of life and she remains an inspiration to us.

2 February, Wednesday, The Presentation of the Lord
Luke 2:22–40

Sometimes older people have an insight into life and into other people that is the fruit of long experience. Life has taught them what is important and what is not so important. In today's gospel reading, we find two older people who express a great insight into the child of a young married couple. Simeon declares the child to be God's salvation, a light to enlighten the pagans and to bring glory to Israel. Anna announces that this child will fulfil the hopes of all who have looked forward to the deliverance of Jerusalem. Simeon made his declaration to the child's parents, and Anna made hers to a larger group. They both speak to all of us today about the true identity of Jesus. As Mary and Joseph present Jesus to God in the Temple, in a sense, Simeon and Anna present Jesus to all of us by what they say about him. Perhaps, on this day, we might remember and give thanks for all those who presented Jesus to us, especially the older members of our family and our community. We bless and light candles on this day in response to Simeon's recognition of Jesus as the light to enlighten all people. God's light has shone and continues to shine upon us through Jesus, the light of God's love, God's truth and God's life. It is a light that has the power to overcome the darkness that can easily hang over us, especially the darkness of fear and of death. The second reading declares that Jesus shared in our flesh and blood so that by his death he might set free all those who had been held in slavery by the fear of death. On this feast, we open our lives and hearts afresh to what Saint John Henry Newman calls God's 'kindly light', which has shone so abundantly upon us through the life, death and resurrection of Jesus.

3 February, Thursday, Fourth Week in Ordinary Time
Mark 6:7–13

There comes a time in life when we need to let others do what we have been doing. We have to let go so that others can take on. None of us can keep doing what we have been doing for ever. We need the wisdom to know when to entrust some of our responsibility, some of our work, to others. We find that happening in both of today's readings. As David comes towards the end of his life, he passes on his role as king, his responsibilities to God's people, to his son Solomon. In the gospel reading, Jesus entrusts the twelve whom he had earlier chosen with a share in his mission. They had spent time with him and now he is ready to send them out as his ambassadors to preach what he has been preaching and to engage in his healing ministry. This happened reasonably early on in Jesus' public ministry. We might be tempted to think that, like David, Jesus would have waited until nearer the end of his life before entrusting a share in his mission to others. However, it seems that for Jesus this task of entrusting to others a share in his work couldn't wait any longer than was absolutely necessary. The Lord desperately needs us to share in his work today. As members of his body, the Church, we are his feet, his arms, his legs, his eyes, his ears, his mouth, his heart and mind. As the Lord once expressed himself through his physical body, he now expresses himself through all of us, his ecclesial body. The Lord needs us all if his work is to continue today, and just as he sent out the twelve in pairs, in six groups of two, he sends us out not as individuals but with others. He can work through us most effectively when we work together, pooling our gifts and resources.

4 February, Friday, Fourth Week in Ordinary Time
Mark 6:14–29

It could be said that some of the worst traits of human nature are on display in today's gospel reading. There is Herod who, contrary to the Jewish Law, married his brother Philip's wife. Herod knew John the Baptist to be a good and holy man, and yet, to save face he succumbed to his wife's request to have John beheaded. Herodias, Herod's wife, had wanted to kill John the Baptist for a long time for objecting to her marriage and she seized her opportunity when it came. Herodias' daughter coolly brought the head of John the Baptist on a dish to her mother. Herod's birthday feast turned into a grisly celebration of the death of a man of God. There is a moral darkness at the core of today's gospel story. Yet, if the three people in the foreground of this gospel story exemplify some of the worst of human nature, the light of God's goodness was there as well, even if in the background, offstage, as it were. There was the good and holy John the Baptist in Herod's dungeon. He had been faithful to his mission to preach God's word, even to powerful people like Herod, although that meant risking his life. Then, there were the disciples of John the Baptist, who, as soon as they heard of John's cruel fate, made haste to give him a dignified burial, even if he hadn't had a dignified death. At the heart of sin and moral darkness, goodness and holiness are always to be found, sometimes in the background, away from the main stage. Saint Paul assures us that where sin abounds, grace abounds all the more. In his letter to the church in Philippi, he called on them to shine like stars in the world. Therein lies the calling of each one of us. We are to let the light of the Lord's goodness, love and beauty shine in our sometimes dark world, holding firm to the conviction that the darkness will never overcome the light.

5 February, Saturday, Fourth Week in Ordinary Time

Mark 6:30–34

Jesus had sent out the twelve to share in his mission. According to today's gospel reading, after returning to him from that mission, he insists that they come away with him to a lonely place all by themselves to rest. Jesus knew that the harvest was great and that the labourers were few, but he also appreciated the need for the labourers to rest from time to time. There was a time to be active in God's service and there was a time to step back from activity and rest. In this gospel reading, Jesus is consecrating the value of rest. God can speak to us when we rest in ways he cannot speak to us when we are active. There are times in life when we are less active, perhaps as we get older or as our strength weakens due to illness. This can be an opportunity to listen more attentively to what the Lord may want to say to us. If we have a tendency to be more of a Martha person, this can be an invitation from the Lord to become a little more like her sister Mary, who sat at the Lord's feet and listened to him speaking. Jesus' planned time of rest for himself and his disciples never materialised because the crowd guessed where they were heading and got there ahead of them. The gospel reading says that when Jesus saw the crowd, far from being annoyed at this unexpected interruption of his plans, he had compassion on them. The word 'compassion' in the Bible is from the same root as the word 'womb'. Jesus is portrayed as responding to the crowd with a mother's anguished love for her struggling children. The Lord remains a compassionate presence in all our lives today. It is often when we step back from our various activities to spend quiet time with the Lord that we come to experience more fully his compassionate presence among us.

7 February, Monday, Fifth Week in Ordinary Time
Mark 6:53–56

Pilgrimage has always been part of our life of faith. People go on pilgrimage to places that are considered blessed in some way because of their relationship to the Lord or to Our Lady or to one of the saints of the Church. The primary place of pilgrimage for the people of Israel was Jerusalem and, in particular, the Temple in Jerusalem. Today's first reading explains why the Temple was such an important place of pilgrimage. It was there that the Ark of the Covenant was placed, containing the two stone tablets of the covenant God made with Israel through Moses, the stone tablets on which were written the Ten Commandments. As a result, the Temple was understood to be the place where the Lord had chosen to dwell in a special way. People went on pilgrimage to the Temple in Jerusalem because they believed they were going on pilgrimage to the Lord. In the gospel reading, we find people going on pilgrimage to Jesus. When Jesus stepped out of the boat by the shore of the Sea of Galilee, they journeyed towards him from wherever they lived so as to touch him and be healed of their infirmities. We are all on a pilgrimage towards the Lord. Our life is a pilgrimage towards the heavenly city of Jerusalem, which is filled with the Lord's presence. In the course of our earthly pilgrimage, we make smaller pilgrimages that express the essence of our earthly pilgrimage. We might go on pilgrimage to Rome, to Assisi, to Lourdes, to Knock or even to the Holy Land. In a sense, every time we are present at Mass, physically or virtually, we are going on a little pilgrimage. Like the people in the gospel reading, we are journeying towards the Lord. These smaller pilgrimages help to keep us focused on the Lord as we travel our earthly pilgrimage towards the heavenly Jerusalem.

8 February, Tuesday, Fifth Week in Ordinary Time
Mark 7:1–13

The beginning of today's gospel reading has a contemporary feel to it. The Pharisees and scribes were complaining that Jesus' disciples were eating with unclean hands, without washing them. We have all got used to washing our hands frequently since the onset of the Covid-19 pandemic. The hand-washing that so preoccupied the Pharisees and scribes had to do not so much with physical cleanliness but ritual cleanliness, which is more difficult for us to understand today. The Bible prescribed hand-washing rituals only for the priests who worked in the Temple in Jerusalem, but the Pharisees wanted to extend these hand-washing rituals to daily life because they held that all Israel was a priestly people. These regulations of the Pharisees for daily life were not in the Bible but were part of what they called the 'tradition of the elders'. In reply, Jesus criticises the Pharisees for giving more importance to these human traditions than to the commandment of God. Jesus is reminding us that we can be overly preoccupied with non-essentials, in religious matters as much as in other areas of life. In the religious sphere, we can easily attribute the greatest importance to something that in God's eyes is not so important, while failing to take seriously what really does matter to God. The life, death and resurrection of Jesus reveals what matters most to God, a way of life that reflects the love that is within the heart of God.

9 February, Wednesday, Fifth Week in Ordinary Time
Mark 7:14–23

In today's first reading the Queen of Sheba visits King Solomon in response to all she has heard about him. She wasn't disappointed. In fact she declares the reality to be much greater than the rumour:

'for wisdom and prosperity you surpass the report I heard'. Sheba has been identified with south-western Arabia, modern-day Yemen, or with modern-day Ethiopia. Jesus makes reference to this incident in the first Book of Kings, declaring that the Queen of the South 'came from the ends of the earth to listen to the wisdom of Solomon, and see, something greater than Solomon is here'. Jesus spoke these words in response to those who were looking for a sign from him; they were failing to appreciate the signs of God's presence that were already clearly visible in his ministry, including in the wisdom of his teaching. In today's gospel reading, Jesus gives expression to some of his wisdom, declaring that what makes a person ritually 'unclean' in God's presence is not certain kinds of food they may eat but what resides in the person's heart. More than once in his teaching, Jesus invites people to look beyond externals and appearances to the human heart. The widow who put two copper coins into the Temple treasury would have been regarded less favourably than those who put in much larger sums. Yet Jesus, looking at the heart, recognised that the generosity of this widow was of a completely superior quality to that of others, because the little she gave was everything she had to live on. In the parable of the Pharisee and the tax collector, the Pharisee who was pleased with his exemplary life was less acceptable to God than the tax collector who publicly confessed himself to be a sinner, because the heart of the latter was more open to God. Jesus encourages us to look beyond appearances to the heart, in our own regard and in regard to others.

10 February, Thursday, Fifth Week in Ordinary Time
Mark 7:24–30

In the gospels, Jesus normally responds immediately to requests for help, especially to parents who come to him to heal their sick children. Today's gospel story is unique in showing Jesus very reluctant to respond to the request of a pagan woman on behalf of her daughter. Jesus is in the region of Tyre, which was a predominantly pagan city, although having a strong Jewish presence. Jesus' words to the woman suggests that he sees his mission as predominantly to his own Jewish people initially: 'The children should be fed first.' It is only after his death and resurrection that he will engage in a mission to pagans, through those Jews who have come to believe in him. As Paul says in his letter to the Romans, the Gospel 'is the power of God for salvation to everyone who believes, to the Jew first and also to the Greek'. However, this Gentile woman is not prepared to wait. She is absolutely determined to change Jesus' timetable. Like others before her in the Scriptures, Abraham, Moses, Job, she argues with the Lord. She acknowledges that in the eyes of Jews she may be a Gentile 'dog', but she observes that some dogs are almost members of the family and eat at the same time as the children, making the most of the children's untidy eating habits, as their crumbs fall to the ground. In the end, Jesus grants her request; he changes his plan and responds to her human need. According to the Book of Genesis, Jacob wrestled with God. The story of the pagan woman confirms that sometimes our relationship with the Lord can take the form of a wrestling match or an argument, and the Lord seems to be at ease with that.

11 February, Friday, Fifth Week in Ordinary Time
Mark 7:31–37

After Jesus heals the deaf man with an impediment in his speech, he calls on his friends who brought him to tell no one about this work of healing. Of course, the friends of the man couldn't contain themselves and they published it widely. As a result, people remarked of Jesus, 'He has done all things well.' Jesus is often portrayed in Mark's Gospel telling people not to broadcast some healing work he had just done. We might wonder why. Surely God's good work done through Jesus needs to be publicly proclaimed. Perhaps Jesus didn't want people following him for the wrong reasons, thinking that he was a just a miracle worker and always wanting him to do more of the same. There is so much more to Jesus than a miracle worker. When he hung from the cross he seemed anything but a miracle worker. Yet the love that moved Jesus to respond to the sick and broken with compassion was the same love that led him to the cross. He was crucified because he had come to reveal God's fatherly and motherly love for all, especially for those whom the religious leaders of the time considered sinners. The Lord's love did not discriminate. What discriminated was how people responded to his love that knew no boundaries. Some found such a love unsettling. We follow Jesus, our Lord, in response to his love for us. His love will not always work miracles in our lives. Sometimes we will find ourselves on the cross with him. At such times, his love for us isn't any less, even though we may be tempted to think it is. His love is always at work in a life-giving way in our lives, until eventually it will bring us to a sharing in God's life of love in eternity.

12 February, Saturday, Fifth Week in Ordinary Time
Mark 8:1–10
The kinds of questions we ask can either open up possibilities or close them down. In the gospel reading, Jesus and his disciples are faced with a hungry crowd in a deserted place. The disciples' question seemed to close down any hope of feeding them. 'Where could anyone get bread to feed these people in a deserted place like this?' Jesus' question was much more hopeful. 'How many loaves

have you?' Jesus was already looking at the possibility of feeding the crowd with just the meagre resources that were available to him. He went on to feed the crowd with seven loaves and a few small fish. The limited resources on their own would not have been enough to feed the crowd, yet without those resources Jesus could not have fed the crowd either. The evangelist is reminding us that the Lord can work powerfully through what we might consider very limited resources. Indeed, he needs them if he is to continue his work of shepherding God's people. The Lord wants us to ask the kind of questions that create space for him to work through us. It is worth paying attention to the kind of questions we ask. Are they coming from a place of trusting hope in the Lord or are they coming from a place where I feel it is all down to me? The Lord is always asking us to take seriously the gifts and resources he has given us, even if they seem small compared to the task that faces us. He also asks us to place them at his disposal, trusting that he will work with them in ways we could never anticipate.

14 February, Monday, Feast of Saints Cyril and Methodius
Luke 10:1–9

Cyril and Methodius were brothers who were born in Thessalonica in northern Greece in the ninth century, sons of a prominent Christian family. Because many Slavs came to that part of Greece, they became proficient in the Slav language. They were noted linguists and scholars and went on to become monks. In response to a request from the leader of Moravia to the emperor in Constantinople, Cyril and Methodius were sent to preach the Gospel in Moravia, which corresponds to modern-day Czech Republic, Slovakia and parts of Hungary. In their efforts to do this they translated the Scriptures and the liturgical texts into the local Slav language. They understood that only if the sacred texts were in the vernacular could they bring the Gospel to the local people. In the process of translating they invented a new alphabet, from which the present Slav alphabet is derived. Today this alphabet is called Cyrillic, after Cyril, and is the basis of the Russian, Ukrainian, Bulgarian and Serbian alphabet. For that reason they are regarded as the founders of Slavonic literature. Because of opposition to their work, they had to leave Moravia, and at the invitation of the pope they travelled to Rome. The pope approved of their work in Moravia and created the two brothers bishops. Cyril died in Rome in 869, and he is buried in the Irish Dominican church of San Clemente near to the Colosseum, where an ancient fresco depicts his funeral. Methodius returned to Moravia where he preached the Gospel in spite of continuing opposition to his mission, including opposition from local bishops who objected to his use of the vernacular. Worn out by his labours, he died in 885. Pope John Paul II, a Slav pope, declared them co-patrons of Europe on 31 December 1980. A few years earlier he had spoken of the brothers as ideal examples of the true missionary spirit, faithful to the tradition that shaped them, yet striving to understand the peoples to whom they were sent, and adapting the tradition accordingly. In the language of today's gospel reading, they were wonderful labourers in the Lord's harvest. In that reading, as the Lord sends out seventy-two labourers, he calls on the seventy-two to pray to God, the Lord of the harvest, to send more labourers into the harvest. We are all called, each in our own way, within our own sphere of influence, to be among those labourers the Lord so keenly desires. We all have some gift through which the Lord can work for the coming of his kingdom. If we use our gifts in the service of the Lord, then he can say through us, in the words of the gospel reading, 'the kingdom of God is very near to you'.

15 February, Tuesday, Sixth Week in Ordinary Time
Mark 8:14–21

It is clear that Jesus is very frustrated with his disciples in today's gospel reading. He warned them against the yeast of the Pharisees and of Herod, 'yeast' being a traditional symbol of evil and wickedness. The disciples interpreted him in a very literal way, presuming he was giving out to them because they did not bring enough bread in the boat. This was shortly after Jesus had fed the multitude in the wilderness with bread. They seem to have been on a totally different wavelength from Jesus. Jesus' litany of questions to his disciples expressed his exasperation at them. 'Do you not yet understand? Have you no perception? Are your minds closed?' It is as if Jesus was saying, 'What do I have to do or say to get through to you?' I suspect the risen Lord continues to struggle with us, his disciples, today. We are not always on his wavelength. Like the disciples in the boat, we can be overly bothered about what is not important and we can fail to appreciate what the Lord is actually doing for us and asking of us. We continue to have eyes that do not see and ears that do not hear. Those first disciples had a long way to go before their eyes were finally opened. It would be after Easter before this happened. Even then, there was much for them to learn from the Lord. We all have a long way to go when it comes to seeing what the Lord wants us to see, hearing what he wants us to hear and opening our minds to what he wants us to understand. What is important is that we stay faithful to this journey of discovery, always having the humility to recognise that, in the words of Paul, 'now we see as in a mirror dimly', and always having the openness of the child to keep receiving what the Lord is trying to show us.

16 February, Wednesday, Sixth Week in Ordinary Time
Mark 8:22–26

It is striking the number of times in the gospels that people bring someone to Jesus who would never have been able to go to Jesus without the support of others. Earlier in Mark's Gospel a paralysed man was carried to Jesus by four friends, and a little later into his ministry people brought a deaf man with an impediment in his speech to him. In today's gospel reading people bring a blind man to Jesus asking that Jesus would touch him. All of these scenes remind us that people have brought us all to Jesus and we, in turn, are asked to bring others to Jesus. We never come to Jesus on our own. We need a community of faith if we are to encounter the Lord. Today's healing story is unique in the gospels in that Jesus struggled to heal the man of his blindness. When Jesus laid his hands on him initially, the blind man began to see, but he did not see clearly. Jesus needed to lay his hands on the blind man a second time before he could see plainly and distinctly. At this point in Mark's Gospel, Jesus is struggling to open the eyes of his disciples to see his true identity and what being his disciple entails. It is only in the light of Jesus' resurrection that they will finally see clearly. There is always some blindness in our lives with regard to Jesus and to what he is asking of us. The Lord can struggle to open our eyes too. Like the blind man in the gospel reading, we often need people who see more clearly than we do to show us the Lord and to help us to see more clearly what he is asking of us. There may also be times when we are asked by the Lord to become such a person for someone who is struggling to see.

17 February, Thursday, Sixth Week in Ordinary Time
Mark 8:27–33

None of us wants to hear the news that someone who means a great deal to us is going to suffer and die. When we are close to someone, we are deeply impacted by all that happens to them. We can sympathise with Peter's reaction to Jesus' announcement that he was to suffer grievously, be rejected and be put to death. We might find ourselves a little shocked by Jesus' response to Peter, 'Get behind me, Satan.' Is Jesus not being a little hard on Peter here? He may have his faults, but surely he is not Satan? After his baptism, Jesus was driven into the wilderness by the Spirit, where he was 'tempted by Satan'. Jesus knew a temptation of Satan from experience. Peter's rebuke of Jesus had an echo of Satan's earlier temptations. Perhaps Jesus experienced Peter's temptation to take a path that did not involve such deadly conflict as very enticing. Because it was such a powerful temptation, he needed to confront it powerfully, hence the strength of his rebuke to Peter. Jesus could avoid the way of the cross, but only by being unfaithful to his mission of proclaiming God's kingdom, with all that entailed. The proclamation of God's kingdom would threaten all who had a kingdom of their own to protect. The temptation to think in a merely human way rather than in God's way is very strong for all of us. Peter reveals ourselves to us. We all struggle to follow the Lord's way, the way of loving service of others without discrimination, even if it entails the way of the cross for us. Yet Jesus assures us that his way, regardless of the cost, is always the way of life, for ourselves and for others.

18 February, Friday, Sixth Week in Ordinary Time
Mark 8:34–9:1

In today's first reading, Saint James says very clearly that genuine faith will always find expression in loving deeds. Similarly, Saint Paul in his letter to the Galatians speaks of faith working through love. In faith we attend to the Lord, we entrust ourselves to him, we open ourselves to his presence and his Spirit, and his Spirit then bears the fruit of love in our lives. The closer we come to the Lord in faith, the closer we will come to others in love. Jesus is the supreme example of faith working through love or expressing itself in love. He entrusted himself faithfully to God his Father and this trusting faith in God found expression in a life of love for others, in his willingness to die to himself, to renounce himself, so that others might have life to the full. This is what Jesus calls for from his followers in today's gospel reading. Those who follow him in faith are to give expression to their faith in him by their willingness to renounce themselves in the loving service of others. 'If anyone wants to be a follower of mine, let him renounce himself'. Jesus also says in that gospel reading that those whose faith in him finds expression in the self-renouncing love of others, far from losing themselves, will find their true selves. 'Anyone who loses his life for my sake, and for the sake of the gospel, will save it'. The more we grow into the person of Jesus the more we become our true selves. The more we allow the risen Lord to live out in us his faith in God that finds expression in the loving service of others, the more we will become the fully human persons that God desires us to be.

19 February, Saturday, Sixth Week in Ordinary Time
Mark 9:2–13
There is a striking contrast in today's gospel reading between the glorious scene on the mountain and the conversation Jesus had with his disciples when they came down the mountain. On the mountain, Peter, James and John had an experience of Jesus in glory. His intense communion with God on the mountain left him transfigured. It was such a striking moment that Peter exclaimed, 'Rabbi, it is wonderful for us to be here', and he suggested a way of prolonging this entrancing experience: 'Let us make three

tents, one for you, one for Moses and one for Elijah.' It was a powerful experience of Jesus as Son of God. When they came down the mountain, the conversation was not about glory but about suffering and death. With reference to John the Baptist's execution by Herod, Jesus says, 'they treated him as they pleased'. Jesus also speaks of himself as the Son of Man who is to 'suffer grievously and be treated with contempt'. On the mountain, the disciples had heard a voice from the cloud saying to them, 'This is my Son, the Beloved. Listen to him.' It can't have been easy for the disciples to listen to Jesus speak about himself in this dark and ominous manner. The gospel reading captures something of the rhythm of our own lives as human beings, and as followers of the Lord. There will always be light and darkness there. There will be moments when we have a strong sense of the Lord's presence and we will say, 'it is wonderful for us to be here', and other moments when we find ourselves facing into struggle and suffering of one shape or form and perhaps wondering where the Lord has gone. Yet the Lord is with us in those valleys of darkness just as much as he is with us on the bright mountain top. God was present to Jesus on the hill of Calvary as much as he was present to him on the Mount of Transfiguration. God and his Son are present in all our Calvary moments too. The light of the Lord's presence always shines in our darkness, and is always stronger than the darkness.

21 February, Monday, Seventh Week in Ordinary Time
Mark 9:14–29

In today's first reading, James refers to the negative consequences for others of a purely self-seeking ambition. He declares that such an ambition leads to 'disharmony and wicked things of every kind'. Not all ambition is self-seeking; there is good ambition too. The saints were people who were ambitious to do God's will at all times by opening themselves to the workings of the Holy Spirit, the Spirit of the risen Lord, in their lives. In that first reading, James suggests that we are to be ambitious for the wisdom that comes down from above, the wisdom of God. He says that such wisdom makes for peace and is kindly and considerate, full of compassion, showing itself by doing good. The issue is not ambition in itself, but what we are ambitious for. The Lord's Prayer could be understood as Jesus' teaching on what we are to be ambitious for. We are to seek after the coming of God's kingdom, the doing of God's will, what we need for each day, daily bread, forgiveness for our sins, and strength when our faith is tempted or put to the test. In the gospel reading, we find another kind of worthy ambition. A father is ambitious for the welfare of his seriously disturbed son, which brings him to Jesus and his disciples. When Jesus says to him, 'Everything is possible for anyone who has faith', he displays a further ambition: 'I do have faith. Help the little faith I have.' He is ambitious for the deepening of his faith. At the end of the gospel reading, Jesus suggests a further worthy ambition for his disciples. When they ask why they were not able to heal the boy, Jesus says to them, 'This is the kind that can only be driven out by prayer', suggesting that they need to have an ambition to be more prayerful. Today's readings might prompt us to pray that our ambition for ourselves and for others would conform to the Lord's ambition for us all.

22 February, Tuesday, Feast of the Chair of Saint Peter
Matthew 16:13–19

In today's gospel reading, Jesus is portrayed as giving Peter a very distinctive role. He is to be the foundation stone of the Church, the community of believers, holding it together in unity. He is given keys, symbolic language for some kind of authoritative role in the Church. The language of binding and loosing suggests the nature of this authoritative role. It is a teaching role with the authority to declare which elements of Jesus' teaching are binding and which are not. Peter is to interpret the message of Jesus for the Church. Within our own Roman Catholic tradition, we consider this role of Peter to reside in the bishop of Rome, the pope. In every age the Church looks to the pope as the focal point of unity for all disciples of the Lord and as the authoritative interpreter of the message of Jesus for the Church and the world. There have been good and bad popes in the history of the Church. In recent decades we have been very fortunate to have popes who have been faithful to the role given to Peter in today's gospel reading. Jesus was willing to give Peter this role because Peter had displayed a deep insight into the identity of Jesus: 'You are the Christ, the Son of the living God'. This was a God-given insight, because, as Jesus said to him, 'It was not flesh and blood that revealed this to you but my Father in heaven.' Peter's unique understanding of Jesus was the basis of the authoritative role Jesus went on to give him. Whereas Peter's role was unique, the question of Jesus is addressed to us all: 'Who do you say I am?' It is a very personal question asked of each one of us, a question that calls us to renew our faith in Jesus, recognising him as Son of God and Lord of our life. Such a faith insight into Jesus is always God-given; it is the work of the Holy Spirit in our lives. It is the Spirit who leads us to the complete truth about Jesus. In so far as we come to know Jesus as he truly is, our own faith will be authoritative, in that it will empower others to believe. As our own relationship with the Lord deepens, the Lord will work through us to lead others to him.

23 February, Wednesday, Seventh Week in Ordinary Time
Mark 9:38–40

There is a great deal of human wisdom in the letter of James. In today's first reading James says to those who are making all sorts of plans for the future, 'You never know what will happen tomorrow ... the most you should say is, "If it is the Lord's will, we shall still be alive to do this or that".' The Covid-19 pandemic taught us how unpredictable the future can be for all of us. We could never have imagined such a massive and prolonged disruption to our normal way of living. Many of us learned during that time to appreciate all that is of value in our lives that we might previously have taken for granted. In his letter to the Philippians Saint Paul wrote, 'whatever is true, whatever is honourable, whatever is just, whatever is pure, whatever is pleasing, whatever is commendable, if there is any excellence and if there is anything worthy of praise, think about these things'. The time of pandemic may have helped many of us to become more aware of all that Paul refers to. In the gospel reading, Jesus calls on his disciples to recognise whatever is commendable, whatever is worthy of praise, even if it is to be found beyond their own narrow circle. The disciples wanted to stop someone trying to do a work of healing in Jesus' name because he wasn't one of Jesus' disciples. Jesus had a very different perspective from that of his disciples. He appreciated the working of the Holy Spirit wherever it was to be found, recognising that 'the Spirit blows where it wills'. We are all invited to recognise and rejoice in whatever is commendable and worthy of praise, wherever it is to be found.

24 February, Thursday, Seventh Week in Ordinary Time
Mark 9:41–50

Jesus sometimes spoke in a way that was intended to shock people, and today's gospel is an example of that kind of speech, with its reference to cutting off hands and feet and tearing out eyes. Jesus is referring to those faults and shortcomings that are very close to us, so close that they can be depicted as parts of our bodies. He is concerned with forces within ourselves that lead us astray and need to be dealt with. Jesus spoke initially about the possibility of any one of us leading others astray, becoming an obstacle to bring down one of these little ones, in the language of the gospel reading. He then goes on to speak about the very real danger of leading ourselves astray, allowing forces within us to shape our lives in ways that lead us away from God. The implication is that if we don't allow ourselves to be led astray we will be less likely to lead others astray. How we are in ourselves determines how we relate to others. Jesus goes on to use a further image or metaphor, that of salt. 'Have salt in yourselves.' Far from causing others to fall, we are to be like salt in the community, preserving and enhancing what is best in others. Jesus recognises in that gospel reading that salt can become insipid, losing its ability to preserve and flavour. That is the danger that Jesus is warning us against. A small quantity of salt can flavour a large amount of food. Jesus is suggesting that a relatively small number of faithful disciples can have a huge impact for good in the world.

25 February, Friday, Seventh Week in Ordinary Time
Mark 10:1–12
In today's first reading, James makes reference to the patience of Job. The phrase 'the patience of Job' has made its way into mainstream English. At the beginning of the book of Job, Job experiences great affliction, losing property, family members and his own personal well-being. In the midst of it all, he remains faithful to God and loving to others. In that first reading, James refers to the patience of Job to encourage members of the community to be patient with each other, not to be constantly making complaints about each other. James goes on to declare that the Lord is kind and compassionate. Our patience with each

other's failings is a reflection of the Lord's patience with us, his kindness towards us and his compassion for us in our distress and our failings. The Lord who is kind, compassionate and patient towards us also has high ideals for us, and that is highlighted by today's gospel reading. Jesus' vision for marriage is of a man and woman coming together in love and remaining one in love for life. Such a vision was not compatible with the Jewish divorce law of the time, which allowed a man to divorce his wife on sometimes very flimsy grounds. The Lord's vision for our lives is demanding, but it is a vision that is worthy of our dignity as human beings created in God's image, and that is possible for us if we rely on the Lord's help. When we fall short of the Lord's vision for our lives, he is patient with us, full of kindness and compassion towards us. Yet he will continue to hold out his vision for our lives, a vision of a love between human beings that reflects God's love for us. It is a vision worth striving for, even if we fail to live up to it many times in the course of our life journey.

26 February, Saturday, Seventh Week in Ordinary Time
Mark 10:13–16

The scene in today's gospel reading is one of my favourite scenes in all of the gospels. The interaction between parents, children, Jesus and the disciples has always intrigued me. Parents try to bring their children to Jesus for him to bless them. Jesus' disciples try to prevent the parents from doing this. Jesus indignantly rebukes his disciples and insists that the children be allowed to come to him. He then pointedly tells his disciples that unless they become like the very children they are turning away from Jesus they will not enter the kingdom of God. Finally, Jesus does what he and the children's parents wanted; he puts his arms around the children, lays his hands on them and gives them his blessing. Jesus showed more respect for the children and their parents than his disciples did. It is a gospel passage that reveals, beyond any doubt, just how important children were to Jesus. If his ministry was primarily to adults, children meant a great deal to him nonetheless. He was clear that they were as entitled to receive God's blessing from him as any adult. Jesus' conviction of this was not the norm in that culture where children were valued more as adults in waiting than for themselves. On the social scale of the time, they were just above slaves. Today's gospel reading calls on us to share Jesus' desire to bring children into the realm of God's blessing. As followers of Jesus, we are to be channels of God's blessing to our children, mediating God's life-giving love to them all.

28 February, Monday, Eighth Week in Ordinary Time
Mark 10:17–27

The opening words of Jesus' reply to the rich man in today's gospel reading has always intrigued me. The man addressed Jesus as 'Good master', and in reply Jesus says to him, 'Why do you call me good? No one is good but God alone.' Jesus seems to be saying that not even he can fully express the goodness that is God. Yet, we believe that Jesus is the fullest revelation of God's goodness possible in a human life. On the basis of what Jesus says, we would have to hold that there is even more to God's goodness than Jesus has revealed. If Jesus is the fullest revelation of God's goodness in a human life, we are all called to reveal something of God's goodness in our own lives. The man who ran up to Jesus with his burning question was clearly a good man. He declared to Jesus that, from his earliest days, he had kept all of God's commandments that Jesus quoted. The commandments Jesus quoted concern how we relate to others; they are the second section of the Ten Commandments. The first section of the Ten

Commandments concern how we relate to God, the very first commandment being that we should have no other god than the Lord God. This is where the man left something to be desired. He was very attached to his wealth, he served his wealth, it had become something of a god for him; he couldn't leave it when Jesus asked him to. Jesus saw his predicament as one to which we are all prone. That is why Jesus turned to his disciples after the man left to warn them of the powerful attraction of possessions. The first commandment is perhaps the hardest of all to live by. We are all prone to allowing something less than the one, true God to become god in our lives.

1 March, Tuesday, Eighth Week in Ordinary Time
Mark 10:28–31

Today's gospel reading follows immediately after the scene where the rich man walked away sad from Jesus because he was unable to respond to Jesus' call to leave everything and follow him. Seeing this, Peter, at the beginning of today's gospel reading, asks Jesus, 'What about us? We have left everything and followed you.' Peter and the other disciples did not have as much to leave as that man who had initially run up to Jesus and who is described as a man of great wealth. Peter, Andrew, James, John and even Matthew the tax collector were not men of great wealth, yet they did leave everything to follow Jesus. Peter, Andrew, James and John left their fishing business and Matthew left his tax-collecting business. They left their livelihoods to follow Jesus. Jesus did not ask everyone he met to leave everything to follow him. Mary and Martha were followers of Jesus and they had their own home where they offered Jesus hospitality. Yet everyone who wants to follow Jesus has something to leave. We all have something in our lives that can and does hinder us from living as the Lord's followers.

It might be some excessive attachment, or some habit that draws us away from the path the Lord wants us to take, the path of life. Leaving and following go together. However, the more important movement is following, following the one who has come that we may have life and have it to the full. If we follow him joyfully and rely on his daily presence to us, then we will find the freedom to leave whatever we need to leave so as to keep following him more closely.

2 March, Ash Wednesday
Matthew 6:1–6, 16–18

The first line of the first reading for the season of Lent is in the form of an invitation from God, 'Come back to me with all your heart, fasting, weeping, mourning … turn to the Lord your God again, for he is all tenderness and compassion.' We are hearing there the fundamental call of Lent. The call involves firstly a recognition that we are sinners, that in various ways we have turned away from God. It also involves a recognition that the God we have turned away from is a God of tenderness and compassion who longs for our return. In today's second reading Saint Paul goes further and reminds us that the God from whom we have turned away has sought us out and continues to seek us out in the person of his Son Jesus. 'For our sake, God make the sinless one into sin, so that in him we might become the goodness of God.' What a powerful statement that is! God sent his Son to become like us so that we might become like God. God in his Son journeyed towards our sinful condition so that we might journey towards God's goodness. The ashes that we wear on this day tell the world that we are sinners. Yet, those ashes we received are in the shape of a cross, which proclaims that we believe in a God whose love is stronger than our sin. As Paul declares in his letter to the Romans, 'God demonstrates his love for us, in that while we still were sinners, Christ died for us.' The three practices of almsgiving, prayer and fasting that Jesus speaks about in the gospel reading are three traditional ways of responding to God's love for us in Christ, three ways of journeying towards God who has journeyed towards us. They are three ways of responding to that call of God at the beginning of the first reading, 'Come back to me with all your heart'. These three Lenten practices are closely interlinked. Fasting is in the service of prayer and almsgiving. We die to ourselves so as to live more fully towards God and our fellow human beings.

3 March, Thursday after Ash Wednesday
Luke 9:22–25

Sometimes the shortest phrases or sentences can be the most powerful and thought provoking. There is a powerful short phrase in today's first reading, 'Choose life'. In recent times we have tended to set pro-choice and pro-life over against each other. However, this phrase, 'choose life', brings them together. To be human is to choose; in that sense there is no alternative to being pro-choice. The only real question is, 'What am I to choose?' Today's first reading calls on us to choose the supreme value in God's eyes, which is 'life'. It goes on to identify choosing life with living in the love of the Lord, obeying his voice, clinging to him. To choose life is to choose God. In the words of the reading, 'in this your life consists'. In choosing God we choose life, because God is the God of life, the giver of life, the source of all life. For us Christians, choosing God means choosing God's Son, Jesus. In the gospel reading, Jesus says that those who follow him, who choose him, will save their life. If we love the Lord, cling to him, follow him, we will find life. Jesus acknowledges that following him will often require us to renounce ourselves, to lose our life, to take up our cross. Following the Lord will often mean dying to our tendency to put ourselves and our own well-being first, so as to be freer to give ourselves in love to others, putting their well-being before our own. This was the way of the Lord and it is the way that his Spirit within us inspires us to take. The dying involved in taking this way will always bring life to ourselves and to others. In taking this way, we will be choosing life.

4 March, Friday after Ash Wednesday
Matthew 9:14–15

In the gospel reading, Jesus says to those who criticise his disciples for not fasting that his ministry is not the time for fasting. Why is it not the time for fasting? It is because Jesus' short public ministry was too joyful a moment in God's dealings with humanity. It had something of the quality of a wedding celebration. Jesus, the bridegroom, expects those who attend on him to be joyful rather than mournful. He asks, 'Surely the bridegroom's attendants would never think of mourning as long as the bridegroom is still with them?' There would come a time when the bridegroom would be taken away, when Jesus would be put to death. That would be a time of mourning, and fasting would be appropriate. However, that time of mourning would be short-lived. On the third day after his crucifixion Jesus would be raised from the dead and the celebratory mood of his public ministry would be restored. Indeed, it would be greatly enhanced, because from now on death would have no power over Jesus. It is worth reminding ourselves that even in this season of Lent we are living in the light of that first Easter. There is a place for fasting in the Christian life but it shouldn't be of such a nature that it leaves us and others miserable. The bridegroom is still very much with us and he is constantly inviting us to the wedding feast of the Lamb. In the first reading, Isaiah reinterprets the Jewish practice of fasting as fasting from all forms of behaviour that are detrimental to others and, more positively, being proactive in regard to the full human flourishing of others. It means 'to break unjust fetters ... to let the oppressed go free ... to share your bread with the hungry and shelter the homeless poor'. The practice of fasting has morphed into the Jewish practices of almsgiving, acts of justice and loving kindness that serve the well-being of others. Jesus would agree with Isaiah that this is the kind of fasting that is always in season and that we are all called to practise every day.

5 March, Saturday after Ash Wednesday
Luke 5:27–32

The question of the Pharisees and their scribes to Jesus reveals what they thought of tax collectors, 'Why do you eat and drink with tax collectors and sinners?' 'Sinners' were those who were perceived as regularly breaking God's Law, and tax collectors were presumed to be among this group. From the perspective of those who thought of themselves as religious at the time, Jesus was keeping strange company. He was living on the religious margins, and he was calling people from these margins, such as Levi, to belong to the group he was gathering around him to share in his work in a special way. Jesus responded to his critics by declaring that his primary concern was to heal the sick, the spiritually sick as well as the physically sick, and to call sinners back home to God. A few chapters later in Luke's Gospel, the same criticism would be levied against Jesus by the Pharisees and the scribes, this time in the form of a statement rather than a question. 'This fellow welcomes sinners and eats with them.' On that occasion, Jesus responded to the criticism by telling the parables of the lost sheep, the lost coin and the lost sons. The younger son had sinned spectacularly against heaven and before his father, yet, the father never lost hope that he would come back home and he scanned the horizon for his return, seeing him 'while he was still far off'. Jesus was very aware of those who were 'far off', on the spiritual edge. He had a special desire to seek them out and assure them that God continued to love them. We can all find ourselves far off from God from time to time, having gone our own way. Today's gospel reading assures us that, even when we are far off, we are never far from the Lord's heart. He is always calling us home. Indeed, he does more; he invites himself to our table in the hope that we will accept his self-invitation.

7 March, Monday, First Week of Lent
Matthew 25:31–46

It is striking how many times in the gospels Jesus identifies himself with others, especially with those who would have been considered without status or honour in his culture, such as children. On one occasion he said, 'whoever welcomes one such child in my name welcomes me, and whoever welcomes me welcomes not me but the one who sent me'. On another occasion he said to his own disciples, 'whoever welcomes you, welcomes me, and whoever welcomes me welcomes the one who sent me'. His disciples, for the most part, would not have been among the powerful and honourable of the time. In today's gospel, Jesus identifies himself with the hungry, the thirsty, the stranger, the naked, the sick and the imprisoned. Jesus seems to be saying to us that he comes to us in a special way through the brokenness, vulnerability and lowliness of others. He is also implying that he comes to others through our own brokenness and vulnerability. The two groups in today's gospel reading were assessed very differently but each group asked the same series of questions, 'When did we see you hungry ... ?' One group was serving the Lord without realising it and the other group was neglecting the Lord without realising it. We often don't recognise the Lord in the brokenness and suffering of life, whether it is the brokenness and suffering of others or our own. Today's gospel reading invites us to become more aware of the Lord's presence in weakness, vulnerability, failure and distress.

8 March, Tuesday, First Week of Lent
Matthew 6:7–15
In the gospel reading Jesus contrasts the prayer he gives to his disciples with the babbling of pagans. The reference is to pagans who seek to manipulate the gods by an abundance of words and sounds. Jesus reveals a God who cannot be manipulated or controlled in that way. On the contrary, in coming before God we open ourselves to God, we surrender before God. That attitude towards God is at the core of the prayer that Jesus gives us in today's gospel reading, which is in many ways a prayer of surrender. In that prayer Jesus teaches us to pray for the coming of God's kingdom, not ours, the doing of God's will on earth, not ours. He teaches us to recognise our dependence on God for what is most important, forgiveness for our sins, sustenance for body and soul, strength when evil puts us to the test or tempts us. It is a prayer that acknowledges who we are in relation to God, sons and daughters of a loving Father who desires all that is best for us. In some ways, it is a prayer of trust. It is only to someone we fully trust that we could say, 'your kingdom come, your will be done'. As well as being a prayer of surrender and trust, it is also a prayer of petition. Jesus is showing us what to ask for when we come before God in our need. All our prayers of petition are to be shaped in some way by this primordial prayer of petition. It is also

a prayer of intercession. It is a prayer that is prayed in the plural, not the singular. We address God as our Father. We ask our Father to forgive all of us our sins, to give all of us our daily bread and to stand by all of us when evil lurks at the door and tests us. It is a communal prayer; we are praying for one another. The language of the prayer is 'our', 'us' and 'we'. Here is a prayer which is at the same time a lesson on how to pray, coming from the one Teacher.

9 March, Wednesday, First Week of Lent
Luke 11:29–32

In the gospel reading Jesus remarks on the fact that even though he is greater than Solomon and Jonah, Solomon and Jonah drew a greater response than Jesus was drawing. They both received a more impressive hearing than Jesus did. The first reading is from the prophet Jonah. Rather than a series of messages, as are most of the prophetic books, this prophetic book is a very engaging and often amusing story. Jonah was a reluctant prophet, but God kept pushing him to go to the Ninevites, Israel's traditional enemies. Eventually, Jonah had no choice but to preach the message of God's loving favour to them. The response of the Ninevites to Jonah's message was extraordinary. Everyone from the king down – including the animals! – put on sackcloth and ashes and renounced their sinful behaviour. The author of this book was reminding the people of Israel that the Spirit of God can move in the hearts of people beyond the boundaries of Israel. This was at a time when the people of Israel were tending to turn in on themselves in a self-congratulatory way and away from the sinful nations. The author was saying that God was not the God of Israel in any narrow sense, but that God's reach extended to all of humanity, including Israel's enemies. Just as the pagan Ninevites responded to a Jewish prophet, so the pagan Queen of

Sheba responded to the Jewish king, Solomon. Jesus too revealed a God who wanted to draw together all the nations. Like Jonah, he came not just for Israel but for all humanity. He is greater than Jonah in that through his life, death and resurrection he drew people to himself from north, south, east and west, and he became the cornerstone of a new spiritual temple in which the distinction between Jew and non-Jew, slave and free, male and female was no longer significant. We are all part of that spiritual temple, and we are invited to keep looking to Jesus as one who is greater than all the wise people and prophets that came before him or have come after him.

10 March, Thursday, First Week of Lent
Matthew 7:7–12
The first reading is one of the great prayers of petition in the Jewish Scriptures. Esther prays to God out of a sense of deep distress and isolation, 'Reveal yourself in the time of our distress … for I am alone and have none but you, Lord.' It is often when our need is greatest that we petition God with the greatest urgency. The really difficult moments in life reveal to us our vulnerability, our need for help beyond ourselves. In the gospel reading, Jesus encourages us to petition God, not just when our need is desperate but at all times. He literally says, 'Keep on asking … keep on searching … keep on knocking'. Our prayer of petition will not always be responded to by God in the way that we hoped. Saint Paul pleaded with the Lord repeatedly to take from him what he calls a 'thorn in the flesh'. His prayer was not answered as he had hoped; he was left with his 'thorn', yet his prayer was not in vain either. Through petitioning the Lord Paul came to realise that God was working powerfully through this thorn in his flesh. God's power was being made perfect in weakness, as Paul said. Even when our prayer of

petition is not answered in the way we want, it is never in vain. Our prayer of petition will always open us up to the Lord's working in our lives. In that sense, when we ask we will always receive, and when we knock the door will always be opened. God gives what the gospel reading calls 'good things' to those who petition him in prayer. In today's responsorial psalm, the psalmist prays, 'On the day I called, you answered; you increased the strength of my soul'. When we petition God out of our need, God will always strengthen our soul. In the words of Saint Paul, we will be strengthened in our 'inner being with power through his Spirit'.

11 March, Friday, First Week of Lent
Matthew 5:20–26
In today's gospel reading, Jesus speaks about virtue. He calls for a virtue that goes deeper than the virtue of the scribes and the Pharisees. The Jewish Law embodied virtuous ways of living and relating to others. However, Jesus has come to form in people a virtue that is more radical than the virtue of the Jewish Law. He seeks a virtue that is more deeply rooted in the human heart. The adjective 'radical' is from the Latin word for 'root'. Jesus gives an example of this more radical or more deeply rooted virtue in today's gospel reading. Whereas the Jewish Law prohibits someone from taking the life of another person, Jesus prohibits the deeply rooted anger that finds its most deadly expression in the killing of someone. The first act of killing mentioned in the Bible, Cain's killing of Abel, sprang from anger. Cain was angry with his brother. Jesus is concerned about human behaviour. He often speaks about the need to do the will of his heavenly Father. However, he is even more concerned about the deep-seated emotions and the underlying attitudes that give rise to behaviour. Jesus wants to renew the human heart, knowing that from such

deep-seated renewal a new way of living will arise, one that conforms to God's will for our lives. Jesus came to pour the very Spirit of God into our lives, into our hearts, so that we can live as God desires us to live. The ultimate source of the deeper virtue that Jesus calls for is the Holy Spirit. Each day we need to keep praying, 'Come Holy Spirit, fill my heart, renew my heart.' Then, the face of the earth will begin to be renewed.

12 March, Saturday, First Week of Lent
Matthew 5:43–48

We have all been noticing a stretch in the evenings in recent weeks. The days are noticeably getting longer. The sun is rising earlier and setting later. The sun does not discriminate between people. In whatever part of the world it shines, it shines on all. Jesus was very observant of nature; it often spoke to him of God and of God's relationship to us. In today's gospel reading, Jesus speaks of God our Father in heaven causing his sun to shine on bad people as well as good. The sun shining on all spoke to Jesus of the indiscriminate nature of God's love. Just as the sun cannot but shine, even when there are clouds in the sky, so God cannot but love and that is because, as the first letter of Saint John says, 'God is love'. There is no more or less in God's love. God does not love us more at some time in our lives than in others and God does not love some people more than others. God's love is constant and unconditional and makes no distinctions between people. According to Jesus, this is what God's perfection consists in. When he says in today's gospel reading, 'your heavenly Father is perfect', he is really saying, 'God is perfect Love'. We don't have to make God love us. God's love is always shining upon us, even in the dark times of our lives, when the storm gathers. What today's gospel reading calls upon us to do is to receive this unconditional, indiscriminate love of God and then to reflect it to others. We are to be perfect in the way God is perfect, to love in the way God loves, and this means loving the bad as well as the good, loving our enemies as much as we love our friends. Jesus calls on us to be nothing less that God-like in our love of others. It is an extra-ordinary calling and we can answer it only with the help that only God can give, with the help of God's Spirit, the Holy Spirit. We need to keep on receiving the Spirit of God's love, the Holy Spirit, if we are to love others with the love of God, in the way God loves them.

14 March, Monday, Second Week of Lent
Luke 6:36–38

In today's gospel reading we find a number of short, pithy, memorable sayings of Jesus, including, 'Give, and there will be gifts for you.' Jesus is suggesting that when we give to others, we will usually receive more than we give. It is as if giving to others opens up a space in our lives for God to be generous with us. Jesus is the supreme example of his own teaching, 'Give, and there will be gifts for you.' He gave everything for others out of love, even to the point of accepting death on a cross. His self-emptying gift of himself resulted in gifts being given to him by God and through him to all of humanity. God raised Jesus to new life and in that new life he became the cornerstone of a new spiritual building, the Church, the community of believers. In giving all, he seemed to have lost all, yet, in reality, he had gained all. At times, it can seem that when we give to others, when we serve them in love, we are losing all, we are missing out in some way. In reality, we are always receiving more than we are giving. In giving ourselves to others in loving service, God is giving to us in ways we may not fully understand or appreciate at the time. In the words of the gospel reading, a 'full measure, pressed down, shaken together, and running over' is being poured into our lap. Our giving to others always involves some kind of dying to ourselves, yet that dying is life-giving both for ourselves and others. As Jesus says elsewhere, the seed that falls to the ground and dies bears much fruit, or, as Saint Paul says in his second letter to the Corinthians, 'the one who sows bountifully will also reap bountifully'.

15 March, Tuesday, Second Week of Lent
Matthew 23:1–12

We haven't tended to interpret Jesus' words in today's gospel reading literally. He says, 'you must call no one on earth your father', yet we speak of our male parent as our father, and within the Roman Catholic tradition, priests have been called 'father'. Jesus also says, 'nor must you allow yourselves to be called teachers', yet we refer to those who impart knowledge in our classrooms and lecture halls as teachers. Saint Paul speaks about the presence of teachers in the first local churches. The prohibition of the titles 'father' and 'teacher' is really in the service of a more fundamental point, namely, 'you only have one Father, and he is in heaven', and 'you only have one teacher, the Christ'. We are all sons and daughters of one heavenly Father and we are all pupils or disciples of one teacher, Jesus. This makes for a very egalitarian understanding of Church. Even those with a teaching role in the Church are pupils of Christ, and all of us in the Church, regardless of role, are sons or daughters of God. We are all trying to sit at the feet of the Teacher and we are all trying to live as children of our heavenly Father. There should be no vying for positions within the Church, because, in virtue of our baptism, we all have the same relationship with God and with Jesus, and, anyway, as Jesus says in today's gospel reading, greatness in the Church is defined in terms of service, 'the greatest among you must by your servant'. Within the Church, we are called to serve one another in various ways, so that we enable one another to be faithful disciples of our one teacher and faithful sons and daughters of our one heavenly Father.

16 March, Wednesday, Second Week of Lent
Matthew 20:17–28

Jeremiah's question in today's first reading is one that resonates in every age. 'Should evil be returned for good?' Jeremiah expected the answer 'no' to his question, as would we. However, Jeremiah's own experience did not bear out that answer. He was trying to do good by proclaiming God's word to the people yet all he got in response was 'evil', people's deadly hostility. Jesus was God's goodness personified. He gave expression to that goodness in all he said and did, yet he experienced the terrible evil of death by Roman crucifixion. In today's gospel reading, Jesus warns the twelve that this is the fate that awaits him in Jerusalem. They seem incapable of hearing what he is saying. 'Should evil be returned for good?' Instead of the grim future that Jesus announces, the twelve are envisaging a glorious kingdom, and James and John are pre-booking the best seats in it, through their mother. The other ten are indignant that James and John are getting in ahead of them. Jesus has to bring all of them back down to earth. Jesus continues to proclaim the coming of God's kingdom but it is not a kingdom of this world. He will not be like the 'rulers' and 'great men' 'among the pagans'. Jesus' kingdom is the kingdom of God's all-embracing love of humanity, and powerful people have been experiencing such a kingdom as a threat to their own little fiefdoms. The disciples need to learn that following this kind of king will mean becoming the loving servant of others, after the example of Jesus, and this will entail drinking the cup that he has to drink. Jesus calls all of his disciples, all of us, to share in his self-emptying service of all, without discrimination. This is what constitutes greatness in the kingdom that Jesus is seeking to establish.

17 March, Thursday, Feast of Saint Patrick
Luke 5:1–11

Some time ago I climbed Croagh Patrick for the first time in the company of my sister, Catherine, and brother-in-law, Patrick, who died a few years ago on the feast of Saint Joseph. They both lived in Southern California. Patrick, who was from the United States, was determined to climb Croagh Patrick. He was recovering from cancer at the time, and, in spite of a very bad back, he wanted to make this climb in thanksgiving for having come through his surgery and treatment so well, and also as a prayer of petition for God's ongoing help. We managed to get to the top, just about. The Croagh Patrick climb is one expression of the cult of Saint Patrick that has continued down to our time. We venerate Patrick today because he spent himself in proclaiming the Gospel on this island, bringing Christ to huge numbers of people.

It is evident from his two writings that have come down to us that Patrick came from a reasonably privileged background. His father was a town counsellor who had a comfortable house with many servants. Patrick says that he was born free, of noble rank. Suddenly, his personal and communal landscape changed radically. At the age of sixteen, he was taken captive with others and brought to Ireland. As he says, he found himself among strangers. Gone were his comfortable home, his loving family, his freedom. He was now a slave, with no rights or protection. He was lost, without friend or future. It is hard to imagine the impact of such a traumatic experience on one so young. Yet, as he wrote his Confession in his old age, he recognised the great gifts that came to him during this painful and lonely time of exile. Although his grandfather was a priest, and Patrick had been baptised, he acknowledged that as an adolescent he 'did not know the true God'. He said he had turned away from God. However, in exile, while herding sheep in all kinds of weathers he had the most extraordinary spiritual awakening. Looking back, he spoke of the 'great benefits and graces the Lord saw fit to confer on me in my captivity'. He spoke of the Lord's 'wonderful gifts, gifts for the present and for eternity, which the human mind cannot measure'. He went on to say, 'my faith increased and the spirit was stirred up so that in the course of a single day I could say as many as a hundred prayers, and almost as many in the night'.

Many years later, he finally broke free of his captivity and made his way home to his family. Having been profoundly touched by God in the years since he left his family, he was now sensitive to the presence and the call of God in his life. Some years after returning home, he heard the Lord's call to return to the land of his former captivity to preach the Gospel. He trained for the priesthood and arrived back in Ireland, this time as a free man, or, perhaps more accurately, as the Lord's slave or servant. He spoke of himself now as a 'stranger and exile for the love of God'. He wrote of 'the people to whom the love of God brought me'. His mission in Ireland was fraught with dangers and difficulties of all sorts, including at times opposition from leading members of the Church in Britain who had authorised his mission to Ireland. Yet his two writings are full of a strong sense of God's protective and guiding presence in his life. He was very aware of all the Lord was doing through him, in spite of setbacks. He wrote, 'I am very much in debt to God, who gave me so much grace that through me people should be born again in God and afterwards confirmed.' He asked, 'What return can I make to God for all his goodness to me? What can I say or what can I promise to my Lord since any ability I have comes from him?' Writing towards the end of his life, Patrick could see the many ways the Lord had worked powerfully through his painful experience of exile as an adolescent. Because of that traumatic experience of loss, the Gospel was brought to what Patrick called 'the most remote districts beyond which nobody lives and where nobody had ever come to baptise, to ordain clergy or to confirm the people'.

Patrick's life teaches us to be attentive to the ways that the Lord may be surprisingly present in situations of great struggle that seem devoid of any value at the time. Whereas it is never the Lord's desire that misfortune should befall us, when it does come our way he is always there with us, working among us and within us for our good and the good of others. Perhaps our very vulnerability at such times can make us more attentive to what the Lord may want to say to us. Patrick's experience of exile made him alert to the Lord's call at different moments of his life. Our own experiences of exile and loss, whatever form they may take, can help to make us more alert to the Lord's loving purpose for our lives. Our own personal circumstances may prompt us to place a distance between ourselves and the Lord, just as Peter in the gospel reading asked Jesus to leave him. However, the Lord can turn all the circumstances of our lives, including our failures, to a greater good, if we entrust ourselves to him as Peter did, and as Patrick did.

18 March, Friday, Second Week of Lent
Matthew 21:33–43, 45–46
The parable that Jesus speaks in today's gospel reading is largely a story of rejection. The owner of the vineyard sends two lots

of servants to collect the produce of the vineyard, but they are rejected, and some of them are killed. Then he sends his son in the full expectation that the tenants would respect him, but he too is killed. Jesus was really referring there to his own experience of rejection by many of his contemporaries, a rejection that would eventually end with his crucifixion. He is the stone rejected by the builders that he mentions in the gospel reading. Yet rejection does not have the last word. As Jesus says, quoting one of the psalms, the stone rejected by the builders became the keystone. God raised his rejected Son from the dead and made him the foundation or the keystone of the Church. Any experience of rejection can leave us deflated; we can be tempted to give up. The parable suggests that God is not like that. In the face of rejection, God just keeps working away; he takes the experience of rejection, the rejected stone, and builds something new upon it. We are being reminded that God is always at work, even in the most unpromising of situations. The God of Jesus Christ is the God of life, who works in a life-giving way even in situations of death. Our refusal to receive the Lord's coming, the Lord's presence, does not in any way diminish his energy to work among us for the coming of God's kingdom. God sees rejection as an opportunity to work afresh. Perhaps we all have something to learn from God in this regard.

19 March, Saturday, Feast of Saint Joseph
Luke 2:41–51

On 8 December 2020, Pope Francis issued an apostolic letter called *With a Father's Heart*, in which he recalls the 150th anniversary of the declaration of Saint Joseph as Patron of the Universal Church. To mark the occasion of this apostolic letter, Pope Francis proclaimed a 'Year of Saint Joseph' from 8 December 2020 to

8 December 2021. In the letter, Pope Francis describes Saint Joseph in a number of very striking ways – as a beloved father, a tender and loving father, an obedient father, an accepting father; a father who is creatively courageous, a working father, a father in the shadows. He wrote the letter against the backdrop of the Covid-19 pandemic, which, he says, has helped us to see more clearly the importance of 'ordinary' people who, although far from the limelight, exercise patience and offer hope every day. In this, the pope says, they resemble Saint Joseph, whom he describes as 'the man who goes unnoticed, a daily, discreet and hidden presence', yet who played 'an incomparable role in the history of salvation'. It is true that Joseph is a discreet presence in the Gospel story. He doesn't feature at all during the public ministry of Jesus, suggesting that he may have died before Jesus began his public ministry. However, he was there during the crucial formation years of Jesus' life. Like any parent, he worried about his young son growing up. In today's gospel reading, we find Joseph and Mary worried when they discovered their son was lost. When they finally found him, the young Jesus said to them, 'Did you not know that I must be busy with my Father's affairs?' When Jesus said, 'my Father', he was referring to God, not Joseph. Joseph had to learn to let go of his son to God's plan for his life, even though that often left him confused, as in today's gospel reading: 'they did not understand what he meant'. Joseph had an important role to play in Jesus' life, but he had to let him go to God from Jesus' early years. Joseph's life reminds us that we all have some role to play in God's greater purpose. There is something we can do that no one else can do. We are often called to be a Joseph figure for others, being there for them but knowing when to let them go to God's purpose for their lives.

21 March, Monday, Third Week of Lent
Luke 4:24–30

There is quite a lot of anger in today's readings. In the first reading, the king of Israel is enraged because he thinks that the king of Syria is trying to pick a quarrel with him by sending Naaman to him to be healed of his leprosy. It was the prophet Elijah who persuaded the king to move beyond his anger, declaring that he, Elijah, could cure Naaman of his leprosy. When Elijah asks Naaman to bathe seven times in the River Jordan, it is Naaman's turn to fly into a rage. It was his servants who persuaded him to move beyond his anger and do what Elijah asked of him. In the gospel reading, the people of Nazareth are enraged because Jesus identifies himself with Elijah and Elisha, two prophets who ministered to individuals beyond the boundaries of Israel. On this occasion, there was no one present to persuade the people of Nazareth to move beyond their anger and listen carefully to Jesus. They wanted to throw Jesus to his death, but Jesus somehow managed to slip away. We can be angry for various reasons, but it isn't always right to act out our anger. We are blessed if we have people around us who help us to see that our anger is propelling us in a direction that won't serve us well. Jesus' way of revealing God often made people angry. He proclaimed a God who welcomes all sorts, sinners and tax collectors, people from outside Israel, even from Israel's traditional enemies, such as the Syrians. In the parable of the prodigal son, the older son was angry that his father was throwing a feast for his younger, rebellious, son. The older son was being asked to journey into the father's unconditional love. It is a journey we are all asked to make. We are asked to accept a God who passionately loves those we find very difficult to love, and then to reveal something of that indiscriminate love of God in our lives.

22 March, Tuesday, Third Week of Lent

Matthew 18:21–35

It can be helpful to pay attention to the questions that we find on the lips of the gospel characters, whether on the lips of Jesus or of those with whom he interacts. Today's gospel begins with one such question, on the lips of Peter. He asks Jesus, 'Lord, how often must I forgive my brother if he wrongs me?' It is a question that Jesus' teaching on the importance of forgiveness must have moved him to ask. Is there a limit to forgiveness? Peter proposes an answer to his own question: 'seven times'. In the Jewish tradition, the number 'seven' was the symbol of perfection. Peter must have been confident that the answer 'seven' would have been acceptable to Jesus. Instead, Jesus answers, 'not seven but seventy-seven times'. Poor old Peter was probably sorry he asked the question in the first place! As so often, Jesus explains himself by telling a story. The first part of the story is one of limitless forgiveness. The amount the servant owed the master was astronomical. He asked for time to pay it back, but several lifetimes would not have been long enough to pay it back. The master simply cancels the debt. Jesus is suggesting that there is nothing calculating about God's forgiveness. If we ask for it, God grants it, even though our debt to God, the weight of our sin, is enormous. The second part of the parable suggests that receiving God's boundless forgiveness requires us to pass on that forgiveness to others. In this, the servant failed. A lower-ranking servant asked for time to pay off a small debt; it could easily have been paid off over time, but time wasn't given to him. Forgiveness was denied. If God gives forgiveness when we ask for it, we must stand ready to freely pass on God's forgiveness when others ask for it of us.

23 March, Wednesday, Third Week of Lent
Matthew 5:17–19

In today's gospel reading, Jesus declares that he has not come to abolish the Law or the Prophets but to complete them. Jesus recognised all that was good and valuable in his own Jewish tradition; he came to enhance and complete that goodness and value. He didn't found a new religious movement from zero. He came to bring his Jewish tradition to a full flowering. Jesus was sensitive to the thread of grace in the story of his own people. He was aware that the Holy Spirit had always been at work in his own religious tradition. This same Spirit now filled Jesus' life and his desire was to pour out that Spirit afresh on all. Jesus teaches us to respect what is good in our own past religious tradition. It is true that the Church is always in need of renewal. There is much in the Church's past that we can be rightly critical of, yet there is also much that is good and valuable in the story of the Church. In the course of the Church's history, holiness and sin are to be found side by side. What is true of the Church's past is true of the Church's present. Jesus' parable of weeds sown in a field of good wheat suggests as much. Yet the message of Jesus is that the weeds will not choke the wheat in the end. Saint Paul puts it very succinctly when he says that where sin abounds, grace abounds all the more. The Spirit that filled the life of Jesus is at work in the Church today, and in our own lives as members of the Church. Our calling is to allow the Spirit to guide us, to shape us, to enlighten us, so that all that is good and valuable in our Church's tradition and in our personal tradition can be brought to completion in our own time and place.

24 March, Thursday, Third Week of Lent
Luke 11:14–23

We are all aware from experience that different people can see the same reality and, yet, interpret it in very different ways. In today's gospel reading, Jesus gives speech to a man who had been dumb. When some of the people saw this, they were amazed. They recognised the presence of what Jesus calls 'the finger of God'. When others saw Jesus' healing, they had a very different response. They concluded that the power at work in his ministry was an evil power; they saw the hand of Satan rather than the finger of God. The gospel reading invites us to ask, 'How sensitive am I to the presence of God, to the working of the Lord?' Jesus' use of the expression 'finger of God' is intriguing. We use our fingers to attend to the details of life. Jesus is perhaps suggesting that God is present in the details of life. God can even be present in those aspects of life that we might be tempted to dismiss as completely negative. Saint Paul once referred to a thorn in his flesh. His perspective on this aspect of his life was completely negative; he referred to it as a messenger of Satan. He pleaded with the Lord to be rid of it. Yet, in his prayer, he heard the Lord say to him, 'my power is made perfect in weakness'. He came to see that the Lord was working powerfully through something he had dismissed as coming from Satan. He recognised that what he had considered an evil was in reality a blessing. There is no indication in the gospel reading that those who dismissed what Jesus was doing as the work of Satan subsequently came to recognise there the finger of God. The Lord can come to us in ways we do not always expect and, as a result, we can fail to recognise him. Like Paul, it is often only when we bring some situation to the Lord in prayer that we begin to see how the Lord may be at work there.

25 March, Friday, Feast of the Annunciation
Luke 1:26–38
There is a lot of very concrete information at the beginning of today's gospel reading: Galilee, Nazareth, Joseph of the house

of David, Mary. There is reference to a very particular place, Nazareth in Galilee, and to a very particular couple in that place, Joseph and his betrothed, Mary. It was that particular couple in that particular place at a particular moment in time whom God chose in a special way for the sake of all of humanity. It was to that couple in that place at that time that God's Son was entrusted for all of us. The gospel reading concludes with the confident declaration, 'Nothing is impossible to God.' Yet the one thing that God cannot do is force our consent. God's purpose for our lives was dependent on the consent of this particular woman in this particular place at a particular moment in history, and on the consent of her spouse, Joseph. Mary's consent to God's messenger allowed God's purpose to come to pass for all of us. In a certain sense, at the moment of the annunciation, Mary represented us all; we all waited for her to say 'yes' to God on all our behalf. All of humanity's deepest aspirations were focused on this particular woman, place and time. At the annunciation, God's call met with the complete human response, 'Let what you have said be done to me.' Luke is here presenting Mary as the exemplary disciple, the one who hears the word of God and keeps it. Because of her exemplary response to God, she became a source of blessing for all of humanity. If we can enter in some way into her response to God's call, we too will be a source of blessing for others.

26 March, Saturday, Third Week of Lent
Luke 18:9–14
How we pray can say a great deal about the kind of person we are. Today's parable is a story of two men who prayed in the Temple. The prayer of the Pharisee was a prayer of thanksgiving. He thanks God for the way he lives his life, recognising God as the source of his good living. It is a perfectly acceptable form of prayer.

However, it had one fatal flaw. In praying, he passed judgement on a fellow worshipper, thanking God that he was not a sinner like the tax collector standing some distance away. In life the Pharisee looked down on the tax collector as his moral inferior and his prayer reflected that judgemental attitude. His prayer displayed a love of God but it was devoid of love for his fellow worshipper, his neighbour. Failing to fulfil what Jesus called the second great commandment, to love our neighbour as ourselves, he failed to live the first commandment, loving God with all his being. The prayer of the tax collector was shorter; it was a prayer of petition in which he acknowledged that he was a sinner and asked God for mercy. He judged himself and nobody else, and in his poverty of spirit he entrusted himself to the loving mercy of God. Jesus declares that it was the tax collector's prayer that was acceptable to God and it was he who went home at rights with God. The parable reminds us that when we come before the Lord in prayer, there is to be no room for comparing ourselves favourably with others, for looking down on others. Rather, we come before the Lord in prayer always aware of our own spiritual poverty and need, entrusting ourselves to the Lord as one who, in the words of today's first reading, can 'bring us back to life'.

28 March, Monday, Fourth Week of Lent
John 4:43–54

In the gospels Jesus is often portrayed as wary of a faith that is dependent on signs and wonders. He never responds to those who ask him for a sign from heaven before they will believe in him. Those who ask him for signs and wonders seem unaware of how Jesus himself is the great sign from God, in all he says and does. The wariness of Jesus before a signs-based faith is reflected in today's gospel reading when he says to the court official who came to ask him to cure his seriously ill son, 'So you will not believe unless you see signs and wonders.' However, the court official immediately demonstrated that he had a faith that was not based on signs and wonders. When Jesus said to him, 'Go home, your son will live', we are told that the court official believed what Jesus had said and started on his way. He believed the word of Jesus, without waiting to see if what Jesus promised would come to pass. Here was a faith that was rooted in the word of Jesus and was not dependent on seeing signs and wonders. The faith of this man represents the kind of faith we are all called to have. We have the word of Jesus in the gospels. We are asked to believe in Jesus on the basis of that word, the inspired account of what Jesus said and did. We listen to the word of the Lord and we respond in faith. We do not ask for a more spectacular sign as a precondition of our faith. The journey of faith will often take us to places that seem barren of any sign of the Lord's presence. It took Jesus to the cross where he cried out, 'My God, my God! Why have you forsaken me?' Yet, no matter where our faith journey takes us, the living word of the Lord will always be our faithful companion, and at every step of that journey we can say with Peter, 'You have the words of eternal life.'

29 March, Tuesday, Fourth Week of Lent
John 5:1–3, 5–16

The paralysed man in the gospel reading seems to have been very alone in his illness. He lay beside a pool in Jerusalem that was believed to have healing properties, if one entered the water after it was disturbed. However, this paralysed man says to Jesus, 'I have no one to put me into the pool when the water is disturbed.' There was never anyone around when he needed to be carried. There was another paralysed man in the gospels who was nowhere near as isolated in his illness as this man. He had four friends who carried him to Jesus, even to the point of creating a hole in the roof above Jesus to lower him down, because the crowds around Jesus were too great. Illness can be very isolating. To be ill without friends is especially isolating. However, Jesus entered this man's isolation, without being invited. He saw him, knew his situation, went over to him and addressed him directly. Having first asked him, 'Do you want to be well again?' Jesus healed this desperate man of his paralysis, without the need to lower him into the water. Jesus befriended him in a manner that no one else had. We are being reminded that when we feel isolated, because of illness or some other reason, the Lord is always by our side, working to raise us up from whatever we are struggling with. Jesus' question to him, 'Do you want to be well again?' may seem strange to our ears. Yet, perhaps Jesus needed to know if he still had the hope of being cured after being ill for so long. The Lord will always respond to our hopes.

30 March, Wednesday, Fourth Week of Lent
John 5:17–30

There is a very striking statement at the beginning of today's gospel reading, 'My Father goes on working, and so do I'. This was in response to the religious leaders who were critical of Jesus for working on the Sabbath by healing the man who had been paralysed for thirty-eight years, at a pool near the Sheep Gate in Jerusalem. The work that Jesus and his Father are always engaged in is that of giving life to others, 'As the Father raises the dead and gives them life, so the Son gives life to anyone he chooses ... For the Father, who is the source of life, has made the Son the source of life.' God goes on working through his Son in a life-giving way. It is reassuring to know that God and the risen Lord go on working to bring life to all. We may not be able to work, for one reason or another. When we do work, we may feel that our work is not bearing any good fruit. Yet God and his Son never cease to work among us and through us. Just as the sun cannot but shine, so God and the Lord cannot but work. The Lord does not rest from his labours on our behalf, no more than a mother rests from her labours on behalf of her child, in the imagery of today's first reading. The Lord calls on each of us to become the instruments of his labour on behalf of others, to allow him to work through us for the present and ultimate well-being of others. If we trust in the Lord, listening to his words, then he will be working through us, even at those times when we seem incapable of much work.

31 March, Thursday, Fourth Week of Lent
John 5:31–47

We are all aware of the increase in daylight in recent weeks. We look forward to more light. In the gospel reading Jesus speaks of John the Baptist as a lamp alight and shining and of those who knew him as enjoying the light that he gave. Jesus is saying that something of God's light shone through John the Baptist. Yet, in this Fourth Gospel, it is only Jesus who is declared to be the light of the world. Jesus does not only reflect the light of God; he is the light of God. The relationship of John the Baptist to Jesus is akin to the relationship between the moon and the sun. Jesus is the source of God's light and John the Baptist reflects this light to others. I was reading the Confession of Saint Patrick recently. Towards the end of that text, Patrick says, 'This sun which we see rises daily at God's command for our benefit, but will never reign, nor will its brilliance endure. Those who worship it will be severely punished. We, on the other hand, believe in and worship Christ the true sun who will never perish, not will anyone who does his will. They will remain for ever as Christ remains for ever.' Patrick wrote those words in a setting where the sun was worshipped. In another of the gospels, Jesus speaks of God who 'makes his sun rise on the evil and on the good'. God has given Jesus, his Son, to all people, without distinction or discrimination. Our calling is to open our lives to God's light shining through God's Son and, like John the Baptist, to reflect something of this light to others, especially to those who live in darkness and the shadow of death.

1 April, Friday, Fourth Week of Lent
John 7:1–2, 10, 25–30
The Book of Wisdom from which our first reading came was written less than a hundred years before the coming of Jesus. It is probably closer to the time of Jesus than any other book of the Old Testament. In our reading, the author places a little speech on the lips of those who were hostile to people of faith, those who took their Jewish faith seriously. They begin by saying, 'Let us lie in wait for the virtuous person'. They go on to say, 'the very sight of him weighs our spirits down'. They conclude by declaring, 'Let us condemn him to a shameful death'. The early church recognised in this speech a prophecy of what was to happen to Jesus. He would be condemned to a shameful death by those who could not stand the sight of him. In today's gospel reading, we sense the growing hostility to Jesus. We are told that the Jewish authorities 'were out to kill him'. As a result, the ordinary people of Jerusalem ask of Jesus, 'Isn't this the man they want to kill?' The gospel reading ends with a reference to Jesus' opponents wanting to arrest him. We might be tempted to ask, 'Why such hostility towards one who is so good? Why are people plotting to kill someone who came so that everyone may have life and have it to the full?' The phenomenon of violence towards the innocent, the just, the good,

is one we will always struggle to make sense of. Goodness does not always have its reward in this life. However, the message of Jesus, and Jesus' life and death, shows us that those who keep trusting in God and remain faithful to his ways will experience God's vindication. God will not ultimately abandon his faithful ones, those who are faithful to the ways of his Son whom he sent into the world for our sakes.

2 April, Saturday, Fourth Week of Lent
John 7:40–52
At the beginning of John's Gospel, Nathanael asked the question in relation to Jesus, 'Can anything good come out of Nazareth?' Something of that same attitude is to be found among the Pharisees at the end of today's gospel reading: 'Prophets do not come out of Galilee.' Both are examples of what we would call prejudice, prejudging someone, judging someone before giving them a fair hearing. This is the criticism that Nicodemus levels against his fellow Pharisees in the gospel reading: 'Surely the Law does not allow us to pass judgment on a man without giving him a hearing and discovering what he is about?' Earlier in John's Gospel, Nicodemus, a leading Pharisee, had given Jesus a hearing, even though he was perplexed by what Jesus said to him. We are all too familiar in our own day with the phenomenon of prejudice and its often very deadly consequences. The temptation to prejudge someone is always real for all of us. We can all find ourselves at times asking the question, 'Can anything good come out of … ?' substituting some place or some other reality for 'Nazareth'. The portrait of Jesus in all the gospels is of someone who, in the words of Nicodemus, gave people a hearing to discover what they were about. That is how the risen Lord relates to each one of us today. He takes it for granted that good can come out of us all, and he

works to bring to pass that potential for good in all of us. This is not only how the Lord relates to us, but it is also how he would like us to relate to each other.

4 April, Monday, Fifth Week of Lent
John 8:12–20

At this time of the year, the days are getting noticeably longer. There is an increasing amount of daylight over darkness. We are aware that with the growing of the light, there is also an increase of life. Many of us feel more alive now that the days are getting longer. Nature is also beginning to come alive again with the longer days and the increase in light. When Jesus speaks about 'the light of life' in today's gospel reading, we have no difficulty recognising the relationship between light and life. Jesus had just declared himself to be 'the light of the world'. He brings the light of God into the world. He reveals God's glory, God's powerful presence, by what he says and what he does, and, especially, by his death and resurrection. Having revealed himself to be the light of the world, he promises that those who follow him will never walk in darkness but will have the light of life. In bringing the light of God into the world, he also brings the life of God into the world. Jesus brings a light and a life from another world into this world. He promises that if we follow him, if we open ourselves, to his presence, then this life-giving light of God will shine upon us. We often pray that eternal light would shine upon those who have died and that they would inherit eternal life. In today's gospel reading Jesus is promising this eternal light and life here and now to those who believe in him and who follow in his way. In and through our relationship with the Lord, we can already begin to experience something of eternal life within this earthly life.

5 April, Tuesday, Fifth Week of Lent
John 8:21–30

In today's first reading, from the Book of Numbers, we are told that the people lost patience on the journey through the wilderness from Egypt to the Promised Land. They were glad to escape slavery in Egypt, but the journey towards freedom was proving difficult. Unlike in Egypt, food and drink were in short supply. The people began to wish they had never left Egypt, 'Why did you bring us out of Egypt to die in the wilderness?' It was a worthwhile journey, but it was also a very testing one. Whenever we set out on a worthwhile personal or communal journey, there will often be times when we wonder if we might have been better off just staying where we had been. 'Why did we leave where we were to set out for something new?' Yet, such moments of questioning, of self-doubt, are not necessarily a sign that we should never have set out in the first place. Any worthwhile journey will bring us face to face with our limitations. Whenever we set out on some journey in response to what we consider to be the Lord's call we will find ourselves being tested. Our faith in the Lord will often be put to the test. Like the people of Israel in the first reading, we will find ourselves asking, 'Why?' Jesus set out on a very significant journey at the moment of his baptism in response to God's call. He was certainly put to the test many times along the way. Yet he could say in today's gospel reading, 'He who sent me is with me, and has not left me to myself.' We can each make our own those words of Jesus. The Lord who prompts us to keep setting out anew on the journey of discipleship is always with us. He does not leave us to ourselves, but sustains us along the way.

6 April, Wednesday, Fifth Week of Lent
John 8:31–42

I have always been struck by that statement of Paul in his second letter to the Corinthians, 'Now the Lord is the Spirit, and where the Spirit of the Lord is, there is freedom.' Paul suggests that the Holy Spirit is the source of true freedom. When we allow the Spirit to shape our lives, when we are led by the Spirit, we enjoy the glorious freedom of the children of God. For Paul, the Holy Spirit is the Spirit of God's love, and the fruit of the Spirit in our lives is love. The person in whom the Spirit bears the fruit of love is the truly free person. If the love of the Spirit came spontaneously to us, then we would be fully free. In that sense, Jesus was the fully free human being, because his whole life was shaped by the Spirit and was one great act of love. Jesus, who gives the Holy Spirit to us, is the source of our true freedom. As he says in the gospel reading, 'if the Son makes you free, you will be free indeed'. The more the Lord lives in us through the Spirit, the freer we will be to love others as the Lord loves us, and such a life of love is a truly free life. Some may be of the view that the closer we come to the Lord, the more we will lose our freedom, the more restricted our life will become. However, the opposite is the case. Jesus frees us to be the person that God created us to be and desires us to be, an image and likeness of God, who is Love. Freedom consists not so much in being free to do what we want, but in being free to do what God wants and desires for us. It is Jesus, through the Spirit, who gives us this freedom.

7 April, Thursday, Fifth Week of Lent
John 8:51–59

The prophet Isaiah speaks of Abraham as the rock from which the people of Israel were hewn. No one in the whole story of the people of Israel was greater than Abraham. The question that the Jewish leaders put to Jesus was almost in disbelief, 'Are you greater than our Father, Abraham?' It was as if they were saying to Jesus, 'You can't seriously be claiming to be greater than our Father, Abraham?' Jesus replied, as one whose Father was God, 'My glory is conferred by the Father.' As Son of God, Jesus is indeed greater than Abraham. As the Son who was with God in the beginning, before anything or anyone was created, Jesus was certainly greater than Abraham. 'Before Abraham ever was, I am'. There was so much more to Jesus than to Abraham. It comes as no surprise that on hearing such talk, the Jewish authorities picked up stones to stone him. The claims that Jesus was making for himself were experienced as a threat to the religious tradition of the time. The claims that Jesus makes for himself in the gospels, especially in the Gospel of John, can never be fully contained by any religious tradition, including our own Christian tradition. There is always more to Jesus than we can give expression to in our own religious tradition. That 'more' need not be experienced as threatening in any way, but rather as a source of consolation. The Lord is more loving, more merciful, more just, more powerful, than we could ever imagine. Because the Lord is more than we could ever imagine him to be, we can entrust ourselves to his care and guidance with total confidence. If we do that, especially when times are dark, we will discover that the Lord will not disappoint us or let us down.

8 April, Friday, Fifth Week of Lent

John 10:31–42

In today's gospel reading Jesus is accused of blasphemy by the Jewish leaders. 'You are only a man and you claim to be God.' That indeed would have been considered blasphemy. Yet that statement expresses the full mystery of Jesus, the mystery of the incarnation. Yes, he is only a man, but he also claims to be God, and not only claims to be so but is so. Jesus is God in human form. We believe that he reveals God to us in a way that no other human being has ever done or will ever do. In the gospel reading Jesus declares, 'Believe in the work I do, then you will know for sure that the Father is in me and I am in the Father.' Jesus was saying, 'Look at the good works I do and then you will recognise that I am God in human form.' Jesus revealed God by what he said, but above all by what he did, by his works. In John's Gospel, from which we are reading this week, the greatest of Jesus' works was his passion and death. It was above all in and through his passion and death that Jesus revealed God most fully, the God who so loved the world that he gave his only Son. As we reflect on the passion and death of Jesus this coming Holy Week we will be looking upon not just a broken human being but upon the fullest human expression of God.

9 April, Saturday, Fifth Week of Lent
John 11:45–56

In today's first reading, the prophet Ezekiel has a vision of God gathering together his scattered people under one king-shepherd, David. Ezekiel's reference to 'one shepherd for all' reminds us of the words of Jesus in John's Gospel, 'There will be one flock, one shepherd', a saying that has inspired the ecumenical movement, especially since the Second Vatican Council. Today's gospel reading, from John's Gospel, suggests that Jesus' death was in the service of this unifying work. The evangelist declares that Jesus died 'to gather together in unity the scattered children of God'. Jesus' death and resurrection were the fullest expression of Jesus' unifying work. Jesus would go on to declare in this gospel, 'When

I am lifted up from the earth, I will draw all people to myself.' According to this gospel, Jesus' death was the revelation of God's love for the world. 'God so loved the world that he gave his only Son.' It was also the complete expression of Jesus' love for his disciples, and, through them, for the world. 'No one has greater love than this, to lay down one's life for one's friends.' The cross was an explosion of love, of God's love for the world through Jesus, and it is in the nature of all authentic love to unite, to create communion, to gather people together. All of the baptised, regardless of their church affiliation, can gather at the foot of the cross in response to the drawing power of Jesus' love. As we allow ourselves to be drawn to Jesus, we will discover that we are drawn closer to each other, we become one in the Lord. This Holy Week we are invited to allow the Lord's love to draw us closer to himself and to those from whom we are estranged in any way.

11 April, Monday in Holy Week
John 12:1–11

In today's gospel reading, Mary, the sister of Lazarus, anoints the feet of Jesus. A few days later, Jesus will wash the feet of his disciples. Mary's service of Jesus, anointing his feet, anticipates the way that Jesus will serve his disciples at the Last Supper. Mary's service of Jesus was her grateful and loving response to Jesus' act of raising her brother Lazarus from the dead. She experienced the Lord's service of her family in a very personal way, and, now she serves the Lord in return. Having received something precious from the Lord, the gift of life for her beloved brother, she now wants to give something precious back to the Lord. Her gift was precious in financial terms. Judas declares that it was worth 300 denarii, which was the equivalent of a year's wages for a day labourer at that time. Jesus appreciated Mary's gift not so much for its financial value, but because of its timely quality. Jesus was just about to enter into his passion and death, and Mary anointed Jesus to strengthen him for this ordeal that lay ahead. As Jesus declares in the gospel reading, 'She had to keep this scent for the day of my burial.' Mary's gesture of loving service was a response to Jesus' loving service of her family, and it strengthened him for his loving service of all humanity that lay ahead, which would cost him his life. The action of Mary portrays what is at the heart of our lives as followers of Jesus. Like her, we too have been graced by Jesus' loving service of us and, like her, we seek to give back to the Lord from what we have received from him. Our lives, in that sense, are to be an act of loving service of the Lord, in gratitude for his service of us.

12 April, Tuesday in Holy Week
John 13:2–33, 36–38

The scene in today's gospel reading has a certain dramatic quality. Immediately after washing the feet of his disciples, Jesus solemnly announces, 'One of you will betray me.' The disciples wondered who Jesus might be talking about. In a final gesture of affection towards Judas, Jesus offers him a piece of bread that he had dipped in the dish. This is the moment when Judas confirms his decision to betray Jesus to the authorities. In the words of the gospel reading, 'Satan entered him'. Judas then left the company of Jesus and the other disciples and went out into the night; he left the company of the light and went out into the darkness. Judas intended to betray Jesus and he did not move from his intention. Peter was also present at the table. He would go on to deny Jesus. However, it is clear from the gospel reading that he never intended to deny Jesus. He declares to Jesus, 'I will lay down my life for you.' With Peter, it was a case of the spirit being willing but the flesh being weak. Judas' spirit was weak. Most of us belong with Peter. We have good intentions but we don't always follow through on them. We want to be faithful to the Lord by what we say and do, but we fall short in various ways. We can take encouragement from Peter's story after his denial of Jesus. The risen Lord appeared to him and gave him the opportunity to renew his faithful love and then gave him an important mission: 'Feed my lambs, feed my sheep.' The Lord comes to us in our own times of weakness, and not only offers us the opportunity to renew our following of him but continues to entrust us with a share in his work.

13 April, Wednesday in Holy Week
Matthew 26:14–25

In today's first reading, the prophet Isaiah speaks of the Lord as giving him a disciple's tongue to reply to the wearied and as waking him every morning to hear, to listen like a disciple. It is the listening like a disciple that allows him to speak like a disciple. A disciple's ear makes possible a disciple's tongue. A disciple was someone who sat the feet of the Master and listened attentively and then lived accordingly. We are all called to be disciples in that sense. We develop a disciple's ear, a readiness to listen ever more deeply to what the Lord is saying to us through his word. As we grow in our listening ability, we will be enabled to speak like a disciple, to have a disciple's tongue, and to live like a disciple. In the gospel reading, the disciples show a willingness to listen like disciples and to put what they hear into practice. Having listened to Jesus' instructions about making preparations for the Passover, they respond fully to those instructions. Yet, as the passion of Jesus unfolds, they will not behave as disciples. Judas will betray Jesus, Peter will deny Jesus publicly and all the other disciples will desert him at the time of his arrest. Jesus entered into communion with them at the last supper, sharing himself with them under the form of bread and wine. Almost immediately afterwards, however, they broke communion with him, some of them in very dramatic fashion. None of us lives as the Lord's disciple all the time. We can all break communion with the Lord, especially when remaining in communion with him becomes costly. Yet the Lord keeps calling us back to listen like a disciple; he continues to offer us a disciple's tongue so that we can reply to the wearied, and he will keep giving us a share in his Spirit to help us in our weakness. All he asks is that we keep returning to him when we lose our way. If we do so, we will always find him waiting for us, for, in the words of today's psalm, 'the Lord listens to the needy'.

Easter Triduum, 14–16 April

18 April, Easter Monday
Matthew 28:8–15
Two emotions are attributed to the women in today's gospel reading in response to the message they heard from the empty tomb that Jesus who had been crucified has been raised from the dead. They were 'filled with awe and great joy'. Easter can continue to generate a sense of awe in us today. The message of Easter is truly awe inspiring. God brought his Son through death into a new and glorious life, a life that allows him to remain with us all to the end of time. As risen Lord, he invites us to draw from his risen strength at every step of our life's journey and when that journey comes to an end he assures us that we will come to share even more fully in his risen life. This awe-inspiring message can continue to give us hope today, especially when we find ourselves in situations that are threatening and disturbing. The second emotion attributed to the women is 'joy'. Even though we might retain something of

the women's sense of awe before the Easter message, we might struggle to share their joy. Many people have little to be happy about. Yet there is a joy that we can experience deep within us, even when we have little reason to be happy in the human sense. This is the joy that Saint Paul says is the fruit of the Holy Spirit. The Spirit is the Spirit of God's love that has been poured into our hearts. The sense of being deeply loved by the Lord, even when life is extremely difficult, can leave us joyful. When Paul wrote to the church in Philippi from prison, his situation at the time was dire; he could have been executed at any time. Yet throughout that letter he says, 'I rejoice', and he calls on the embattled community of disciples in Philippi to rejoice. The source of Paul's joy is that sense he had of the loving nearness of the risen Lord. He gives expression to his sense of the Lord's nearness towards the end of that letter when he says, 'I can do all things through him who strengthens me'. Perhaps we could make those words of Paul our own. As we repeat them to ourselves, we will find ourselves relying more on the Lord and less on ourselves, and that will help to keep us going.

19 April, Easter Tuesday
John 20:11–18
Those who have a back or front garden often consider themselves very fortunate. As the weather improves, it is very therapeutic to go out into the garden and 'potter around', as my father used to say. At this time of the year, gardens are places of new life. Shrubs are coming into bud, grass is beginning to grow and some flowers are starting to show their colour. According to John's Gospel, the tomb where Jesus was buried was in a garden. When the risen Lord appeared to Mary Magdalene near to the empty tomb, she initially thought he must be the gardener. There is some relationship between

the work of the risen Lord and the work of a gardener. The gardener tends the ground so that it bears the life of nature. The risen Lord tends the human person so that he or she bears the life of the Spirit. It was only when this stranger called Mary by her name that she recognised his true identity. He was not the gardener; he was the Lord whose body she had been seeking and for whom she had been weeping. The light of the risen Lord's presence penetrated the darkness of her grief. She would go on to say to the other disciples, 'I have seen the Lord'. Like Mary, we don't always recognise the presence of the Lord in our lives. She was blinded by her grief. We too can be blinded by grief, or anxiety or remorse or despondency. There was something about the way the Lord came to Mary that made her think that he could have been the gardener. The Lord often comes to us in very simple and ordinary guises, calling us by name, as he called Mary by name. We need to pray for eyes to see the Lord's presence and ears to hear his very personal call to us. He comes to us every day as light into our darkness, as he came to Mary in the depths of her loss and grief, and he sends us out to say with our lives, 'I have seen the Lord.'

20 April, Easter Wednesday
Luke 24:13–35

The way the Lord related to the two disciples on the road to Emmaus reflects how he relates to all of us. They were walking in the wrong direction, away from Jerusalem. The Lord walks with us, even when we are walking in the wrong direction. He invites us to tell him our story, and he listens carefully to it. He tries to give us the fuller picture, he helps us to see the crucial bit of the story we may be missing, and, in that way, he prompts us to take a better direction. The Lord always meets us where we are, very often in our brokenness, but he also works to lead us beyond where we are. He listens to and respects the stories we tell, but he is always trying to open us up to that bigger story of God's life-giving work among us. We hear that bigger story in the Scriptures. It was the Scriptures that Jesus opened up for the two disciples in order to tell them that bigger story, which does not end in death, but in glory. We hear and experience that bigger story of the Scriptures, above all, in the Eucharist. It was while he was at table with the two disciples and broke bread with them that their eyes were opened. The Lord journeys with us to lead us towards life, but he needs some openness on our part as well. At a certain moment in the Lord's journey with the two disciples, they took a crucial initiative; they pressed Jesus to stay with them. 'It is nearly evening and the day is almost over.' It was in response to their initiative that the Lord joined them at table. The Lord will always take the initiative towards us but he looks to us to take some initiative towards him. It is significant that the two disciples said, 'Stay with us', and not 'Stay with me'. The initiative we take towards the Lord is always one we take with other disciples. We reach out towards the Lord, who journeys with us in the company of our fellow pilgrims, those who are stumbling along the path of discipleship with us. This Easter season is a good time us all to pray, 'Stay with us, Lord.'

21 April, Easter Thursday
Luke 24:35–48

According to the beginning of today's gospel reading the disciples were talking together about all that had been happening since the women found the tomb of Jesus empty. The two disciples were telling their story of what had happened to them while they were walking to Emmaus. Others were sharing how the Lord had appeared to Simon Peter. It was while they were sharing their experiences of the Lord together that suddenly the risen Lord appeared among them. They didn't have to go looking for him, no more than the two disciples on the road to Emmaus or Simon Peter had to go looking for him. No, the risen Lord looked for them; he came to them; he stood among them, with his greeting 'Peace be with you'. That is how the risen Lord relates to us all. We don't have to go looking for him. He comes to us. He might come to us while we are walking along, like the two disciples on the road to Emmaus; he might come to us while we are grieving, as he came to Mary Magdalene. He might come to us while we are talking with and listening to other disciples, other people of faith, as in today's gospel reading. The risen Lord is always coming to stand among us, wherever we are, whether we are in church or at home, or out walking. He comes to stand among us, whatever our frame of mind or heart, whether we are sad or excited or puzzled. The initiative is always with the Lord, rather than with us. All we can do is to respond to his initiative towards us. He comes; we respond. Our response can evolve over time. In today's gospel reading, the initial response of the disciples to the Lord's coming was one of alarm and fright; that response gave way to joy, and then to loving service as they offered the Lord some food. Our response to the risen Lord's coming to us and standing among us is never a full response, at least not in this earthly life. There is always another step we can take in response to the Lord's coming, and the Lord will help us to keep taking that step.

22 April, Easter Friday
John 21:1–14
In today's gospel reading we find the disciples going back to their work as fishermen in the aftermath of Jesus' crucifixion. The journey they set out on when Jesus called them from their fishing by the Sea of Galilee had come to an end. Now they could only

go back to where they had been before Jesus called them. There can be times in our own lives when we feel that we have gone backwards rather than forwards in our relationship with the Lord. Perhaps something happens in our lives that undermines our faith and our hope. Yet, in the gospel reading, the journey of faith that the disciples thought had come to an end was, in reality, only beginning. Their Lord who had been crucified was alive with a new and risen life. He came to his disheartened disciples and renewed his call to them. That call took the form of a simple invitation, 'Come and have breakfast.' It was an invitation to a renewed communion with him. It was that renewed communion which would be the basis of the renewed call to go forth and become fishers of people, shepherds of the Lord's flock. In those moments when we feel that we have gone backwards and that our faith has grown weak, the Lord comes to us too. As he did for those disciples by the Sea of Galilee, he invites us into a renewed communion with him. One of the ways we respond to that invitation is through our presence at the Eucharist, where the Lord says, 'Come and eat.' We may drift from the Lord in various ways but he is always calling us back into communion with himself and from that communion he sends us out as his messengers of Easter hope.

23 April, Easter Saturday
Mark 16:9–15

In today's gospel reading, the evangelist Mark gives us a list of some of the appearances of the risen Lord to his disciples. He mentions the Lord's appearance to Mary Magdalene, his appearance to the two disciples on the road to Emmaus, and his appearance to the eleven disciples in the setting of a meal. A fuller account of these appearances is to be found in the other gospels. There were many other appearances of the risen Lord, according to the gospels, and according to the earliest witness to the appearances, the apostle Paul. He lists in his first letter to the Corinthians the Lord's appearances to Peter, and to the twelve, to more than 500 of the brothers and sisters at the same time, to James, to all the apostles, and, finally, to himself, on the road to Damascus. The tradition of the appearances of the risen Jesus to his followers was an inspiration to the early church, especially to those who did not have such a privileged experience. The Lord's appearances to so many remains an inspiration to us all. It was those appearances that allowed the first disciples to understand why the tomb of Jesus was empty on the third day after his crucifixion. It was empty because he had been raised to a new and glorious life, in which his body was transformed. According to today's gospel reading, when Mary Magdalene told the other disciples that the Lord had appeared to her, they did not believe her, and when the two disciples told the other disciples that the Lord had met them on the road to Emmaus, they did not believe them either. When the Lord himself appeared to this wider group of disciples, he reproached them for refusing to believe these reports. Sometimes good news can be harder to believe than bad news. This Easter we are invited to renew our faith in the good news of Easter. The Lord is risen from the dead. He thereby reveals to us our own ultimate destiny, which is to share in his risen life beyond this earthly life. As risen Lord, he is also present with us throughout our earthly life, empowering us to live in the same self-giving way as he did, the way that leads through death to new life.

25 April, Monday, Feast of Saint Mark, Evangelist
Mark 16:15–20
The first letter of Peter was written from the church of Rome to churches that are now in modern-day Turkey. There is an ancient

tradition that locates the writing of the Gospel of Mark in the city of Rome and identifies the evangelist Mark as a disciple of Peter. The first reading from the first letter of Peter and the gospel reading from the Gospel of Mark have a theme in common. In the first reading, Peter assures the churches he is addressing that even though they are having to suffer for their faith, the Lord 'will see that all is well again; he will confirm, strengthen and support you'. The Lord is with his struggling churches to keep them faithful to the end. In the gospel reading, the risen Lord sends out his disciples to proclaim the Gospel to the whole world, and the evangelist then says that as they went out to preach everywhere, the Lord was 'working with them and confirming the word by the signs that accompanied it'. The risen Lord is with his disciples, working with them and confirming them. The message of the Lord working with and confirming his disciples is present in both readings. This is a message we need to hear today. Whenever we strive to be faithful to the Lord's ways, whenever we seek to witness to him, we can always be assured of the Lord's confirming presence. We understand the Sacrament of Confirmation as the moment when we confirm our baptism. However, the more fundamental confirmation is the Lord confirming us as we strive every day to follow in his way. The Lord is always working with us to confirm, strengthen and support us in our efforts to answer his call in today's world.

26 April, Tuesday, Second Week of Easter
John 3:7–15

In today's gospel Jesus says, 'the wind blows wherever it pleases'. In other words, the wind does not blow in accordance with our wishes. When it comes to our relationship with the wind, it is the wind, not us, that has the upper hand. Some days we have a cold wind from the north or the east. Other days we have a warm wind from the south. Most days in this part of the world we have a damp wind from the west. We have to accept the wind that comes our way. We can harness the wind to some extent, to generate electricity, but that is dependent on the strength of the wind, over which we have no control. The wind is a mysterious force which we cannot simply manage to suit ourselves. In the gospel reading Jesus makes a comparison between the wind and the Holy Spirit. Indeed, in the language Jesus spoke and in the language in which the gospels were written the one word could be translated either wind or Spirit. If the wind is mysterious and beyond our control, the Spirit of God is even more mysterious and beyond our control. The Spirit comes from God and goes to God and God is always beyond us, beyond our understanding and our control. However, the Spirit can enter a human life and we know what a Spirit-filled life looks like. Jesus is the one on whom the Spirit came down and remained and his life is pre-eminently Spirit-filled. The risen Lord continues to pour out his Spirit into our hearts so that our lives may be Spirit-filled. Paul portrays such a Spirit-filled life when he says in his letter to the Galatians that the fruit of the Spirit is 'love, joy, peace, patience, kindness, generosity, faithfulness, gentleness, and self-control'. Elsewhere Paul suggests that a Spirit-filled life is also a prayerful life. In his letter to the Romans he says, 'We do not know how to pray as we ought, but that very Spirit intercedes with sighs too deep for words.' It is the Spirit in us who does the praying. The Spirit may be mysterious, but when the Spirit takes shape in a human life we recognise the Spirit's attractiveness. It is the attractiveness of God, whose love is beyond human comprehension.

27 April, Wednesday, Second Week of Easter
John 3:16–21

The Gospel of John frequently refers to Jesus as light. On one occasion, Jesus says of himself: 'I am the light of the world.' In today's gospel reading, Jesus says with reference to himself, 'Light has come into the world.' In one of the most memorable statements of the New Testament the gospel reading declares that the light that has come into the world in the person of Jesus is the light of God's love. 'God loved the world so much that he gave his only Son so that everyone who believes in him ... may have eternal life.' The light of Jesus is not the probing light of the grand inquisitor that seeks out failure and transgression with a view to condemnation. Indeed, the gospel reading states that God 'sent his Son into the world not to condemn the world'. The light of Jesus, rather, is the inviting light of God's love, calling out to us to come and to allow ourselves to be bathed in this light, and promising those who do so that they will share in God's own life, both here and now and also beyond death. At the beginning of our gospel reading, Jesus speaks of himself as the Son of Man, who must be lifted up. It was on the cross that Jesus was lifted up, and it was above all at that moment that the light of God's love shone most brightly. Those who attempted to extinguish God's light shining in Jesus only succeeded in making that light of love shine all the more brightly. God's gift of his Son to us was not in any way thwarted by the rejection of his Son. God's giving continued as Jesus was lifted up to die, and God's giving found further expression when God lifted up his Son in glory and gave him to us as risen Lord. Here indeed is a light that darkness cannot overcome, a love that human sin cannot extinguish. This is the core of the Gospel.

28 April, Thursday, Second Week of Easter

John 3:31–36

In today's gospel reading, John the Baptist says of Jesus, 'He whom God has sent speaks God's own words.' Jesus speaks God's own words because he is the Word of God in human flesh. In the opening verses of his gospel, John the evangelist declared, 'The Word became flesh and lived among us.' We reflect deeply on all that Jesus said and did, on the whole of his life, on his death, resurrection and ascension, because we know that it is through Jesus that God has spoken the most powerful and clearest word he could ever speak. We are not in the dark about God, wondering who God is and what God is like. In the language of this Fourth Gospel, it is Jesus, 'who is close to the Father's heart, who has made him known'. Jesus came among us, full of God's grace and truth, God's gracious love and faithfulness, and we are invited to keep receiving from this fullness of God in Jesus. He has given us so much from his fullness that a lifetime is not long enough to receive it all. According to today's gospel reading, God gives the Spirit to Jesus without reserve. God gave all to Jesus without reserve, and what Jesus received from God he has given to us, without reserve. However, there will always be a reserve in our receiving. We struggle to empty ourselves sufficiently to receive all the Lord wants to give us. We spend our lives learning to receive like little children. The greater our capacity to receive from the Lord's fullness, the greater will be our ability to give as we have received. As Jesus received all from God and gave what he received to us, so Jesus looks to us to receive all from him and to give what we receive to one another. We are to keep receiving from Jesus his word, his Spirit, his love, so that, like Peter in the gospel reading, we can witness to him before others.

29 April, Friday, Feast of Saint Catherine of Siena

Matthew 11:25–30

Catherine (1347–1380) was a truly extraordinary woman. She was born in tumultuous times. The Black Death prowled the land; armies fought each other on behalf of their client-cities; the pope had left Rome for Avignon. She came from a prosperous family and her parents wanted her to marry well. However, she felt strongly called to live as the bride of Christ. She lived a life of solitary prayer for three years before re-joining her family and working with the sick, the poor, prisoners and plague victims. After a powerful, ecstatic experience of Christ in 1374, she commenced her public role, mediating in an armed conflict between the city of Florence and the Avignon-based papacy. She travelled to Avignon to Pope Gregory XI, insisting that he return to Rome. Her mission was a surprising success. However, shortly after his return to Rome, Gregory died. The College of Cardinals elected Urban VI, who turned out to be a distastrous pope. The cardinals, regretting their choice, elected another pope, Clement VII, but failed to persuade Urban to retire. The Church now had two rival popes. Catherine remained loyal to Urban, judging that, for all his faults, he had been validly elected. Shortly before her death she had a vision in which it seemed as if the Church, like a mighty ship, was being placed on her back. She died at the age of thirty-three. Catherine was both a mystic and a woman of the world, who served those in greatest need and involved herself in the great issues of Church and state of the day. The gospel reading is very suited to her feast. Jesus speaks both as a mystic and as one who serves those who are overburdened. He blesses God his Father, as one who knows the Father in a way no one else does, while also acknowledging that his Father knows him as no one else does. Jesus also speaks as one who invites all who are overburdened to come to him for rest. His intimate relationship with God flows over into a loving and caring relationship with all who struggle under heavy burdens. Catherine, like Jesus, was a mystic in action. We are all called to be mystics in action, people who are called into an intimate relationship with God and his Son and who are then sent to live out of that relationship by bringing God's rest and loving presence to all who are in need of it.

30 April, Saturday, Second Week of Easter
John 6:16–21

There is a sense in which we are always trying to get to the other side, like the disciples in the boat who were trying to reach the other side of the Sea of Galilee. We often feel the call to move beyond where we are, to reach for a different shore. We set out and we can then find ourselves struggling. In the gospel reading, darkness came over the disciples in the boat, and they found themselves facing into a strong wind and having to sail through a sea that was getting rougher. When we take on some new enterprise, when we go in a new direction of some kind, we will sometimes find ourselves battling with the equivalent of a strong wind and a rough sea, with a kind of darkness coming over us. It was at that moment, when they were battling with the elements, that the disciples saw Jesus coming towards the boat, saying to them, 'It is I. Do not be afraid.' The Lord comes to us all in our moments of struggle, when we sense our vulnerability, our frailty, when a darkness of spirit threatens to engulf us. As risen Lord he is there with us at those moments in all his risen power, calling on us not to be afraid but to trust in his presence. Once the risen Lord spoke to the disciples, they seem to have reached the shore they were making for immediately. The Lord's presence to us and our awareness of his presence always makes the journey to the other side, the far shore, seem that bit shorter.

2 May, Monday, Third Week of Easter

John 6:22–29

There tends to be a restlessness in all of us. That restlessness drives us to make contact with other people; it often leads us to set out on a journey of one kind or another, whether it is a physical journey or an inner journey. There is something of the searcher, the seeker, in us all. At the deepest level of our being, we are searching for God. It was Saint Augustine who said that our hearts are restless until they rest in God. In today's gospel reading, the people of Galilee set out to look for Jesus. He had fed the multitude in the wilderness; this had made a great impression on them. Jesus was pleased that they came looking for him, but he wanted to refine their search. They looked for him as the giver of bread; Jesus wanted them to look for him as the giver of food that endures to eternal life. As Christians, we are all searching for Jesus in some sense. The gospel reading invites us to pay attention to why we are searching for him. What are we looking to him for? What do we expect from him? Perhaps, like the people of Galilee, our expectations are too small. What Jesus can offer us, more than anything else, is eternal life, a sharing in God's own life. This sharing in God's life begins here and now for those who turn to Jesus in faith, and comes to fullness in the life beyond death.

3 May, Tuesday, Feast of Saints Philip and James

John 14:6–14

Today we celebrate the feast of two of the twelve apostles, Philip and James. According to the Fourth Gospel, Philip was from the same town as Andrew and Peter, Bethsaida on the north shore of the Sea of Galilee. James is identified as the brother or cousin of Jesus. After the death and resurrection of Jesus, he became the leading member of the church in Jerusalem. In today's first reading from the first letter to the Corinthians, Paul lists James as one of those to whom the risen Lord appeared. In today's gospel reading, Philip makes a request of Jesus: 'Lord, let us see the Father and then we shall be satisfied.' He recognises in that request that only God can satisfy the deepest longings of the human heart. We will never be fully satisfied until we see God. We look forward in hope to seeing God face to face beyond this earthly life. It is only then that the deepest hungers and thirsts of our hearts will be completely satisfied. Earlier in that first letter to the Corinthians, Paul had said, 'now we see in a mirror, dimly; but then we will see face to face'. For the moment, we have to make do with seeing in a mirror dimly, a poorer form of seeing to that which awaits us in eternity, the seeing face to face. Yet, even this seeing in a mirror dimly is potentially a very rich form of seeing. In the gospel reading, Jesus says to Philip, 'To have seen me, is to have seen the Father.' There is a very real sense in which we see Jesus, the risen Lord, in this earthly life, and through him see God. We see the Lord as he comes to us in his word and in the Eucharist, the breaking of bread. We see him in each other, particularly in the broken and vulnerable. We see him in creation. It was Joseph Mary Plunkett who wrote, 'I see his blood upon the rose / and in the stars the glory of his eyes; / His body gleams amid eternal snows, / His tears fall from the skies.' If our eyes were opened, we would see the Lord in his many guises and we would begin to experience in the here and now something of that rest and peace which is the fruit of seeing God face to face in eternity.

4 May, Wednesday, Third Week of Easter

John 6:35–40

In today's gospel reading, Jesus says, 'whoever comes to me I shall not turn away.' It is a statement that reveals the welcoming nature of the Lord's presence. Those who come to him will find a welcome from him. The opening invitation of Jesus in this gospel is 'Come and see'. He invites people to come to him and he promises those who do so that he will never turn them away. In this he is being true to God's will, which is, according to the gospel reading, that all who see the Son and believe in him shall have eternal life. It is as the source of life, as the one who can satisfy our deepest hungers and thirsts, that Jesus invites people to come to him, while assuring them that they will never be turned away if they do come. It is said of Saul in the first reading that he worked for the total destruction of the Church. Saul sought to destroy all who responded to the welcoming invitation of Jesus. There will always be forces in our world that are hostile to our coming to Jesus. Yet the later experience of Saul suggests that not only does the Lord welcome those who come to him but he seeks out those who are hostile to him. Saul eventually came to Jesus because Jesus went after him. The Lord who welcomes us when we come to him also seeks us out when we walk away from him. When we don't come to him, he comes after us, not in anger but in love. He is always driven by God the Father's will that all should see the Son and believe in him and so have eternal life.

5 May, Thursday, Third Week of Easter
John 6:44–51

The portrayal of the Ethiopian in today's gospel reading suggests that he was engaged in a spiritual search. He had been on pilgrimage to Jerusalem. People who go on pilgrimage are often seeking to know God more fully. On his way home from the pilgrimage, he continued to engage in his spiritual quest, reading from the prophet Isaiah. It is notable that the text says that Philip heard him reading Isaiah the prophet. The Ethiopian was not reading silently to himself; he was reading aloud. This was how people usually read the Scriptures at that time, even when they were alone. His reading of the passage gave rise to a question to which he sought an answer from Philip. 'Tell me, is the prophet referring to himself or someone else?' When Philip then proclaimed the Gospel to him, the Ethiopian took a further initiative on his spiritual quest, again in the form of a question, 'Look, there is some water here; is there anything to stop me being baptised?' Having been baptised by Philip, the Ethiopian went on his way rejoicing. Even though the Lord drew near to the Ethiopian through Philip, the Ethiopian himself was drawing near to the Lord through his reading of the Scriptures, his questioning spirit and his request for baptism. In the gospel reading, Jesus says, 'No one can come to me unless drawn by the Father who sent me.' God the Father is always drawing us to his Son, as he drew the Ethiopian to Jesus through Philip. Yet we ourselves need to take our own steps towards the Lord, the kind of steps the Ethiopian took, if the drawing of the Father is to bear fruit in our lives. Even though God's quest for us is the more fundamental one, we need to be engaged in our own quest for God. The story of the Ethiopian shows that if we seek the Lord we will find him, because the Lord is always seeking us.

6 May, Friday, Third Week of Easter
John 6:52–59

There is a wonderful painting of the scene in today's first reading, the call of Paul, in a church in Rome by the artist Caravaggio. The artist does not depict the risen Lord, only the impact of the risen Lord on Paul. Paul is lying on the ground with his arms raised towards the heavens as light falls on him from above. A large horse stands behind the prone Paul, occupying the centre of the painting. The painting conveys a sense of this powerful figure now rendered helpless before the risen Lord. In his weakness, he is ready to be redirected by the Lord. The helplessness and weakness of Paul is conveyed in the first reading by the depiction of the blind Paul having to be led by the hand into the city of Damascus, a city he had expected to be riding into confidently and authoritatively. Yet the Lord had wonderful plans for this almost helpless figure. As the Lord said to Ananias, 'This man is my chosen instrument to bring my name before pagans and pagan kings and before the people of Israel.' It was as if Paul had to become like a little child, needing to be led, before the Lord could work through him with great power. Indeed, Jesus said that unless we become like little children we cannot enter the kingdom of heaven. Sometimes, it is our very weakness that gives the Lord scope to work through us most fully, whereas when we are over-confident and too sure of our own ability and success we can block the Lord from working through us. We don't draw life from ourselves but from the Lord. In the gospel reading, Jesus declares, 'Whoever eats me will draw life from me'. We need to be in communion with the Lord if our presence in the world is to be truly life-giving in the way Jesus' presence was. Even when we cannot eat the Lord's body and drink his blood in the Eucharist, we can still remain in communion with him. We can open our hearts and souls to his presence wherever we are. When we do that, like Paul, we too can become the Lord's chosen instruments to bring his presence into the lives of others.

7 May, Saturday, Third Week of Easter
John 6:60–69

There are several stories in the gospels about Jesus calling people to follow him and their responding to his call immediately. In today's gospel reading, however, we find the opposite happening. Disciples who have been with Jesus for some time left him and stopped going with him. They objected to Jesus' insistence on the need for his disciples to eat his body and drink his blood. 'This is intolerable language. How could anyone accept it?' They rejected Jesus' teaching on the Eucharist. It must have been discouraging for the remaining disciples to see other disciples leaving Jesus. We all feel a little sad when people no longer gather for the Eucharist in the same numbers as in the past. We miss the presence of younger people especially. Perhaps sensing the impact of the loss of some disciples on the remaining disciples, Jesus turns to the twelve and asks them 'What about you, do you want to go away too?' It is a question that is addressed to each one of us, especially when our faith feels undermined by the actions of others. Jesus must have been very heartened by the response of Peter on behalf of the others: 'Lord, who shall we go to? You have the message of eternal life, and we believe, we know that you are the Holy One of God.' We are all invited to make our own that response of Peter whenever we too may be tempted to leave the community gathered around the Lord in the Eucharist. Our presence is all the more important when others have left. The willingness of any one of us to remain is an encouragement to everyone else. Like the early churches at the beginning of today's first reading, we need to build each other up by remaining in communion with the Lord and living out of this communion in our day-to-day lives.

9 May, Monday, Fourth Week of Easter
John 10:1–10

In John's Gospel Jesus often makes a statement about himself beginning with the two little words 'I am'. He says, 'I am the bread of life'; 'I am the light of the world'; I am the resurrection and the life'; 'I am the good shepherd'; 'I am the way, the truth and the life'; 'I am the vine'. In today's gospel reading, Jesus says

'I am the gate.' Gates usually do two things, they keep people out and they let people in. They stop people and they let people through. When Jesus says 'I am the gate', he is thinking of a gate in this second sense, as letting people in or through. When he says 'I am the gate,' he immediately adds, 'anyone who enters through me will be safe.' One of the things Jesus is saying is that he is the gateway to God; he is the gateway to the fullness of life that only God can give. 'I have come,' he says,' that you may have life and have it to the full.' Jesus is the gate, and when we come and go through him we will find that fullness of life that Jesus gives us from God. By saying that he is the gate, Jesus wants us to interact with him, to go in and out through him. He wants us to be constantly keeping in touch with him. We do this through prayer and through the Sacraments, especially the Sacrament of the Eucharist. He promises that if we constantly interact with him, we will find true life, not just at the end of our earthly lives but here and now in the midst of our day-to-day lives.

10 May, Tuesday, Fourth Week of Easter
John 10:22–30

It is a great gift to be able to recognise the good that the Lord is doing through someone or some group and then to encourage it along. This is what we find Barnabas doing in today's first reading. News reached the church in Jerusalem that something unexpected was happening. In the city of Antioch, the Gospel was being preached to pagans, and they were responding in large numbers. Up until that point, the church had been Jewish Christian; the disciples of Jesus were all Jews. The church in Jerusalem needed to check out this new and unforeseen development, and they sent Barnabas to Antioch. The first reading says that when Barnabas got there, 'he could see for himself that God had given grace, and this pleased him', and he went on to give encouragement to what was happening. The Lord was moving the young church in a new direction and Barnabas recognised this and supported it. Every so often the Lord prompts the Church to take a new step beyond where it has been. He calls on us to break new ground, to grow in new ways, as individual believers and as a community of faith. At such times, we need people like Barnabas who recognise that the Lord is behind this new direction and who encourages us to trust that the Lord is present in what is happening. In the gospel reading, Jesus, speaking as the good shepherd, says, 'The sheep that belong to me listen to my voice.' We are always trying to listen to the Lord's voice so as to discern where he is leading us, the new directions that he is taking us in. There is always another step that the Lord is calling us to take. He can be speaking to us through new and unforeseen situations. We all need something of the vision of Barnabas to see how the Lord is working in such unexpected and unplanned developments.

11 May, Wednesday, Fourth Week of Easter
John 12:44–50
In the gospel reading, Jesus speaks as one who is open and responsive to what God his Father wants: 'What the Father has told me is what I speak.' He is able to speak what God has told him because he listens to God. In the first reading, the early Church is portrayed as doing what the Holy Spirit wants. They are able to do what the Holy Spirit wants because they listen to the Holy Spirit. The church in Antioch recognises that the Holy Spirit is asking them to send two of their leading members on mission, Barnabas and Saul. Even though it was a sacrifice to give away such important members to the mission field, they did so in response to the prompting of the Holy Spirit. In every age the Church is

called to be responsive to the Holy Spirit in the way that Jesus was responsive to God the Father. The call on the churches of Asia Minor in the Book of Revelation is addressed to the churches in every age and place. 'Let anyone who has an ear listen to what the Spirit is saying to the churches.' The prayer of listening is a vital form of prayer for the Church and for every member of the Church in every age. The Lord continues to speak to each of us today through the Holy Spirit. A good way to begin our prayer is by saying the prayer of the young Samuel in the Jewish Scriptures, 'Speak, Lord, your servant is listening.'

12 May, Thursday, Fourth Week of Easter
John 13:16–20

The saying of Jesus in today's gospel reading, 'No servant is greater than his master', is found in more than one setting in the Fourth Gospel and its setting determines its meaning. In our gospel reading, Jesus said those words just after he washed the feet of his disciples. He was saying to his disciples, that if he, the master, washed their feet, they must wash each other's feet. Jesus washed the feet of his disciples so as to send them out to love others as he has loved them. That is the essence of our baptismal calling. Jesus exercised his Lordship in humble, loving service, and we, his servants, are to take him as the pattern of our living. One of the disciples whose feet Jesus washed did not go out to share the love he had received. Judas rejected Jesus' love. As Jesus says in the gospel reading, 'Someone who shares my table rebels against me.' Judas shows us the capacity in us all to turn away from Jesus' offer of his love and the call it implies. Yet Jesus identifies very closely with those who do receive the gift of his love and who allow themselves to be sent out by the Lord to share the love they have received. He says in the gospel reading, 'Whoever welcomes the one I send welcomes me.' In the Gospel of John, Jesus is the Sent One, the one sent by God the Father to bring God's love to the world. However, as disciples of Jesus we are all 'sent ones', sent by him to bring the love we have received from him to others. Whenever we seek to be true to that identity, we become the Lord's ambassadors. He identifies with us in a very personal way, such that those who welcome us welcome him. It is a sobering thought that the Lord wants each one of us to be his personal presence to others. In receiving the Lord's love into our lives and sharing it with others, we become the Lord's presence to others. There is no higher calling than this.

13 May, Friday, Fourth Week of Easter
John 14:1–6

Today's gospel reading is one you will hear many times when a funeral takes place. It is one of the most frequently chosen gospel readings for funeral Masses. On the night before his own death, in the context of the Last Supper, which Jesus shared with his disciples before his crucifixion, Jesus speaks about the many-roomed house of God his Father towards which he is journeying. He is reminding his troubled disciples that the Roman cross will not be his final destination. Beyond that shameful death there is the heavenly house of God his Father where he will be received with great honour and glory. Even on the night before his own death, Jesus is not only thinking of himself; he is thinking of others, of his own followers. He assures them that the heavenly house of God his Father is not only his own ultimate destination but it is also the final destination of his disciples. At the end of their earthly lives he promises to come to them and take them to that heavenly house so that where he is they may be too. Where Jesus is going, his disciples will follow; to that extent, he is the goal of their journey. This is a very reassuring message for all of us. That is why Jesus begins what he has to say with those very reassuring words, 'Do not let your hearts be troubled'. As well as declaring himself to be the goal of our earthly journey Jesus also declares himself to be the way to that goal: 'I am the way.' He is our present way and our future hope.

14 May, Saturday, Feast of Saint Matthias
John 15:9–17

According to today's first reading, when the early Church looked for a replacement for Judas to complete the group of the twelve, they wanted to know whom the Lord had chosen. The disciples chose two candidates they thought would be suitable, Joseph and Matthias, but in prayer they sought which of these two the Lord had chosen: 'Show us which of these two you have chosen.' The Lord was choosing one and not the other, and the Church prayerfully discerned that Matthias was the Lord's choice. There is another sense in which each one of us is chosen by the Lord. That is clear from today's gospel reading. Jesus is speaking to his disciples, who, in John's Gospel, represent disciples of every generation. He says to them, 'You did not choose me; no, I chose you.' The Lord's choice of us is prior to our choice of him. To put that in other terms, the Lord loves us before we love him. The Lord loves us first. His love for us is a given, as he says at the beginning of the gospel reading, 'As the Father has loved me, so I have loved you.' The Lord's love for us is a constant, and our task, according to the gospel reading, is to remain in the Lord's love. The Lord's love for us remains, endures, and it falls to us to remain in his enduring love. According to Jesus in the gospel reading, we remain in his love by living his one commandment to love one another as he has loved us. We might have expected Jesus to say, 'You remain in my love by loving me.' Instead, he says, 'You remain in my love by loving one another as I have loved you.' The Lord's love for us is to empower us to love one another with his love. This is our fundamental baptismal calling. According to Jesus in the gospel reading, when we love one another as the Lord loves us we will enter into the Lord's own joy, which is the completion of every human joy. We don't find happiness by seeking happiness directly but by opening ourselves to the Lord's love for us and then by seeking to share that love with each other.

16 May, Monday, Fifth Week of Easter
John 14:21–26

When Paul is speaking to a pagan audience in today's first reading, he tells them that the living God did not leave them without evidence of himself in the good things he did for them, such as abundant rain, the growth of crops, sufficient food. It can be helpful for us to recognise the presence of the living God in the good things in our own lives, especially when we have so many not-so-good things to come to terms with. Even in the midst of struggle and loss, good things can be found, and all such good things are little reminders of the presence of the living God. The really good thing in our lives that the living God has given us is God's own Son, Jesus. In the gospel reading, Jesus makes the extraordinary statement that if we love him, he and his heavenly Father will come to us and make their home with us. It is quite something to reflect on how Jesus and God the Father want to make their home with each one of us. We speak of our parish church as God's house, God's home. Yet Jesus is reminding us that each one of us can become a church, in the sense that God and his Son can make their home in us. We can each become the house of God, the home of God. It is through the Holy Spirit that Jesus and God the Father make their home in us.

At the end of the gospel reading, Jesus says that God the Father will send us the Advocate, the Holy Spirit, to remind us of all Jesus said to us. In one of his letters, Paul refers to the baptised as temples of the Holy Spirit. It is good to ask ourselves, 'Do I think of myself as a home for God and Jesus, as a temple of the Holy Spirit?' 'When I do think of myself in this way, what impact does it have on me?' Elsewhere in John's Gospel, Jesus suggests that this awareness can bring us a peace the world cannot give.

17 May, Tuesday, Fifth Week of Easter
John 14:27–31
I am very struck by the resilience of Paul and Barnabas in today's first reading. They had preached the Gospel in Lystra, but Paul's enemies stoned Paul and dragged him outside the town, thinking he was dead. What did Paul do? He went straight back to Lystra! After a short while, he and Barnabas went on to the next town, Derbe, and preached the Gospel there. Then they went back to Lystra again and, according to our reading, they put fresh heart into the disciples there, encouraging them to persevere in the faith. In the very town where Paul nearly lost his life, he put fresh heart and gave great encouragement to the disciples. What was done to Paul could have left him very discouraged, but, instead, he became a source of encouragement to others. There is a similar portrayal of Jesus in the gospel reading. He is speaking on the evening of the Last Supper. He knows that his enemies, including one of his own disciples, are gathered to launch him into his passion and death. As Jesus says in the reading, 'the prince of this world is on his way'. He had good reason to be discouraged. Instead, there he is, giving encouragement to his disciples: 'Do not let your hearts be troubled or afraid,' he says to them, and he goes on to say, 'I am doing exactly what the Father told me.' It was Paul's

close relationship with the risen Lord that allowed him to give encouragement to others when so many were against him, and it was Jesus' relationship with God, his Father, that enabled him to give encouragement to others, when so many were against him. There can be many human reasons for us to get discouraged. However, what keeps us hopeful, what enables us to encourage others, is our relationship with the Lord. If we keep opening ourselves to the Lord's presence, then we will experience what Jesus calls in the gospel reading, 'my own peace ... a peace the world cannot give', and, like Paul and Jesus, we will be able to put fresh heart into others and encourage them on their journey.

18 May, Wednesday, Fifth Week of Easter
John 15:1–8

There is always a temptation to put limits on God, to say, in effect, that God cannot do this or that unless this or that happens. We find such a scenario in today's first reading. Some Jewish Christians from Jerusalem came down to the church in Antioch and told converts to the faith from paganism, Gentile Christians, 'Unless you have yourselves circumcised in the tradition of Moses, you cannot be saved.' They were saying, in effect, 'Much as God would like to include you among those who will inherit eternal life, he is powerless unless you have yourselves circumcised.' We don't have to go back as far as the Acts of the Apostles to find such a mindset. In living memory, we have allowed ourselves to think that we cannot find favour with God unless we follow certain rules or rituals or long-standing customs. However, God cannot be boxed in like that. Today's gospel reading is taken from the Gospel of John; earlier in that gospel Jesus says to Nicodemus, 'the Spirit blows where it chooses'. Because God is all loving towards us, God is completely free in our regard in a way we can never understand. God's love towards us has been fully revealed in Jesus. In one of his letters, Paul speaks about 'the love of Christ that surpasses knowledge'. Because our relationship with the Lord is one of love, there is nothing mechanical about that relationship, whereby if we do one thing, he becomes free to do something else. There is nothing less mechanical than the image of the vine and the branches that Jesus offers us in today's gospel reading. It is a vibrant, living, dynamic image. If Jesus is the vine and we are the branches, it is difficult to know where the vine ends and the branches begin. Jesus invites us to make our home in him, as he makes his home in us. He desires an intimate relationship with us, a relationship of love. It is an empowering relationship, just as the vine empowers the branches to bear fruit. As we grow in our relationship, our friendship, with the Lord, something of his love that surpasses knowledge will become visible in our own lives.

19 May, Thursday, Fifth Week of Easter
John 15:9–11

In today's gospel reading Jesus speaks about the joy he desires for his disciples, for all of us. He tells his disciples that 'I have said these things to you so that my joy may be in you and your joy may be complete.' Jesus is not speaking about any old joy, but about what he terms 'my joy', the joy that Jesus himself has. It may seem strange to us that Jesus can speak about his joy on the very night before he faces into his crucifixion. Clearly his joy is something so deeply rooted that not even the prospect of his painful death on the next day can take it from him. In fact, his joy is rooted in the great conviction that he has of the Father's love for him, 'As the Father has loved me, so I have loved you.' He remains in that love by doing what God asks of him, and this is the source of his joy. Jesus declares in that reading that as the Father has loved him, he has loved us, and as he remains in his Father's love, we are called to remain in the Lord's love. The Lord loves us with an infinite and faithful love. We remain in the Lord's love by trying to live as the Lord calls us to live, and that is the source of our joy. By remaining in the Lord's love we come to share in the Lord's own joy. Saint Paul can be a very good model for us in this regard. He wrote a letter to the Philippians from prison, and yet it is full of joy. Paul was someone who shared in the Lord's own joy because he was convinced of God's love for him and he remained in that love by seeking to do what the Lord was asking him to do, even though that meant time in prison. Jesus and Paul both teach us that true joy does not result so much from our physical circumstances but from our relationship with the Lord, our conviction of the Lord's love for us and our struggle to live and to love as he calls us to live and love.

20 May, Friday, Fifth Week of Easter
John 15:12–17
One of the great blessings in life is friendship. Many friendships form naturally. People who have something in common are drawn to each other and become friends, sometimes for life. Many people make friends through sport or through a walking group or film club or bridge club. They share a common interest and they become friends. There is another form of friendship where people chose to befriend someone with whom they may have little in common. They do so out of a deeper kind of love than natural friendship. Someone may befriend another person they share little with on the natural level, simply because otherwise that person would have no friends. This is the kind of friendship that Jesus is talking about in the gospel reading, when he says to his disciples, 'You are my friends ... I call you friends.' They were probably a very mixed

bunch and it is likely that Jesus had little in common with many of them on a purely natural level, yet he befriended them. He befriended Judas, for example, washing his feet at the Last Supper along with the feet of all the others. This kind of friendship is inspired by the Holy Spirit. It is the kind of friendship the Lord has with each one of us. To all of us, regardless of our temperament or personal story or failings, he says, 'You are my friends.' Jesus says in the gospel reading that he demonstrates the quality of his friendship with us by sharing with us what is deepest within him, all that his heavenly Father has told him, and he demonstrates his friendship towards us even more powerfully by laying down his life for us. In natural friendships there is always a giving and a receiving between friends. However, Jesus' friendship is pure gift on his part and is not dependent on what he receives from us. 'You did not choose me: no, I chose you.' His friendship with us endures, even though he may receive little in return. Having befriended us in this Spirit-inspired way, he then calls on us to befriend one another as he has befriended us, to love one another as he has loved us. This is the core of our baptismal calling and, in so far as we live out that calling, our lives will bear fruit that will last, in the language of the gospel reading.

21 May, Saturday, Fifth Week of Easter
John 15:18–21
In today's gospel reading Jesus tells his disciples on the night before he died that they can expect the same hatred from the world that he himself has experienced. In that regard, as in others, he remarks that a 'servant is not greater than his master'. We know that Christians are being persecuted in many parts of the world at present. There has been persecution of the Church in China for many decades. In the Maoist era, Catholics were forced to go

underground. Mao's late wife once said, 'Christianity in China has been confined to the history section of the museum. It is dead and buried.' Thankfully, China's Christians have greater liberties now than in the past. Yet, those Catholics who recognise the pope rather than the state-backed Catholic Patriotic Association are liable to persecution and harassment. In a letter written to the faithful of the Catholic Church in China in May 2007, Pope Benedict XVI expressed the hope that 24 May would become a day of prayer for the Church in China. He chose this day because it is the memorial of Our Lady Help of Christians, who is venerated with great devotion at the Marian shrine of Sheshan in Shanghai. The statue of Our Lady Help of Christians at the shrine is very striking. Our Lady holds the child Jesus high above her head; the child's hands are extended straight out to left and right, symbolising his death on the cross and the overcoming of his death with his resurrection. These outstretched arms are also a symbol of love for all humanity. As we approach the memorial of Our Lady Help of Christians, we pray for the Church in China and for all persecuted Christians throughout the world, and we also ask the Lord to make us more courageous in bearing witness to him in our own time and place.

23 May, Monday, Sixth Week of Easter
John 15:26–16:4

In the gospel reading, Jesus, speaking in the setting of the Last Supper, tells his disciples that he is speaking to them in the way he is so that 'your faith may not be shaken'. Jesus was aware that beyond the time of his death and resurrection, his disciples' faith in him would be shaken; it would be put to the test. Looking beyond his immediate disciples, he could also see that the faith of future disciples would be put to the test, your faith and mine. That is why the prayer that he gave us to pray has the petition, 'Lead us not into temptation but deliver us from evil'. Jesus was teaching us to pray for the strength to stand firm in our faith when we are tempted to lose faith in him, when our faith in him is put to the test. There is a line in the first letter of Saint Paul to the Corinthians that has always spoken to me: 'God is faithful, and he will not let you be tested beyond your strength, but with the testing he will also provide the way out so that you may be able to endure it.' Paul is saying there that when our faith is put to the test, the Lord stands by us, and he will give us the strength to endure in the face of the test. One of the ways he stands by us is by giving us the gift of the Holy Spirit. In today's gospel reading, Jesus says that he will send us the Advocate from the Father, the Spirit of Truth. Jesus goes on to say that the Spirit 'will be my witness', and he will empower us to witness to Jesus. We have a wonderful resource in the Holy Spirit when our faith is put to the test for whatever reason. As Saint Paul says in another of his letters, his letter to the Romans, 'the Spirit helps us in our weakness'. When our faith feels fragile, there can be no better prayer to pray than, 'Come Holy Spirit, fill my heart', or, in the words of the Sequence we pray on Pentecost Sunday, a lovely prayer to the Holy Spirit, 'Heal our wounds, our strength renew; On our dryness pour thy dew.'

24 May, Tuesday, Sixth Week of Easter
John 16:5–11

In critical situations, we can be very conscious of what we are losing. We sense the loss of a great deal that means so much to us. As a result, we can find ourselves 'sad at heart' in the words of today's gospel reading. There Jesus is speaking in a critical moment for himself and his disciples. It is the evening of the Last Supper, and the disciples are 'sad at heart' because they sense that they are losing Jesus. He is going from them and will not return.

However, whereas Jesus does not deny the reality of their loss, he tries to show them that something worthwhile is coming out of this loss that wouldn't otherwise happen. He says to them, 'It is for your own good that I am going because unless I go, the Advocate will not come to you'. Jesus' departure to his heavenly Father will make possible the sending of the Holy Spirit ,who will make Jesus present in a new and more wonderful way, not just to these disciples, but to disciples of every generation. Moreover, Jesus says, when the Advocate comes, he will go on the offensive against the opponents of Jesus and his disciples, proving these opponents wrong in their assessment of Jesus and his followers as sinners, and of themselves as being in the right, and, also, in their assessment that Jesus was being judged or condemned by God on the cross. In other words, when the Advocate, the Holy Spirit, comes, he will be a wonderful resource to the disciples, to the church. Yet, because the Advocate is the Spirit of the risen Lord, he cannot come unless Jesus returns to his Father through his death and resurrection. Jesus is assuring his disciples that great good will come out of the tragedy that is unfolding. Even in the midst of tragedy, we can be confident that the risen Lord is working to bring some good out of our affliction. In today's first reading, the affliction of Paul's imprisonment led to the baptism of the jailer and his family. The Lord can work powerfully in situations where we feel powerless and helpless, if we give him the space to do so.

25 May, Wednesday, Sixth Week of Easter
John 16:12–15

The Acts of the Apostles suggests that Paul had a gift for adapting his preaching to his audience. When preaching to Jews, he regularly quoted from the Jewish Scriptures. In today's first reading from the Acts of the Apostles we find Paul preaching to the town council of Athens on the Areopagus. They were enlightened pagans. He took his cue from an altar he noticed that was inscribed, 'To an Unknown God'. He proceeded to tell them that this unknown God had made himself known in the life, death and resurrection of Jesus. As Christians, we recognise Jesus as the one who has made God known. In the words of the first chapter of the Gospel of John, 'No one has ever seen God. It is God, the only Son, who is close to the Father's heart, who has made him known.' As we come to know Jesus, we come to know God, yet,we never come to know Jesus fully in this life. We are always on a journey towards knowing him. This knowing Jesus, which we never fully attain in this life, is not so much an intellectual knowing as a knowing of the heart, a knowing that is the fruit of love. We are always on the way towards that kind of knowing of Jesus. That is why Jesus says in the gospel reading that when the Spirit of truth comes, he will lead us to the complete truth. If Jesus makes God known to us, the Holy Spirit makes Jesus known to us. He leads us to the complete truth, to Jesus who said of himself, 'I am the truth.' Every day, the Holy Spirit works to take us on this journey towards Jesus, the complete truth, if we allow him. It is the Holy Spirit who makes the love of Jesus tangible for us, and it is the Holy Spirit who moves us towards that love of Jesus which brings us to know him ever more fully.

26 May, Thursday, Sixth Week of Easter
John 16:16–20

A married couple, Aquila and Priscilla, feature in today's first reading. They were a Jewish Christian couple who had recently come from Rome to Corinth, and when Paul come to preach the Gospel for the first time in Corinth, he stayed in their accommodation. They were tentmakers like himself. Paul's letters reveal that this married couple hosted a church in their house in Ephesus and later in Rome. They provided the space for believers in these two cities to gather for prayer, for Eucharist, for sharing together. They were clearly an important presence in the early church. They were generous in sharing their resources with other believers and were clearly a great support to Paul. Paul says of them in his letter to the Romans, 'They work with me in Christ Jesus, and ... risked their necks for my life.' Even the great apostle to the Gentiles needed the support of believers like Aquila and Priscilla. In the gospel reading we find Jesus supporting his disciples. He is speaking in the setting of the Last Supper. Knowing that he is facing into his own death, which will impact gravely on his disciples, he says to them, 'You will be weeping and wailing.' Yet, at this moment when he is at his most vulnerable, he seeks to support and encourage his disciples, saying to them, 'Your sorrow will turn to joy', and 'You will see me again.' What Jesus does for his disciples in the gospel reading, the married couple do for Paul in the first reading. We have here an image of what the Church is called to be. We are to be a community of believers who support one another in the faith and encourage one another when times are difficult. The ministry of encouragement and building up of each other is a vital ministry in the Church, and it is a ministry in which we all share, whether we are male or female, young or old, single or married. It is a ministry that the Holy Spirit will always be moving us to undertake. He is the great consoler and comforter, and he inspires and empowers us to be a consoling and comforting presence to one another

27 May, Friday, Sixth Week of Easter
John 16:20–23
At the beginning of today's first reading from the Acts of the Apostles, the risen Lord says to Paul in the course of his mission

in Corinth, 'Do not be afraid to speak out … I am with you.' So many times in both the Jewish Scriptures and in the gospels, the Lord says to people, 'Do not be afraid … I am with you.' Speaking to Paul, the Lord does not make little of the opposition Paul will encounter in preaching the Gospel in Corinth. The Lord's words to Paul, 'Do not allow yourself to be silenced', presupposes that there are people who are trying to silence Paul, and that becomes evident further on in that reading. Some members of the Jewish community drag Paul to the Roman governor in Corinth on trumped up charges. The opposition is real, but the Lord says to Paul, 'Do not be afraid… I am with you.' This is the message that Jesus gives to his disciples in the gospel reading as well. He acknowledges the pain and sorrow that the disciples are experiencing and that lies ahead for them, 'You will be weeping and wailing … you will be sorrowful … you are sad now.' Yet Jesus also says to them, 'I will see you again.' In other words, 'I will be with you.' Because of his presence to them, Jesus says to them, 'Your hearts will be full of joy, and that joy no one will take from you.' In both readings the Lord assures us that his presence to us will help us to get through whatever painful experiences come our way. It is good for us to hear that simple but profound message, especially when times are difficult. We are not on our own. The Lord is with us and he will give us the strength we need. Indeed, according to the gospel reading, in the midst of so much that can understandably make us sad and sorrowful, the Lord can give us a share in his own risen joy because of his sustaining presence to us.

28 May, Saturday, Sixth Week of Easter
John 16:23–28

There is another striking portrayal in the first reading of how the members of the early church supported one another. We are told that Paul continued his journey through the Galatian countryside and then through Phrygia, encouraging all the followers. Then, when a young Jewish Christian named Apollos arrived in the city of Ephesus from the city of Alexandria, the married couple, Aquila and Priscilla, gave him further instruction in the faith. This was the same couple that had offered Paul accommodation in Corinth. When Apollos wanted to cross over from the church in Ephesus to the church in Corinth, the members of the church in Ephesus wrote a letter to the church in Corinth asking believers there to welcome Apollos. When Apollos arrived in Corinth he helped the believers there considerably by God's grace. In the space of a few verses we have a wonderful picture of the members of the early Church supporting and encouraging one another in a whole variety of ways. In the gospel reading, Jesus encourages his disciples in the setting of the Last Supper. He says to them, 'the Father himself loves you.' They, and we, are as much loved by God the Father as Jesus himself is. Jesus draws us into his own loving relationship with God. We can address God the Father in the same intimate way that Jesus does. We don't need Jesus to go to God the Father on our behalf. As Jesus says, 'When that day comes, you will ask in my name; and I do not say that I shall pray to the Father for you, because the Father himself loves you.' We have privileged access to God the Father and we don't need Jesus to intercede for us. Jesus says a great deal in that gospel reading to encourage all of us. It is out of the strength we receive from the encouragement that Jesus gives us that we are enabled to encourage one another in the ways that the members of the early church are portrayed as doing in the first reading.

30 May, Monday, Seventh Week of Easter

John 16:29–33

I have always been struck by the reply of some disciples in Ephesus to Paul's question, 'Did you receive the Holy Spirit when you became believers?' With great honesty they said, 'No, we were never even told there was such a thing as a Holy Spirit.' Paul went on to give them further instruction, and then, laying his hands on them, they received the Holy Spirit. Their answer to Paul's question speaks for many in our world today, perhaps even for many who have been baptised. 'We were never even told there was such a thing as a Holy Spirit.' Those disciples in Ephesus needed instruction in the faith on this very important matter of the Holy Spirit. We all need instruction in the faith. We all have a journey to travel when it comes to understanding our faith and living our faith. In the gospel reading, the disciples speak with great confidence about their understanding of Jesus and their relationship with him. 'Now you are speaking plainly … we believe that you came from God.' Jesus has to puncture their self-confidence, declaring that in a very short time they will desert him, leaving him alone, and each going their own way. When it comes to our relationship with the Lord, we are all learners, like those disciples in Ephesus, and for that we can be grateful. It means that there is so much more to discover about the Lord and his relationship with us and ours with him. Unlike those disciples in Ephesus, we have been told about the Holy Spirit, the Spirit of God the Father and of Jesus. Yet we have so much more to learn about the place of the Holy Spirit in our lives, and we all have a journey to travel in terms of opening ourselves more fully to the guidance of the Spirit. When it comes to our faith, we are always on a journey of discovery and the road ahead is always full of wonderful surprises, as we seek to enter ever more deeply into the mystery of God's loving relationship with us.

31 May, Tuesday, The Visitation of the Blessed Virgin Mary
Luke 1:39–56

The month of May has traditionally been associated with Mary. It is fitting that the last day of May should be a feast of Mary, the feast of her visitation to her cousin Elizabeth. This scene in Luke's Gospel has become the second joyful mystery of the Rosary. The first part of the prayer we know as the Hail Mary is drawn both from the greeting of the angel Gabriel to Mary at the annunciation, 'Hail, full of grace', and from the response of Elizabeth to Mary's greeting at the visitation, 'Blessed are you among women and blessed is the fruit of your womb.' Gabriel was God's messenger to Mary and Mary was God's messenger to Elizabeth. As Gabriel brought good news to Mary, so Mary brought good news to Elizabeth. We are all called to be God's messenger to one another; we are to be good news for each other. According to the gospel reading, in response to Mary's greeting, Elizabeth was filled with the Holy Spirit, and because of the way that Elizabeth received Mary, Mary was filled with a spirit of prayer as she exclaimed, 'My soul proclaims the greatness of the Lord ...'. There was something about the way these two women received each other that allowed the Holy Spirit to come alive within each of them. They were good news for each other. The encounter between these two women can serve as a model for all our human encounters. The quality of Mary's visit to Elizabeth and the quality of Elizabeth's reception of Mary has much to teach us about how to visit others and how to receive the visit of others.

1 June, Wednesday, Seventh Week of Easter
John 17:11–19

In today's gospel reading Jesus prays for his disciples on the eve of his passion and death. Jesus prays that God would protect them from the evil one. This prayer of Jesus for his disciples puts us in mind of one of the petitions in the Lord's Prayer, the prayer that Jesus asked us to pray. In that prayer we pray, 'lead us not into temptation but deliver us from evil or from the evil one'. Jesus' prayer for his disciples is the prayer that we are to pray for ourselves. In praying that his disciples would be delivered from the evil one, Jesus is praying that they would remain faithful to himself, true to himself, true to God and true to their calling as his disciples. Jesus begins his prayer for his disciples by asking God to 'keep those you have given me true to your name'. That is Jesus' prayer for all of us. He prays that we would be true to God's name, true or faithful to the word of Jesus or, to put it more negatively, that we would be delivered from evil, that we would resist the temptation to be unfaithful to the Lord and what he desires of us. This is, in a sense, the fundamental prayer that Jesus prays for us and that he wants us to pray for ourselves. Jesus prays this prayer for us and we are to pray it for ourselves precisely because he does not ask God to remove us from the world of unbelief and hostility, but sends us straight into that world to proclaim the truth of the Gospel.

2 June, Thursday, Seventh Week of Easter
John 17:20–26
The prayer of Jesus in today's gospel reading, 'May they all be one', has been the primary inspiration for the ecumenical movement, especially since the Second Vatican Council. On the night before he is lifted up on the cross to draw all people to himself, Jesus prays for a unity of love among his present and future disciples. He goes on to pray, 'Father, may they be one in us.' He suggests there that the unity he is praying for among his disciples flows from their relationship with himself, Jesus, and his Father. In other words, this unity is not just the result of human effort. It is rooted in our communion of love

with God and God's Son. It is God through his Son, who creates this unity among the disciples of Jesus. Our role is to cooperate with this work of God. God is always at work to bring about a unity, a communion, among the disciples of Jesus that reflects the unity or communion between God and Jesus. That is why Jesus prays in the gospel reading 'that they may be one as we are one'. This is God's work among us today. Towards the end of that prayer, Jesus expresses how God brings about this quality of unity among us, Jesus' disciples. Jesus prays that 'the love with which you loved me may be in them, and so that I may be in them'. When the love of God for Jesus dwells within us, when Jesus himself dwells within us and flows through us, then the unity that Jesus is praying for will come to pass. There is a wonderful vision here of what we are called to be as followers of the Lord. We are to open our hearts to God's love for us in Jesus. We are to allow the person of Jesus to live in us and shape our lives, so that we become one, in the way that God and Jesus are one. Only when this happens, Jesus says in the gospel reading, will the world outside the church come to believe in Jesus as the loving face of God. 'May they all be one ... so that the world may believe it was you who sent me'.

3 June, Friday, Seventh Week of Easter
John 21:15–19
Peter had denied Jesus three times over a charcoal fire just before Jesus' crucifixion. In today's gospel reading, the risen Jesus asks Peter three times, 'Do you love me?' In the setting of a meal that the risen Jesus had with his disciples over another charcoal fire, Jesus was giving Peter the opportunity to reverse his threefold denial. With the threefold question to Peter, 'Do you love me?' Jesus was inviting Peter to make a fresh start. Jesus wasn't going to hold Peter's threefold denial against him. On the contrary,

when Peter answered, 'Yes, Lord, you know I love you', to Jesus' question, Jesus gave him an important role in the Church. 'Feed my lambs, feed my sheep'. Peter was to be the chief shepherd in Jesus' Church; he was to care for the other disciples as Jesus' representative. Peter went on to do great things for the Lord. He would lay down his life for the Lord and his Church; he would show himself to be a good shepherd in the image of Jesus himself. Even though Peter was unfaithful to Jesus, denying him three times, the Lord remained faithful to him. His love for Peter didn't lessen because of Peter's denial. There was never any question about Jesus' love for Peter; the only question was whether Peter continued to love Jesus, which is why Jesus asked him three times, 'Do you love me?' Even though we may fail the Lord in various ways, the Lord will always be faithful to us. He loves us unconditionally. His love for us never ceases, even when we deny him by the way we live, by what we say or do. If we fail the Lord in some way, he will always give us the same opportunity he gave to Peter, the opportunity to renew our relationship with him, our love for him. As risen Lord he comes to us to ask us the question he asked Peter, 'Do you love me?' He asks that question of us in a special way at every Eucharist. At every Mass we have the opportunity to say with Peter, 'Lord, you know everything; you know I love you'. When we renew our love for the Lord in that way, he will call us too, as he called Peter, to shepherd one another, to care for and look out for one another, to show something of the Lord's own faithful love towards one another.

4 June, Saturday, Seventh Week of Easter
John 21:20–25
I have always been struck by the ending of today's gospel reading, which is the ending of John's Gospel. It declares that Jesus did

many other things, apart from what is written in this gospel. Indeed, according to the evangelist, the world could not contain the books that would need to be written to express all that Jesus said and did. This Fourth Gospel gives us a very rich insight into Jesus as God in human form, the Word become flesh. Yet the author acknowledges that there is so much more to Jesus than he has managed to express. The other three evangelists could undoubtedly have written the same about their own gospels. It is good to be reminded that there is more to Jesus than the gospels give us, not less. The identity of Jesus is so rich that it is impossible to express it fully, even in four wonderful gospels that were written under the inspiration of the Holy Spirit. The gospels give us a marvellous insight into who Jesus is and what he said and did, but even that insight falls short of the wonder of Jesus, now risen Lord. Even with the gospels, we have to say with Saint Paul that now we see as in a mirror dimly and it is only then, beyond this earthly life, that we will see face to face. If we are attracted by the Jesus of the gospels, our 'seeing' of him beyond this earthly life will be all the more wonderful. Saint Paul speaks about the breadth and length and height and depth of the love of Christ that surpasses knowledge. We could spend our whole life exploring that love of Christ, and still have a great deal more to discover beyond this earthly life.

6 June, Monday, Blessed Virgin Mary, Mother of the Church
John 19:25–34

Three years ago, Pope Francis inserted the Memorial of the Blessed Virgin Mary, Mother of the Church, into the Church's liturgical calendar, to be celebrated on the Monday after the feast of Pentecost. He was acknowledging that devotion to Mary as mother of the Church is a very ancient tradition. Coming on the day after the feast of Pentecost, reminds us that Mary was present with the disciples at Pentecost when the Holy Spirit came down upon them. According to today's second reading from the Acts of the Apostles, she joined with the twelve apostles and several women in continuous prayer as they all prepared to receive the Holy Spirit who had been promised by the risen Lord. This moment of the coming of the Holy Spirit is often celebrated as the birth of the Church. Men and women were joined together in prayer at the birth of the Church and Mary was in the midst of them in a motherly role. She was the mother of Jesus, but now she was also the mother of Jesus' male and female disciples, the mother of the Church. This is the role that Jesus gives her from the cross in today's gospel reading. At the foot of the cross there is again a little community of men and women, rather, of one man, the beloved disciple, and several women. This beloved disciple who has no name stands in for us all, male and female disciples, and what Jesus says to him he says to us all, 'this is your mother', having just said to his mother, 'Woman, this is your son'. Mary becomes mother of all disciples, mother of the Church, at the foot of the cross. At Pentecost she shows herself a mother by praying with other disciples in preparation for the coming of the Spirit. In the first reading Eve is spoken of as 'the mother of all those who live'. Mary was understood early in the Church as the new Eve, mother of all those who live with the life of her Son, a life received in baptism and nourished at the Eucharist. Mothers tend to pray for their children, and Mary prays for us all, just as she was praying with the disciples in our second reading. In the Hail Mary we recognise this motherly role of Mary when we say to her, 'Pray for us, sinners, now and at the hour of our death.' We all need people to pray for us, and it is reassuring to know that Mary, mother of the Church, our spiritual mother, responds to our request to pray for us.

7 June, Tuesday, Tenth Week in Ordinary Time
Matthew 5:13–16

In Ireland, wherever the land is mountainous or hilly, towns and villages tend to be built in the valleys where there is shelter from the wind and the rain of winter. In Italy, and also in Palestine, where Jesus lived, towns and villages in hilly or mountainous areas tend to be built on top of the hills rather than in the valleys because in the heat of summer the hilltop is a much more pleasant place to be than the valley. The saying of Jesus in the gospel reading reflects that practice; Jesus speaks of a city or a town built on a hilltop. Such a city cannot be hidden; it is visible for all to see. Nazareth, where Jesus grew up, was such a hilltop town, visible from the valley below and the hills around. Jesus was saying to his disciples, and to us, 'like a city on a hilltop you cannot be hidden'. The light of Christ has shone in our hearts; we are to let that light shine, rather than try to hide it. Jesus identifies letting our light shine with the doing of good works, the kind of works that the values of the Beatitudes inspire, the works that are performed by the gentle, those who hunger and thirst for what is right, the merciful, the pure of heart, the peacemakers. Within the circumstances of our own particular lives, we are called to do the good words inspired by the values of the Beatitudes, so that the light of Christ may continue to shine through us today.

8 June, Wednesday, Tenth Week in Ordinary Time
Matthew 5:17–19

The opening statement of Jesus in today's gospel reading, 'Do not imagine that I have come to abolish the Law or the prophets', suggests that there were some who believed that Jesus was doing just that. In reality, he declares, he has come to fulfil the Law and the prophets, in the sense of revealing what truly corresponds to God's will in all of the Law and the prophets. Jesus presents himself in the Gospel of Matthew as the authentic interpreter of the word of God in the Law and the prophets. Because Jesus is Emmanuel, God-with-us, he is uniquely placed to interpret what God is truly saying to us through the Law and the prophets. Jesus insists that the Jewish Law, as he interprets it, is valid 'till heaven and earth disappear'. In the remainder of the Gospel of Matthew, Jesus will highlight what he terms 'the weightier matters' of the Law, which he identifies as 'justice, mercy and faith'. He also highlights the greatest commandments of the Law, the love of God with all one's being and the love of neighbour as oneself. All prescriptions of the Jewish Law must be tested against these two great commandments. Even though much of the Jewish Law no longer applies to us today, Jesus' interpretation of the Jewish Law remains valid for all time. Jesus did not abandon the old but drew out what was best there, recognising that God who now speaks through him also spoke through the traditions of the past. There is always some good in the past, including in our personal past. The Lord is always at work to bring what is best there to full flowering.

9 June, Thursday, Feast of Saint Columba
Matthew 8:18–27
Columcille was born in Gartan, Coountyu Donegal in 521 and was of royal lineage, belonging to a branch of the O'Neill dynasty. He studied under Saint Mobhi in the monastery of Glasnevin, and went on to establish monasteries in Derry, Durrow and possibly Kells. In 563 he left Ireland with twelve companions and founded a monastery on the island of Iona off SW Scotland, which was given to him by the ruler of the Irish Dalriada for the purpose of establishing a monastery. The monastery became a place of learning, with the monks engaged in the copying and

illumination of manuscripts. Columcille remained the rest of his life in Scotland, mainly Iona, returning to Ireland only for occasional visits. He died on June 9, 597. Columcille and his companions preached the gospel in the western part of Scotland. After his death, monks from Iona went to evangelise Northumbria, where they established monasteries at Lindisfarne and Whitby. Columcille and his companions made the word of God fully known wherever they went. During their ministry, they went through many a stormy time, like the disciples in today's gospel reading. Yet, just as Jesus was with the disciples in the storm at sea and brought them through it, he was with Columcille and his companions through all their difficult moments, and they came to discover, like those first disciples, that the Lord was stronger than the storm. Our own following of the Lord won't always be easy; the storms and trials of life will often put our faith to the test. Just as Jesus was asleep in the boat, it can seem to us at such times that the Lord is asleep on our watch. Yet the Lord is always attentive to us. One of the psalms expresses that conviction very well, 'He will not let your foot be moved; he who keeps you will not slumber. He who keeps Israel will neither slumber nor sleep'. The Lord is ever watchful and faithful. It is we who can become faithless or, in the rebuke of Jesus to the disciples in the boat, people of 'little faith'. It is because we are all prone to 'little faith' that we need to keep making our own that prayer of the father of a seriously ill boy which we find in one of the gospel stories, 'Lord, I believe, help my unbelief.'

10 June, Friday, Tenth Week in Ordinary Time
Matthew 5:27–32
The teaching of Jesus in today's gospel reading shows a profound respect for women. Jesus is addressing married men primarily,

saying to them, 'If the law prohibits you to commit adultery against your wife, I prohibit the lustful look that leads to adultery.' Jesus was very aware that how we see people profoundly influences how we behave towards them. Not just individuals but a whole people can be seen as less than human, and then treated accordingly, as we know from the history of the twentieth century. Racism is a form of behaviour that is rooted in a certain way of seeing people. Jesus knew that actions spring from what is in the human heart, the attitudes and values that reside there. Jesus goes on to address married men regarding divorce. It was common practice in the time of Jesus for a married man to divorce his wife for the flimsiest of reasons, thereby leaving his wife vulnerable and exposed. A woman, in contrast, could never divorce her husband under Jewish Law. In prohibiting married men from engaging in casual divorce, Jesus was calling on them to be faithful to their wives in love, to respect them as equals. Jesus' defence of woman against male exploitation in today's gospel reading is in keeping with his defence of all who were vulnerable in his society, the poor, the blind, the deaf, the lame, children, those judged to be possessed by evil spirits. Jesus' attitude of respect for everyone was rooted in his loving relationship with God, his deep conviction that everyone was equally precious in God's sight. The more we open our hearts to the Lord in love, the more we let him into our lives, then the more we will imbibe his loving respect for all. In the first reading, Elijah the prophet lets the Lord into his life more fully. On that occasion the Lord came to Elijah not in the dramatic signs of the mighty wind or the earthquake but in the sound of a gentle breeze. The Lord doesn't overpower us; he comes to us gently, imperceptibly, respecting our freedom. Whenever we welcome his coming and receive him into our hearts, he will send us out, as he sent out Elijah, to bring his life-giving presence to all those we meet.

11 June, Saturday, Tenth Week in Ordinary Time
Matthew 5:33–37

In a court of law people take an oath that they will tell the truth and nothing but the truth. The giving of the oath is a recognition that, left to themselves, witnesses might not always tell the truth. Pressure needs to be applied to people to tell the truth by getting them to swear an oath on the Bible. When Jesus calls on his disciples not to swear at all whether it is by heaven or by God's throne or by the earth, he is calling for a quality of truthfulness in speaking that renders the taking of an oath superfluous. His disciples are to speak truthfully at all times, saying 'yes', when they mean 'yes', and 'no' when they mean 'no'. We recognise in ourselves the tendency to say 'yes' when we mean 'no' and 'no' when we mean 'yes'. Jesus told a parable once of a father and his two sons. He asked his sons to work on his land, and one of them said 'yes' but really meant 'no', because he didn't follow through on his 'yes'. In the past we often used the term 'white lies' to refer to the telling of an untruth that had a certain justification in our eyes. In the gospel reading, Jesus calls upon us to speak the truth at all times. Yet he would have recognised that, sometimes, love for someone requires that we do not tell them the full truth all at once. We sometimes have to judge how much truth people can cope with at any particular time in their lives. It was T. S. Eliot who said that 'humankind cannot bear very much reality'. Out of love for someone, we sometimes have to ask, 'How much truth can this person bear?' There is always a delicate interplay between love and truth. Loving someone means being truthful with them, but perhaps not necessarily giving them all of the truth at the one time. The letter to the Ephesians expresses this interplay of love and truth very well: 'Speaking the truth in love, we must grow up in every way into him who is the head, into Christ.'

13 June, Monday, Eleventh Week in Ordinary Time
Matthew 5:38–42

The question of land is often a contentious one, especially land that has been in a family for generations. The land can have more than a monetary value; the story of a family over many generations can be deeply embedded in a plot of land. In the first reading, when king Ahab offered Naboth the worth of his vineyard in money or even a better vineyard, he replied, 'The Lord forbid that I should give you the inheritance of my ancestors'. Naboth was very aware that his vineyard belonged not just to himself but to the members of his family who went before him. King Ahab went into a kind of a sulk, because he couldn't get his way. His wife, Jezebel, was much more decisive. She arranged for Naboth to be killed, so that Ahab could just go and take possession of the vineyard. She worked on the principle that 'if you want something badly enough and you have the power to get it, then just take it, regardless of the consequences for others'. It is an attitude that is not without its parallels in today's world. It would be difficult to classify such an attitude, such behaviour, in any other way but 'evil'. There is much evil in our world today, as there was in the world of Naboth. How do we deal with evil? Jesus' answer to that question in today's gospel reading may sound very unrealistic to many, and even ineffective: 'Offer the wicked person no resistance.' Surely, we should resist evil and those who embody evil? However, Jesus spoke those words as a comment on what is often called the law of retaliation, 'eye for eye, tooth for tooth'. In other words, evil should be met with evil, the taking of a life with the taking of a life. Jesus went beyond that principal. For him, the response to evil is not more evil but, rather, extraordinary goodness. Jesus responded to the evil that was done to him on Calvary with extraordinary loving goodness, which is why we call the Friday on which he was crucified 'Good Friday'. When Paul was writing to the church in Rome, he made reference to 'those who persecute you', and his call to the church was, 'Do not be overcome by evil, but overcome evil with good.' Jesus was very aware that evil done to people can easily generate more evil. The call to overcome evil with good is one of the most demanding calls of the Gospel, but it is one we can live out in the power of the Holy Spirit.

14 June, Tuesday, Eleventh Week in Ordinary Time
Matthew 5:43–48

In yesterday's gospel reading Jesus calls on his followers not to take vengeance on the enemy. In today's gospel reading, he goes further and calls on us to love the enemy. As one commentator on this passage puts it, 'Who else is left to love, after one has loved the enemy?' The love Jesus speaks of is not just a feeling but finds expression in active service. We might think of the parable of the good Samaritan, in which the Samaritan renders loving service to the injured Jew, who would have been regarded by the Samaritan as an enemy. Such a love of the enemy will also find expression in prayer for the enemy, as when Jesus asked his Father to forgive those who were responsible for his crucifixion. The human tendency is to focus our love on those for whom we have strong feelings of warmth and affection. This is natural, but according to today's gospel reading, it is not exceptional. Jesus calls on us to stretch beyond those our love would naturally embrace. This is one of the gospel texts that does indeed stretch us. Jesus is calling on us to reveal, by our way of relating to others, the God who in love causes the sun to rise on bad people as well as good, and the rain to fall on honest and dishonest alike. This way of life that Jesus calls us towards is only possible in the power of the Holy Spirit, who lives among us and within us.

15 June, Wednesday, Eleventh Week in Ordinary Time

Matthew 6:1–6, 16–18

Three times in the course of the gospel reading Jesus speaks of God as 'your Father who sees all that is done in secret'. Jesus is saying that God sees what humans often do not see. God sees the good we do that others do not get to see. Jesus saw in the way that God sees. He often saw the good people were doing that others never saw. He recognised the generosity of the widow at the Temple treasury. She put in two small copper coins, hardly making a sound as they were dropped into the treasury. She would have gone unnoticed by most people present. However, Jesus noticed her and drew the attention of his disciples to her extraordinary generosity, recognising that in giving the little she gave she was, in reality, giving everything she had. Jesus often saw goodness in people whom others would have written off. He invited himself to the house of Zacchaeus because he recognised that there was more to Zacchaeus than met the human eye. The human eye only sees so much. As the Jewish Scriptures declare, we look at appearances, whereas the Lord looks at the heart. The Lord always sees what is best in us, even when the goodness in our heart or the good we do is below the radar when it comes to human seeing. We are called to live as people who are always before the Lord, aware that the Lord is always seeing us, not with judgemental eyes but with eyes of love, eyes that recognise the good in us that others very often do not see and that, perhaps, we do not even see ourselves.

16 June, Thursday, Eleventh Week in Ordinary Time

Matthew 6:7–15

When it comes to prayer, Jesus declares in today's gospel reading that God the Father knows what we need before we ask him. The prayer of petition, therefore, is not about giving information to

God that God does not already have. It is not a matter of bringing to God's attention something of which God is not already aware. Jesus seems to be suggesting that the prayer of petition is not primarily for the sake of God but for our sakes. To petition God changes us, not God, and the quality of our petitioning God will impact on the quality of the change in us. In today's gospel reading, Jesus teaches us how to petition God in a way that helps to make us the kind of person that God desires us to be. We are to be people who place the doing of God's will before the doing of our own will and who give greater priority to the coming of God's kingdom than to the protection of our little fiefdoms. We are to be people who pray out of a sense of belonging to a community, with the emphasis on 'we' and 'us' rather than on 'I' and 'my'. We are to be people who acknowledge our dependence on God for all that is vital in our lives, our daily bread. We are to be people who are always aware of our need for God's mercy and who stand ready to the give to others the mercy we have received from God. We are to be people who acknowledge that the person God desires us to be is always being put to the test by evil and who therefore recognise our need for God's strength to keep us faithful to his daily call. Here is a prayer which is also a portrait of the person we are called to become as sons and daughters of our heavenly Father and disciples of his beloved Son.

17 June, Friday, Friday, Eleventh Week in Ordinary Time
Matthew 6:19–23

In today's gospel reading, Jesus contrasts two kinds of treasures, treasures on earth and treasures in heaven. He implies that treasures on earth are vulnerable to all kinds of external forces, such as the actions of the thief. In contrast, treasures in heaven are totally secure. Elsewhere in the gospels, Jesus speaks of being rich in the sight of God, which is equivalent to storing up treasures in heaven. Jesus is saying that it is not earthly treasures and possessions that make our life secure but being rich in the sight of God. The one person who was supremely rich in the sight of God was his Son, Jesus, and we are rich in the sight of God to the extent that we are becoming conformed to the image of his Son, in the language of Saint Paul. Jesus shows us what being rich in the sight of God looks like. Rather than storing up treasures for himself on earth, he emptied himself in the service of others. He gave himself away for others and this self-giving reached its completion on the cross. As he hung from the cross, he was supremely poor in the eyes of the world, but supremely rich in the sight of God. In so far as we allow the risen Lord to live out his self-giving love in our lives, we too will be rich in the sight of God and our lives will be truly secure.

18 June, Saturday, Eleventh Week in Ordinary Time
Matthew 6:24–34

At the end of the gospel reading, Jesus makes a distinction between the pagans, who set their hearts on food, drink and clothing, and his followers, who are to set their hearts on the coming of God's kingdom and on God's righteousness, the doing of God's will. That distinction governs all Jesus has been saying prior to this statement. We are not to worry about our earthly life, what we are to eat and drink, and about our body, what we are to wear, to the point where this worry becomes dominant in our lives. It goes without saying that, for those who lack the basic necessities of life, what to eat and drink and how to be clothed will be the dominant concern of their lives, and Jesus is clear in his teaching that we have a responsibility to meet their needs, declaring that what we do or fail to do to them we do or fail to do to him. Seeking first the kingdom of God will often mean feeding the hungry and clothing the naked. However, Jesus seems to be primarily addressing those who are in danger of allowing their concern for material things to become dominant in their lives or, in the language of the gospel reading, those who are in danger of becoming slaves of money. We can be overly anxious about matters that are not of ultimate importance and not anxious enough about what really matters in the Lord's eyes. Such was the anxiety of Martha when Jesus entered her home. Jesus is less concerned with the presence of anxiety in our lives than with the focus of our anxiety. He met many people in the course of his ministry who were anxious about the wrong things. The Lord wants us to allow his own anxiety for the coming of God's kingdom and the doing of God's will to become the dominant anxiety in our lives.

20 June, Monday, Twelfth Week in Ordinary Time
Matthew 7:1–5
We live in a somewhat judgemental society. If someone fails in some way, people can take a certain delight in drawing attention to their failure. In that sense, the message of Jesus in today's gospel reading has a somewhat subversive feel to it: 'Do not judge, and you will not be judged.' Jesus seems to be suggesting that when we judge others, we are leaving ourselves open to God's judgement. Jesus may be implying that when we judge someone, we are doing something that only God can do. We simply do not have the insight into others to judge them fairly or justly. In addition, our own perception of others is restricted because of our own failings. This seems to be the point of the humorous image Jesus uses of someone with a plank in their eye trying to take a splinter out of someone else's eye. Because of all kinds of prejudices and failings in ourselves, we don't see clearly enough to make a sound judgement of others. There is a line in the Jewish Scriptures,

'The Lord does not see as mortals see; they look on the outward appearance, but the Lord looks on the heart.' In John's Gospel, it is said of Jesus, 'He himself knew what was in everyone.' Jesus is considered unique in this regard. No one else knows what is in everyone. Our limited insight into others, arising partly out of our own failings, should make us slow to judge others. Saint Paul was true to the teaching of Jesus in this matter of judging others. He says in his first letter to the Corinthians, 'Do not pronounce judgement, before the time, before the Lord comes, who will bring to light the things now hidden in darkness and disclose the purposes of the heart.' Only the Lord can disclose the purposes of the human heart; we can never get inside the heart of another. It is clear from the gospel reading that Jesus wants us to work on our own failings before focusing unduly on the failings of others. 'Take the plank out of your own eye first.' There is enough there to be going on with, for most of us.

21 June, Tuesday, Twelfth Week in Ordinary Time
Matthew 7:6, 12–14
In using the image of entering by the narrow gate in today's gospel reading, Jesus is suggesting that the way of life he has set before his disciples is a difficult and challenging way. Entering through a narrow gate requires a clear focus and a certain concentration of effort. Jesus is also suggesting that his way will often run counter to the way taken by the great majority. The call of the Gospel, in that sense, will often be experienced as counter to the prevailing culture. For that reason, it will require a conscious decision on our part. The way of the Lord, with all it entails, is a way that needs to be chosen. That choice is always a response to a call, the Lord's call, but it remains a human choice. We may have been baptised into this way of the Lord as infants but as we go through

life we have to choose this way for ourselves. Every day we have to choose to go through the narrow gate, to take the Lord's way. Although the gate is narrow and the way may be difficult, Jesus assures us in the last line of the gospel reading that his way is the way that leads to life. It not only leads to life beyond this earthly life, eternal life, but it leads to life here and now. As Paul says in his second letter to the Corinthians, 'now is the day of salvation'. Jesus offers himself to us as the gate and he promises that all who walk through him will find life to the full.

22 June, Wednesday, Twelfth Week in Ordinary Time
Matthew 7:15–20
There is often a value in disguise. In time of war combatants often need to disguise themselves, especially when they are in enemy territory. The art of spying is heavily dependent on disguise. However, there are settings where disguise is not appropriate and it is to such settings that Jesus refers in today's gospel reading. He warns his disciples against false prophets, those who come claiming to be announcing the word of God but who are actually only announcing their own word. They look as harmless as sheep but in reality they are as dangerous as wolves, so they are not to be trusted. Jesus is reminding us of the uncomfortable truth that people can be more harmful than they appear to be on the surface. Unfortunately, many have made that discovery to their great cost, and continue to do so. How can you recognise genuine goodness, rather than be taken in by the appearance of goodness? Jesus declares very simply but profoundly, 'you will be able to tell them by their fruits'. When the New Testament speaks of 'fruit' in relation to human lives, the reference is always to qualities that reflect the life of Jesus. In John's Gospel the branches of the vine, the disciples of Jesus, bear the fruit of love, the quality of love

that God has for Jesus and that Jesus has for his disciples and for the world. In the letters of Paul the fruit of the Holy Spirit in a person's life is also love, because, for Paul, the Holy Spirit is the love of God poured into our hearts. Those in whom the Spirit bears the fruit of love can be trusted because the good fruit of the Spirit always comes from a good heart, a heart that has been given over to the Lord.

23 June, Thursday, Feast of the Birth of John the Baptist
Luke 1:57–66, 80

The feast of the birth of Jesus coincides more or less with the winter solstice as the light begins to increase, as befits one who said of himself, 'I am the light of the world.' The feast of the birth of John the Baptist coincides more or less with the summer solstice as the light begins to decrease, as befits one who said, 'He [Jesus] must increase, but I must decrease.' In the gospel the crowds at the circumcision of the child John ask the question, 'What will this child turn out to be?' He turned out to be the one who worked to ensure that Jesus would increase, even if that meant that he had to decrease. His calling, his mission, was to make a way for Jesus in people's lives, to prepare people to receive Jesus. Having already received Jesus into his own life, he became the first and most powerful witness to Jesus before others. He was the voice who called Israel's attention to the presence of the Word standing among them, unknown to them. John's role and mission speaks to us of our own role and mission as people who have been baptised into Christ. We too are called to make a way for Jesus, firstly in our own lives, and then in the lives of others. Like John, we are called to create a space for Jesus to increase in our own lives and in the lives of others. Like him, we are to welcome the coming of Jesus into our lives so that we can witness to Jesus before others. John was executed before Jesus suffered his own passion and death. John did not know of the resurrection of Jesus. He died before the coming of the Church, which was born from the death of resurrection of Jesus. In that sense, we are much more privileged than he was. As Jesus says, 'The least in the kingdom of heaven is greater than he.' Yet John remains a shining lamp for us all, as Jesus once referred to him. John reveals the essence of our baptismal calling, which is to witness to Jesus by opening our lives to Jesus' presence and allowing him to increase in us.

24 June, Friday, Feast of the Most Sacred Heart of Jesus
Matthew 11:25–30

In today's gospel reading, Jesus first addresses God in prayer, and then he addresses all who labour and are overburdened. Those were the two fundamental movements in the life of Jesus, towards God in prayer and towards others, especially the burdened, in loving compassion. The heart of Jesus, his sacred heart, was always open to God, and open to others. It was because his heart was so fully open to God that he fully revealed the loving heart of God towards others, especially towards all who were struggling in any way. His prayer to God in today's gospel reading is a prayer of praise, 'I bless you, Father'. He praises God out of a recognition of what is happening in his ministry. Yes, many of those who think of themselves as learned and clever are rejecting his message, his invitation, but many others are welcoming his ministry, those considered mere children by the learned and the clever, those who haven't studied the Jewish Law, who have no impressive credentials to their name, who are not considered honourable or important in the eyes of the world. On one occasion, Jesus said that unless we all become like children we will not enter the kingdom of God. We need to approach the Lord with humility, with a recognition that we need all he has to offer us, and that we have nothing to offer that he needs. This is the attitude of the poor in spirit, to whom the kingdom of God belongs. When we are poor in spirit, humble in heart, then we are more likely to hear and respond to the invitation the Lord offers us in the gospel reading, the invitation to come to him and to find rest for our souls. It is a very personal invitation. Jesus says, 'Come to me', not 'Come to my teaching'. He says, 'Learn from me', not learn from this law code or that set of teachings. It is a call from the Lord's heart to our heart. The prayer of Jesus shows that he had a deep communion with God, but Jesus wants us to have a deep communion with himself, and, through him, with God. It is that loving communion with the Lord which is at the heart of our faith. It is only out of the strength, the rest, received from that loving communion with the Lord that we can live in the loving way the Lord calls us to live. The life of faith, which is a life of love, is a joyful response to an experience of the Lord's love for us. As today's second reading puts it, 'Since God has loved us so much, we too should love one another.' The heart of Jesus, the life of Jesus, reveals God to be love. When we look upon Jesus, we cannot but say, 'God has loved us so much.' Today's feast of the Sacred Heart invites us to welcome that love like children and to allow it to flow through us to bless and grace others.

25 June, Saturday, Twelfth Week in Ordinary Time
Matthew 8:5–17

During the months of lockdown, we became used to things happening at a distance from us. Children and young people were taught at a distance. Parishioners attended Mass at a distance, as they tuned in to parish Masses via parish webcams. In today's gospel reading, Jesus healed at a distance. When a Roman centurion pleaded with Jesus about his seriously ill servant, Jesus was willing to go to this pagan's home, just as he subsequently went to the home of Peter's mother-in-law. However, the centurion did not consider himself worthy to have this renowned Jewish man of God visit his pagan home, and he expressed faith in Jesus' ability to cure his servant at a distance. He believed that Jesus did not need to visit his home in person for him to do his healing work. Jesus could enter his home without having to go there physically. The centurion knew the power of his own word on his subordinates, and he believed that the word of Jesus was much more powerful, powerful enough to heal at a distance. The gospel reading says that Jesus was astonished at the centurion's faith. The centurion symbolises all those pagans who would come to believe in Jesus without having seen or heard him, all those who believed in Jesus without having physical contact with him. In that sense, the centurion represents us all. We believe that the Lord can enter our homes, our lives, without him having to enter our homes physically in the way he entered the home of Peter's mother-in-law. Like the centurion, we believe that the Lord is never really distant from us. He can enter our homes, our hearts, our lives, at every hour of every day. 'Say but the word.' The Lord's word can grace and bless us at any time, in any place. All the Lord needs for that to happen is for us to have something of the centurion's faith, something of his openness of heart and sense of expectancy. Then the Lord will be astonished at us, as he was astonished at the centurion.

27 June, Monday, Thirteenth Week in Ordinary Time
Matthew 8:18–22

The words of Jesus to the two men who wanted to become his followers must have sounded very challenging to them. We are not told how the two would-be followers of Jesus reacted. Did they have a change of mind and heart when they heard what Jesus said to them? Jesus was highlighting two qualities of being a follower of his that remain valid for all time. To the first man, Jesus says that he will be following someone who has nowhere to lay his head. Jesus will always be on the move; becoming his follower is not a settled way of life. Even though we are all settled to some degree, being the Lord's disciples never leaves us completely settled. The Lord is always calling us beyond where we are. He is always prompting us to take some new step in our relationship with him, to deepen our allegiance to him, to grow in our readiness to go where he leads us. What Jesus says to the second man can seem especially harsh to our ears. However, we have to imagine a situation where the man's father has not actually died, but is very elderly. The would-be disciple wants to wait until his father dies and bury him before following Jesus. In response, Jesus says, in effect, 'Now is the time to follow me, not at some indefinite future date.' We can all be tempted to put off following the Lord until sometime in the future. We may be aware that the Lord is calling us to something worthwhile, but we keep putting off our response to that call. Jesus' words remind us that there is an urgency about his call. Today, now, the present moment, is always the ideal time to respond to his call. The two responses of Jesus in today's gospel reading suggest that he doesn't want us to become too settled in our following of him, or to keep postponing our response to his call indefinitely.

28 June, Tuesday, Thirteenth Week in Ordinary Time
Matthew 8:23–27
I like the music of Margaret Rizza and I especially like the chant 'Calm me Lord', whose repeating verse goes 'Calm me Lord as

you calmed the storm; / Still me, Lord, keep me from harm. / Let all the tumult within me cease, / Enfold me, Lord, in your peace.' From earliest times Christians have made a link between Jesus calming the storm in today's gospel reading and the risen Lord calming the storm in our lives. The disciples found themselves in a storm at sea. That external storm caused a storm within. They were frightened, as is clear from their prayer to Jesus, 'Save us, Lord, we are going down.' We can all find ourselves buffeted by some form of external storm. Something over which we have little or no control breaks over us. It often generates an internal storm within us. We feel frightened and powerless, perhaps even hopeless and despondent. Many people had such feelings during the time of the recent pandemic which, like the storm in the gospel reading, broke over us without warning. In such situations, there is often little we can do about the external storm. We have to go through it. However, the Lord can calm the resulting storm within us, if we turn to him in trusting prayer, like the disciples in the boat. Our prayer may take the form of a cry from the depths, 'Save us, Lord, we are going down.' The gospel reading suggests that this is a prayer the Lord always responds to. Our prayer of trust will always open us up to the Lord's steadying influence, allowing us to weather the storm until we reach a place of peace.

29 June, Wednesday, Feast of Saints Peter and Paul
Matthew 16:13–19

Today we celebrate the feast of Saints Peter and Paul. Each of them went through their own times of confinement, of social isolation. There were each imprisoned for their preaching of the Gospel. In the first reading, we heard that King Herod arrested Peter and put him in prison. Yet, according to that reading, Peter in prison was supported by the prayers of the church: 'The church prayed to God for him unremittingly.' The Lord came to him in his imprisonment through the prayers of the faithful. The Lord came to him in an even more dramatic way through an angel who delivered him from his confinement and restored him to the community of faith. Peter declared, 'The Lord really did send his angel and has saved me.' Hopefully, the story of Peter reflects our own experience. When we are confined, socially isolated, the Lord does not isolate himself from us. Even when we cannot come to church, the Lord comes to us. The Lord knows nothing of social isolation. Even when we cannot receive the Eucharist, we can say in the words of today's responsorial psalm, 'Taste and see that the Lord is good.' This was the experience of Saint Paul as well, the other great pillar of the Church. In today's second reading, he writes from prison, fully expecting that he may not get out alive, 'The time has come for me to be gone.' It was a very isolating experience for him. He writes, in a verse omitted from our reading, 'all deserted me'. Yet, like Peter, he experienced the Lord's powerful presence. As he says in today's reading, 'The Lord stood by me and gave me power', and he goes on, 'the Lord will bring me safely to his heavenly kingdom.' Like Peter, he experienced the Lord's sustaining presence when he was at his weakest and most isolated. This is one of the lessons these two great preachers of the Gospel can teach us today. The Lord comes to us in our times of weakness and stands by us in our moments of isolation. No matter what distressing situation we may find ourselves in, the Lord is with us to strengthen and sustain us. Even when we are cut off from those who matter most to us, we are never cut off from the Lord, because he is always true to his name of Emmanuel, 'God with us'. That is why, in the words of today's psalm, every moment of every day, we can 'look towards him and be radiant'.

30 June, Thursday, Thirteenth Week in Ordinary Time
Matthew 9:1–8

It can seem strange to us that the first words Jesus speaks when the paralytic is brought to him are, 'Courage, my child, your sins are forgiven.' We would have expected Jesus to heal him immediately of his physical paralysis. This he went on to do, but Jesus first addresses himself to the man's need for spiritual healing. Jesus recognises that this is as great a need for the man as his need for physical healing. Many of us need some form of physical healing, especially as we get on in years, yet we all need spiritual healing at every stage of our life's journey. Jesus is the great mediator of God's forgiveness to us. He speaks of himself in the gospel reading as the Son of Man who has authority on earth to forgive sins. The title 'Son of Man' is one that Jesus often uses with reference to himself. It is a title that is found only on the lips of Jesus; no one ever uses it of him. It can mean, 'Son of Humanity', and, therefore, highlight that Jesus is human in every respect, like us in all things but sin. The title can also have a more glorious sense. In the Book of Daniel, the Son of Man is a glorious figure to whom God gave an everlasting kingdom. In the time of Jesus, many Jews looked forward to the coming of this glorious, heavenly, Son of Man. The title 'Son of Man' can relate to Jesus in his humanity and in his glorious state. The risen, glorious Lord continues to have authority on earth to forgive sins today. He will always respond to our need for spiritual healing, if we approach him recognising our need for this form of healing. He continues to say to us today what he said to the paralytic, 'Courage, my child, your sins are forgiven.' We all need to hear such words on a regular basis in the course of our lives.

1 July, Friday, Thirteenth Week in Ordinary Time
Matthew 9:9–13

In the first reading today, Amos, in his usual forthright way, speaks of a coming time when there will be a famine of hearing the word of the Lord. People will hunger for the word of the Lord but it will not be there; they will seek the word of the Lord but fail to find it. Because the people have been failing to take the Lord's word to heart, the Lord will stop speaking to them. It is as if Amos is saying that the Lord will withdraw from sinners. However, the gospel reading strikes a somewhat different note. There Jesus shares table with Matthew the tax collector and with other tax collectors and people who would have been classified as sinners. Jesus not only breaks bread with them at table; he also breaks the bread of God's word with them, God's healing and merciful word. In response to the Pharisees who criticise Jesus for eating with sinners, Jesus quotes from one of the prophets, not the prophet Amos, but the prophet Hosea: 'What I want is mercy and not sacrifice.' Jesus reveals a merciful God, who expects others to show mercy too; he reveals a God who does not withdraw his living word from us, even when we show ourselves unworthy of it. Rather, the Lord continues to speak his word of love and light into the darkest and most troubled places of our lives. He keeps offering us the bread of his word to satisfy our deepest hunger. As he does so, he waits for us to take and eat, as Matthew and his companions did.

2 July, Saturday, Thirteenth Week in Ordinary Time
Matthew 9:14–17

In the course of the gospels Jesus speaks of himself in a whole variety of ways, as shepherd, gardener, flute player, sower, king, mother hen, and many more. Each image expresses some aspect of his ministry. In today's gospel reading he speaks of himself as a bridegroom. 'The time will come for the bridegroom to be taken away from them.' Jesus seems to be alluding here to his own death, his crucifixion. If he is the bridegroom, he refers to his disciples as the bridegroom's attendants. These are the people who look after the bridegroom on his wedding day. It would never be expected that such attendants would fast. A wedding day is celebratory; it is a time for eating and drinking. Jesus was defending his disciples against those who accused them of not fasting enough. He was comparing his ministry to a joyful wedding feast to which everyone was invited. He came to proclaim good news; there was a joyful dimension to his ministry. That remains the case today. The Lord remains the bridegroom and, according to Saint Paul, we, the Church, are his bride. There is a lovely beatitude in the Book of Revelation, 'Blessed are those who are invited to the wedding feast of the Lamb'. That beatitude embraces all of us. We are all invited to the wedding feast of the Lord, who is our bridegroom. That feast will be celebrated fully in the kingdom of heaven, but it is already being celebrated in this life. Here and now the Lord is inviting us to share in his joy, the joy of the heavenly bridegroom. It is a joy that comes from knowing that we are deeply and faithfully loved by the Lord. The Lord's love has been poured into our hearts through the Holy Spirit and this joy is the fruit of the Holy Spirit in our lives.

4 July, Monday, Fourteenth Week in Ordinary Time
Matthew 9:18–26

In the gospel reading Jesus is approached by two people who are very different. One is a synagogue official, who has a recognised and important religious role within the community. The other is a woman who suffers from a flow of blood, and who, in virtue of that condition, would have been considered ritually unclean, and, therefore, excluded from the synagogue. Not only are these two people at opposite ends of the religious spectrum of the time, but the way they approach Jesus is very different. The official comes up to him very publicly, bowing low in front of him. The woman secretly touches the fringe of Jesus' cloak, not wanting to be noticed. In spite of their different standing within the community and their different approaches to Jesus, what they had in common was their great faith in Jesus and in his saving power. Jesus responded equally generously to both of these people, healing the official's daughter and healing the woman of her condition. The gospel reading suggests that what matters to the Lord is not our standing in the community or how we approach him, how we pray, but the strength of our faith in him, the quality of our relationship with him. According to the opening line of today's first reading, the Lord lured the people of Israel into the wilderness to speak to their heart. The Lord speaks to the heart of all of us who approach him and he always responds to our plea for help.

5 July, Tuesday, Fourteenth Week in Ordinary Time
Matthew 9:32–38
We would probably all agree with the assessment of the people in today's gospel reading to the healing ministry of Jesus: 'Nothing like this has ever been seen in Israel.' We might even go further and say, 'Nothing like this has ever been seen anywhere.' This was a unique moment in human history when, in this particular time and place, God became God-with-us in the person of Jesus of Nazareth. The opening line of today's responsorial psalm declares, 'Our God is in the heavens; he does whatever he wills.' In Jesus, God was on earth and God's will was being done through Jesus, on earth as in heaven. This indeed was something to be wondered at. Yet, according to the gospel reading, there were some, the experts

in the Jewish Law, who held that Jesus' healing ministry showed the power of Satan at work. The revelation of God's goodness was being interpreted as the working of supreme evil. It is hard to understand how some people could have got Jesus so wrong, yet it is a reminder to us all that our way of seeing can be extremely skewed. We sometimes see what is not there and fail to see what is there. We need to be open to the Spirit of God to recognise the working of God's Spirit among us. As Paul says in his first letter to the Corinthians, 'No one comprehends what is truly God's except the Spirit of God. Now we have received ... the Spirit that is from God, so that we may understand the gifts bestowed on us by God.' Every day we are to invite the Spirit of God into our lives so that we can see more clearly the signs of God's presence and activity all around us.

6 July, Wednesday, Fourteenth Week in Ordinary Time
Matthew 10:1–7

Today's first reading and responsorial psalm call on us to seek the Lord. God, speaking through the prophet Hosea, says, 'It is time to go seeking the Lord until he comes to rain salvation on you.' The psalmist calls on us to 'consider the Lord and his strength; constantly seek his face'. We seek after many things in life, but the Scriptures remind us that at the heart of all our seeking is a seeking of the Lord, who alone can satisfy the deepest hungers and thirsts of our heart. We are to seek a personal relationship with the Lord and the way of life that flows from that relationship. The gospel reading reminds us that when we seek the Lord, he is at the same time seeking us. Having appointed the twelve Jesus calls on them to go to the lost sheep of the house of Israel. Later in this gospel Jesus will say, 'I was sent only to the lost sheep of the house of Israel.' In the Gospel of Luke, Jesus says more broadly,

'The Son of Man came to seek out and to save the lost.' Jesus is like the shepherd who seeks his lost sheep, the woman who seeks her lost coin, the father who seeks out his lost sons. Jesus is always seeking us, especially when we turn from him. When we 'constantly seek his face' we discover that the Lord is constantly seeking us. Our seeking of him is always a response to his seeking us, even when we are not aware of it.

7 July, Thursday, Fourteenth Week in Ordinary Time
Matthew 10:7–15

There is a very motherly image of God in today's first reading from the prophet Hosea. Speaking through the prophet, God says to Israel, 'I was like someone who lifts an infant close against his cheek; stooping down to him I gave him his food.' It is language suggestive of a mother's care for her infant child. The quality of God's love is such that it needs to be expressed in the imagery of both motherly and fatherly love. The best of a father's love and the best of a mother's love give us a glimpse into the nature of God's love. Jesus was the fullest revelation of God's love possible. He speaks of his searching love as like that of a shepherd searching for his lost sheep and a woman searching for her lost coin. He speaks of the kingdom of God as like a farmer who sows a mustard seed in the soil and a woman who took yeast and mixed it in with three measures of flour. There is a male and female dimension to the kingdom of God. In the gospel reading, Jesus sends out the twelve to proclaim that the kingdom of heaven or the kingdom of God is close at hand. They are to give expression in their ministry to both dimensions of the kingdom of God; they are to reveal God's motherly and fatherly love. Such love will show itself especially in their care for the sick and vulnerable. The Church needs to find new ways of expressing the male and female character of God and of God's kingdom. It is only men and women working together in ministry who can begin to give adequate expression to the love of God spoken of by Hosea in our first reading.

8 July, Friday, Fourteenth Week in Ordinary Time
Matthew 10:16–23

At the beginning of today's gospel reading, Jesus makes reference to four different animals, sheep, wolves, serpents and doves. The twelve are being sent out to places where they will encounter great hostility. They will be as vulnerable as sheep before wolves. In dealing with their enemies they are to be as clever and cunning as serpents, so as to protect themselves from unnecessary hostility. At the same time, they are to harm no one, remaining as innocent and as free of malice as doves. The situation of hostility that Jesus describes is true to the experience of disciples today in many parts of the world. The setting in which disciples live today is becoming more hostile, even in those countries that have been culturally supportive of Christianity in the past. Many believers feel more and more like sheep among wolves and are becoming more aware of their need for the cunning of the serpent while remaining free of malice towards those who are hostile to them. Jesus assures his disciples that when the opposition to them is at its greatest, they will not be left to their own human resources alone. The Holy Spirit will be given to them by God, to strengthen them for the ordeal and to enable them to witness to Jesus by what they say and do. The Spirit is given to believers in every age to help them remain faithful when put to the test. In the first reading, God says to the people of Israel, 'I am like a cypress ever green, all your fruitfulness comes from me.' Jesus says the same in different terms, promising us the Spirit from God who will bear the rich fruit of courage and wisdom in our lives when the wolves are at the door.

9 July, Saturday, Fourteenth Week in Ordinary Time

Matthew 10:24–33

You may have recognised a line in today's first reading as very similar to one of our responses at Mass, 'Holy, holy, holy is the Lord of hosts. His glory fills the whole earth.' Many of our responses at Mass are taken from the Scriptures. In a vision, Isaiah heard the angels acclaim God with these words in the Temple in Jerusalem. Isaiah's sense of the holiness of God brought home to him his own sinfulness: 'I am a man of unclean lips.' The closer he came to God, the more aware he became of how unlike God he was. Isaiah was giving expression to a sense of reverence and awe in God's presence, what is sometimes referred to as 'fear of the Lord'. The word 'fear' there doesn't mean what we normally mean by fear. It is that sense of the otherness of God, the holiness of God, which brings home to us our own unworthiness to be in God's presence. In the gospel reading, Jesus calls on his disciples to fear God, in that sense. God is beyond us; God's thoughts are not our thoughts; God's ways are not our ways; God evokes our reverence and awe. Yet this same God became human in the person of Jesus. Jesus revealed God to be beyond us in the sense that God is so much more loving and caring than any human could be. In the gospel reading, Jesus speaks of God as one who cares for the details of his creation, who knows when a humble sparrow falls to the ground. Jesus goes on to say that God's loving care for each one of us is so much greater because we are worth more than hundreds of sparrows. Jesus had a very deep sense of God's loving care for him and he wants us to know that God cares for us all just as much as he cares for his Son. Jesus' sense that God was holding him in the palm of his hand gave him the strength and the courage to do what God was asking of him. Jesus wants us all to be without fear in that sense. Three times in today's gospel reading he calls on us not to be afraid of those who are hostile to our faith. We can be courageous in our witness to Jesus, because God is taking care of us, as he took care of Jesus.

11 July, Monday, Fifteenth Week in Ordinary Time
Matthew 10:34–11:1

In today's first reading, the Lord, speaking through the prophet Isaiah, makes a very powerful statement. He declares that all the worship of the Temple in Jerusalem is unacceptable to him if it is not accompanied by a search for justice and by a readiness to help the oppressed and the most vulnerable. This message is very much in keeping with the two basic commandments of the Jewish Law, which are inseparable one from the other, the commandment to love God with all one's being and to love our neighbour as ourselves, especially our vulnerable neighbour. We give expression to our love of God by worshipping God and by loving those whom God loves. The life of Jesus is in complete harmony with that teaching of the Jewish Scriptures. Jesus was a person of deep prayer and also a person who sought justice for others, who befriended the most vulnerable. In the gospel reading, Jesus says that we are to love him above everyone else; we are to prefer him more even than those for whom we have the strongest natural affection, such as our parents. The Lord is to be our first love. Yet Jesus goes on to identify himself with his disciples declaring, 'Anyone who welcomes you, welcomes me', and saying that 'anyone who gives so much as a cup of cold water' to his disciples will not lose their reward. The Lord comes to us through his followers, especially through those he calls the 'little ones' among his disciples, those most likely to be dismissed as unimportant. Later in Matthew's Gospel he declares that he comes to us through the hungry, the thirsty, the naked, the stranger, the sick, the imprisoned, whether they are his disciples or not. We love the Lord through loving others. We are to worship the Lord in prayer and with our lives. Saint Paul in his letter to the Romans speaks of our 'spiritual worship', which consists in presenting our bodies, our whole selves, 'as a living sacrifice, holy and acceptable to God'. This kind of worship will always find expression both in prayer and in the loving service of others.

12 July, Tuesday, Fifteenth Week in Ordinary Time
Matthew 11:20–24
In the chapter of Matthew's Gospel previous to today's gospel reading, Jesus had said, 'You received without charge, give without charge.' When the Lord gives to us, he looks to us to give to others from what we have received from him. When the Lord gives, we need first to receive from what he gives, and then to give to others from what we have received. That first step of receiving what the Lord gives is vital. We can be slow to receive what the Lord wants to give us. We have to keep learning to receive from him. As Jesus says elsewhere, anyone who does not receive the kingdom of God like a child will never enter it. In today's gospel reading, Jesus bemoans the fact that the inhabitants of Chorazin, Bethsaida and Capernaum were unwilling to receive what Jesus was offering them. God had worked powerfully through Jesus in these towns, yet their inhabitants failed to receive Jesus. God was gifting them through Jesus, yet they did not welcome God's gifts through Jesus, God's gift of Jesus. Today's gospel invites us to ask ourselves, 'How well do we receive all that God is offering us through his Son?' The opening chapter of John's Gospel declares that Jesus came among us full of grace and truth and from his fullness we have all received. Because the Lord is full of God's love for us, there is no limit to how much we can receive from

him. There is always more to receive, and more that we can give from what we have received.

13 July, Wednesday, Fifteenth Week in Ordinary Time
Matthew 11:25–27

At a critical time in Matthew's Gospel when Jesus finds his ministry largely rejected in Galilee, he nevertheless praises his Father, Lord of heaven and earth. Even as Jesus was experiencing rejection from many of the towns of Galilee, he knew there was much to give thanks and praise to God for. There are times in our own lives when nothing seems to be going well for us. We feel disappointment and hurt at how others are relating to us. However, even in such moments, there is always something for which we can give thanks and praise to God. If we look at our situation with the eyes of faith, we will always find some sign of God's grace and favour for which we can give thanks. In his first letter to the Thessalonians, Paul says, 'Give thanks in all circumstances.' He doesn't say give thanks *for* all circumstances but *in* all circumstances. Paul is reminding us that even when our faith in God is being put to the test and we find life a struggle, there is always something for which we can give thanks. In the face of opposition and hostility, Jesus gives thanks to God because in his mysterious plan it is the 'babes' in the field of religion, the poor , the tax collectors, the sinners, rather than the experts in the Law, who are open and receptive to God's revelation of himself through Jesus. It is they who have the poverty of spirit to receive what God is offering. Sometimes, the trials and struggles of life can help us to become more like children, in the sense of opening us up more fully to all the blessings and graces that God continues to shower upon us through Jesus. This is something for which we can certainly give thanks.

14 July, Thursday, Fifteenth Week in Ordinary Time

Matthew 11:28–30

This short gospel reading is one that has spoken powerfully to believers over the centuries. The personal nature of Jesus' invitation is very striking. He does not say, 'Come to my teaching', or 'learn from all I say and do', but, rather, 'Come to me' and 'learn from me'. He calls us into an intimate and personal relationship with himself as one who is 'gentle and humble in heart'. In the next chapter of his gospel, Matthew identifies Jesus with the servant of God who 'will not break a bruised reed or quench a smouldering wick'. He is gentle and humble in the sense of knowing how to receive people in their weakness and vulnerability. He encourages us to turn towards him when we feel crushed or overburdened by life's demands. When Jesus issues an invitation in the gospels, it is often accompanied by a promise. His invitation to come to him is accompanied by a promise of rest. 'Rest' is not simply the absence of activity or work. The Sabbath rest was a time when people were given the opportunity to be renewed in body, mind and spirit. It was a time of refreshment and restoration at all levels of one's being. When the Jews looked forward to the age of the Messiah, they thought of it as a prolonged time of rest in that Sabbath sense. The rest Jesus offers is a fullness of life which is associated with life in God's kingdom. Although fully experienced beyond this earthly life, Jesus offers an anticipation of this rest in the here and now. He promises that those who come to him and learn from him and walk in his way will find what the Fourth Gospel calls a joy the world cannot give, a deeply satisfying sense of refreshment.

15 July, Friday, Fifteenth Week in Ordinary Time

Matthew 12:1–8

One of the questions we can all find ourselves asking from time to time is, 'What does God want?' We may not always manage to do what God wants, but we seek to know what God wants, nonetheless. We believe that it is Jesus who has shown us what God wants, more than any human being who ever lived. In today's gospel reading, he quotes from the prophet Hosea to show us what God wants: 'What I want is mercy, not sacrifice.' According to Jesus, God places a higher value on merciful love towards others than on offering sacrifice in the Temple. Jesus spoke those words from Hosea to the Pharisees who were criticising Jesus' disciples for satisfying their hunger on the Sabbath by picking ears of corn and eating them. They considered this a form of work that was forbidden on the Sabbath. There was a lack of mercy on their part towards the hungry disciples. They allowed their strict interpretation of the Sabbath law to make them judgemental. They needed to be reminded that what God wanted above all was 'mercy', a willingness to make allowances for human weakness, in this case the weakness of the body, the need to satisfy hunger, even on the Sabbath. It is a reminder we all need from time to time. We can all be tempted to judge people unfairly and unnecessarily, not making allowances for human weakness, the same human weakness that is in ourselves. Jesus revealed God to be a God of mercy, which is why he shared table with those considered sinners at the time, people who broke the Jewish Law in various ways, including the Sabbath Law. It led people like the Pharisees to ask, 'Why does this man eat with tax collectors and sinners?' Because we are made in the image of God, Jesus reminds us in today's gospel reading that God wants us to be merciful as God is merciful. If we have received merciful love from God, who are we to refuse it to others?

16 July, Saturday, Fifteenth Week in Ordinary Time
Matthew 12:14–21
The first reading from the prophet Micah refers to 'those who plot evil', and in the gospel reading the Pharisees begin to plot against

Jesus and, as a result, he withdraws from the district where he had been. Jesus is not in the business of plotting against anybody. His ministry is one of merciful love. The gospel reading goes on to interpret Jesus' ministry in the light of a quotation from the prophet Isaiah. Jesus had spoken about himself as 'gentle and humble in heart' (11:29). Such a person does not 'brawl or shout', in the language of the quotation. The primary focus of Jesus' mission was those plotted against in various ways, the afflicted crowds, the 'crushed reeds' and 'smouldering wicks', in the language of the quotation from Isaiah. Pope Francis often speaks about the need for tenderness in our relationships with others. The quotation from Isaiah evokes Jesus' tender love towards the broken and vulnerable. Jesus could be angry when anger was called for, towards his opponents and even towards his own disciples. Towards the most vulnerable, however, he showed tender loving care. Rather than breaking the crushed reed, he helped to mend it. Rather than putting out the smouldering wick, he fanned it into a living flame. Such tender love was the visible expression of the presence of the Holy Spirit in his life. In the words of the quotation from Isaiah, Jesus is the servant whom God has endowed with his Spirit. The risen Lord has poured that same Spirit into all our hearts so that we can become servants in the mould of Jesus, giving expression to his tender love for the weak and vulnerable among us. Like him, we are to care and provide for the crushed reeds and smouldering wicks, those who have lost their vibrancy and whose light has almost gone out.

18 July, Monday, Sixteenth Week in Ordinary Time
Matthew 12:38–42
There are times when the message of the Jewish Scriptures anticipates very clearly the teaching of Jesus. We find an example

of that in today's first reading. The prophet Micah gives a succinct statement of what God wants of us, what God asks of us: 'to act justly, to love tenderly and to walk humbly with your God'. It is a very striking formulation of the two great commandments, to love God with all one's being and our neighbour as ourselves. Walking humbly with our God implies a loving and trusting relationship with God. Acting justly and loving tenderly spells out the meaning of loving our neighbour as ourselves. In the gospel reading, Jesus claims to be greater than the wise men and women of Israel, greater than Solomon, and greater than the prophets of Israel, greater than Jonah. Yet much of Jesus' teaching is in line with the teaching of the wise men and prophets of Israel, especially the prophets. Jesus is in continuity with his Jewish tradition but also goes beyond it. He claims to be bringing it to completion or fulfilment. God has given us the gift of his Son, Jesus, someone greater than all the prophets and wise people of Israel. We are indeed blest to have received such a gift. God's gift of his Son is with us to the end of time. Someone greater than Solomon and Jonah is here, with us, now and every day of our lives. We don't come to Jesus demanding signs from him, like the Pharisees in the gospel reading. The Lord will give us signs of his presence, without us having to ask for them. The most powerful of his signs is to be found in the lives of all those people who are trying to act justly, to love tenderly and to walk humbly with their God.

19 July, Tuesday, Sixteenth Week in Ordinary Time
Matthew 12:46–50

Today's gospel reading is the first mention of Jesus' mother since the story of Jesus' infancy in chapters 1 and 2 of Matthew's Gospel. The last we heard of Jesus' mother, Mary, and of his father, Joseph, was in the setting of the family's escape to Egypt from the murderous intentions of King Herod and their return to Israel after the death of Herod. Joseph then made his home with Mary and Jesus in Nazareth. In the chapter following the one from which we are reading today, when Jesus returns to Nazareth for the first time since his baptism the townspeople will ask, 'Is not this the carpenter's son? Is not his mother called Mary?' In today's gospel reading, Jesus makes clear that he has moved on from his blood family and is in the process of starting a new family of his disciples. The wish of Mary and other members of Jesus' family to speak to Jesus is the opportunity for Jesus to declare who his true family now is, his true mother, brothers and sisters. This must have been a difficult reality for Mary to come to terms with. She had to let Jesus go to God's greater purpose for his life. One of the great challenges of love is having the freedom to let go of the beloved when that is called for. We can assume that Mary had that freedom. Genuine love for another, the love inspired by the Holy Spirit, is always a love that surrenders to God's purpose for the life of the loved one. Mary's love for Jesus was no less when he moved on from his blood family to form a new family of disciples. As members of Jesus' new family, we are called to love others in the same selfless way that Mary loved Jesus.

20 July, Wednesday, Sixteenth Week in Ordinary Time
Matthew 13:1–9
There is a lot of failure in the parable of today's gospel reading. Much of the farmer's work seems wasted. Much of the good seed that he generously scattered fell on unpromising soil and came to nothing. Yet, at the end of the day, enough seed fell on good soil for the harvest to be bountiful. Jesus is suggesting that the experience of failure is never the end of the road. Jesus' public ministry, during which he liberally scattered the seed of God's loving reign,

met with a great deal of failure. Indeed, Jesus' crucifixion was the ultimate expression of failure. Yet Jesus was not discouraged by his experience of failure. He continued to do God's work, confident that God would ensure that, in the end, the harvest would be plentiful, for Jesus and for all who believe in him. Some of the seed Jesus scattered fell on good soil; his presence and ministry met with a generous, even if flawed, response on the part of some. They would become the nucleus of a new community beyond his death. God even worked powerfully through the ultimate failure of crucifixion, raising his Son from the dead and pouring out the Spirit of his risen Son on all who believe in the Gospel preached by the disciples. The harvest turned out to be great, even if the labourers, at times, were few. The parable is a statement of hope, of confidence in the power of God to work in the midst of failure. It encourages us to live with our own experiences of failure, trusting that our failure need never be the end of the road for us, but that God can work powerfully in and through us, in spite of failure.

21 July, Thursday, Sixteenth Week in Ordinary Time
Matthew 13:10–17
The words of Jesus in today's gospel reading suggest that there is a difference between looking and seeing and between listening and hearing. It is possible to look without really seeing and to listen without really hearing. What do we see when we look? What do we hear when we listen? Jesus complains that when many of his contemporaries looked upon him, they did not see him for who he truly was, the one through whom God was powerfully at work and in whom God was uniquely present. When they listened to him, they did not hear his words as words from God. In contrast to many of his contemporaries, Jesus declares his disciples to be 'blessed' because they saw Jesus for who he really was when they looked

upon him, and when they listened to what he said they heard God's word. Jesus reflected in sadness on the failure of many to see and hear, because, in turning towards him with open eyes and attentive ears, they would have been healed by Jesus, in the language of Isaiah whom Jesus quotes. Where do we stand? Is it with many of Jesus' contemporaries or with his disciples? We would all want to be embraced by the beatitude that Jesus addresses to his disciples, 'Blessed are your eyes, because they see, your ears because they hear.' Yet we are aware that we are not always fully attentive to the Lord when he speaks to us and shows himself to us. We are always on the way towards a clearer seeing and a more finely attuned hearing of the Lord who is present among us.

22 July, Friday, Feast of Saint Mary Magdalene
John 20:1–2, 11–18
According to the gospels, Mary Magdalene was one of the women disciples who followed Jesus in Galilee. She stood with the other women looking on as Jesus was crucified. She witnessed the burial of Jesus by Joseph of Arimathea. She went to the tomb with other women early on the first day of the week. It is the Gospel of John that highlights the role of Mary Magdalene on Easter Sunday. The portrayal of Mary Magdalene standing outside the tomb of Jesus weeping, in today's gospel reading, is true to the experience of all who have suffered a painful loss. As a priest, I have witnessed many a person weeping at a graveside. The tears we shed at a graveside flow from our love for the person who has died. We have a profound sense of loss and we are heartbroken. When we love someone deeply, sooner or later our heart will be broken. On that first Easter Sunday, Mary seems to have been alone weeping outside the tomb, yet she was not really alone. The one for whom she wept was present to her, even though she did not identify him.

'She turned around and saw Jesus standing there, though she did not recognise him.' She thought she was seeing the gardener. The risen Lord is always present to us in our moments of sadness and grief, in our times of struggle and distress. Like Mary Magdalene, we don't always recognise the Lord's presence. We can be so absorbed by our grief or by our plight that we struggle to see beyond it. At such times, we often need to find a quiet moment to become aware of the risen Lord's presence, and to hear him speak our name, as he spoke Mary's name to her. It was when the stranger spoke her name that she recognised him as the risen Lord. As Jesus said to Mary Magdalene, the risen Lord has ascended to his Father and our Father, to his God and our God, but he is also present among us and present to each one of us personally, especially in times of loss and struggle. The feast day of Mary Magdalene invites us to allow ourselves to become more aware of the risen Lord's presence and to become more attuned to his addressing us by name.

23 July, Saturday, Feast of Saint Bridget of Sweden
John 15:1–8

Bridget was born in the year 1303. She was the daughter of a wealthy governor in Sweden. When she was thirteen she was married off to a wealthy man. They lived happily together for twenty-eight years and had eight children, four sons and four daughters. She went on to serve as the principal lady-in-waiting to the queen of Sweden. She had a reputation as a woman of great prayer. After her husband's death, Bridget became a member of the Third Order of Saint Francis and devoted herself to a life of prayer and caring for the poor and the sick. She sensed Christ calling her to found a new religious order. She founded a monastery for sixty nuns and twenty-five monks who lived in separate enclosures but shared the same church. She journeyed to Rome in 1349, with her daughter Katerina, to obtain papal approval for her order. She never returned to Sweden. She spent much of the remainder of her life on pilgrimage in Italy. She also made a pilgrimage with her daughter and son to the Holy Land. Along with Catherine of Siena, she worked hard to get Pope Clement VI to return from Avignon to Rome. She was admired for her simplicity of life and her devotion to pilgrims, to the poor and the sick. She experienced visions of various kinds; some of them were of the passion of Christ. She died in her house in Piazza Farnese in Rome in 1373. She was canonised in 1391, less than twenty years after her death. In 1999, Pope John Paul II made her a co-patroness of Europe, alongside Saint Catherine of Siena and Saint Teresa Benedicta of the Cross. In the gospel reading for the feast of Saint Brigid, Jesus, our risen Lord, declares himself to be the vine. 'I am the vine, you are the branches.' It is difficult to distinguish between the vine and its branches. Where does the vine end and the branches begin? When Jesus refers to himself as the vine and to us as the branches, he is giving us an image of the very intimate relationship that he desires to have with us, his disciples. The Lord is intimately involved with his Church. He is in communion with us. That is a given. What Jesus calls for in the gospel reading is that we be in communion with him, that we make our home in him, after the example of Saint Brigid. The image of the vine and the branches also expresses our dependence on the Lord. We need to be in a deeply personal communion with Jesus so as to live off the sap that reaches us from him. We need to live in close contact with him, if we are to be fruitful in the way he wants us to be, in the way Saint Brigid was. It is only in and through our communion with Jesus that we can bear his fruit, the fruit of the Spirit, which is love. We need to nurture a vital contact with him, to ensure that we are a truly life-giving and life-enhancing presence in our world, as Brigid was in the world of her time.

25 July, Monday, Saint James, Apostle
Matthew 20:20–28

According to the gospels, James and his brother John were among the first disciples that Jesus called to follow him. Their father, Zebedee, seems to have had a successful fishing business by the Sea of Galilee, as he had 'hired men' working for him alongside his two sons. James and his brother were present at key events of the public ministry of Jesus, such as his raising of the daughter of Jairus, his transfiguration on the mountain and his distraught prayer in the Garden of Gethsemane. According to the Acts of the Apostles, in the year 44 CE King Herod Agrippa 'had James, the brother of John, killed with the sword' (Acts 12:2). He was the first member of the group of the twelve apostles to be put to death for his faith. According to an ancient tradition James's bones were brought from Jerusalem to Compostela in north-western Spain. His shrine there has been a place of pilgrimage for the past thousand years or more. Of all the passages in the New Testament where James features, today's gospel reading shows him in the least favourable light. The mother of James and John, speaking on their behalf, asks Jesus for seats on his right and left in his kingdom for her two sons. The brothers' preoccupation with worldly honour draws forth Jesus' powerful teaching on what constitutes true honour in his kingdom. 'Anyone who wants to be great among you must be your servant.' James went on to be a great servant of the Church and of the Lord, even to the point of drinking the cup of suffering that Jesus drank. At this point in the gospel story, however, James was still a work in progress. Yet God had begun a good work in him and would bring it to completion. James is an encouragement to us all. Sometimes, like James in today's gospel reading, we can display a side to ourselves that falls short of what the Lord desires for us. Yet such failures need not hold us back from continuing to take the path the Lord is calling us to take or becoming the faithful servant the Lord desires us to be. The Lord knows, in the words of Paul in today's first reading, that we are like earthenware jars holding the precious treasure of the Gospel. Like such jars, we are prone to breaking. Yet, as Paul reminds us in that reading, the overwhelming power to live our baptism to the full comes from God and not from us. The Lord's power is always at work, even in our weakness.

26 July, Tuesday, Seventeenth Week in Ordinary Time
Matthew 13:36–43

Today's first reading from the prophet Jeremiah reflects the darker side of human existence. There is death in the countryside and hunger in the city. The religious leaders, prophets and priests, are at their wit's end. Anguished questions rise up to God. 'Why have you struck us down with no hope of cure?' People's legitimate hopes have been dashed. 'We were hoping for peace, no good came of it! For the moment of cure, nothing but terror!' Yet in the midst of such devastation and darkness of spirit, people have not lost hope in God. 'O our God, you are our hope'. It can be difficult to keep hopeful faith in God when there seems to be no human reason for hope. Yet so often the Scriptures inspire us to keep hoping and trusting in God even when, especially when, 'we are in the depths of distress', in the words of today's responsorial psalm. In the gospel reading, Jesus acknowledges that all will not always be right with the world. What Jesus calls 'the enemy', those opposed to God's good purposes, will sow darnel, seeking to kill off the good seed, but he assures us that in the end God's good purposes will win out, 'the virtuous will shine like the sun in the kingdom of their Father'. God is working and will continue to work through the glorious Son of Man to overcome the forces of evil and ensure the coming of God's kingdom. Saint Paul expressed this conviction very succinctly: 'Where sin abounds, grace abounds all the more.' This is the basis of our hope. Hope is rooted not in anything human but in God's life-giving power, which, in the words of Paul, 'is able to accomplish abundantly far more than all we can ask or imagine'.

27 July, Wednesday, Seventeenth Week in Ordinary Time
Matthew 13:44–46

There is often a gap between finding something of value to us and actually possessing it. In both of the two short parables in today's gospel reading, someone finds a treasure, but having found it does not yet possess it. The man in the first parable, probably a poor day labourer, finds treasure in a field that he wasn't looking for. The man in the second parable, probably a wealthy merchant, finds a pearl of great value that he had been looking for over many years. What these two people from opposite ends of the social spectrum have in common is that, having found this wonderful treasure, they have the freedom to sell everything so as to purchase and possess it. The few resources the poor day labourer had and the many resources the wealthy merchant had seemed of little value compared to the treasure they had found. Jesus is saying that the kingdom of God is like both of those scenarios. The dynamic gift that Jesus brings to us from God is like the treasure hidden in the field and like the pearl of great price. The fullness of this gift from God is in the future, beyond this earthly life, but we can begin to savour it here and now. To the extent that we find and appreciate this wonderful gift for the treasure it is, we will be happy to sacrifice everything else to possess it. We will hold our various possessions lightly and have the freedom to let them go for the sake of this rich gift that Jesus has come to bring us, which is a sharing in his own relationship with God and the way of life it inspires. In his letter to the Philippians, Saint Paul lists all that he once treasured and then he goes on to say, 'I regard everything as loss because of the surpassing value of knowing Christ Jesus my Lord'. Christ was his treasure in the field, his pearl of great price, before whom all else seemed so much loss. The same risen Lord and all he offers us is our treasure, our precious pearl, before whose surpassing value all else pales.

28 July, Thursday, Seventeenth Week in Ordinary Time
Matthew 13:47–53
In the Scriptures, day-to-day human experience is understood to speak about God's relationship with us and our relationship with God. A potter at his wheel speaks of God's ability to reshape our lives when it comes out wrong. God does not give up on us when our lives do not turn out as God desires for us, just as the potter does not give up on the clay when the vessel he is trying to make comes out wrong. God can work on lives that are out of shape, in the sense of not being genuine images of God. Whenever we turn out wrong, we can be tempted to give up on ourselves, closing down a better future for ourselves. At such moments, God's way of looking upon us is very different. God sees the potential for good there, recognising that there is material here to work on. We all need to learn to see ourselves and others more as God sees us. Jesus also saw in the daily event of fishermen catching all kinds of fish an image of how God is relating to people in his own ministry. God, through Jesus, was casting his net far and wide, without discrimination. The Lord was drawing all sorts of people into the

new community he was gathering about himself. He was revealing the God who makes his sun to shine on the bad and the good alike. He shared table with those considered sinners and those regarded as holy. The net of God's abundant love was being cast over all, as the fishermen brought in all kinds of fish. Yet those drawn into the net of God's love would need to open themselves to that love and allow themselves to be shaped by it, as clay is shaped by the potter. There will be a separation, but it will be based not on God's preferences but on how well or otherwise we open ourselves up to God's creative and renewing presence in our lives.

29 July, Friday, Feast of Saint Martha
John 11:19–27

This feast has a certain significance for me because it is the anniversary of my father's death. I was aware that he had a devotion to Saint Martha. There was a novena to Saint Martha over nine Tuesdays, with a candle lit on each Tuesday. A section of the novena prayer read, 'Comfort me in all my difficulties, and through the great favour you enjoyed when the Saviour was lodged in your house, intercede for my family that we be provided for in our necessities.' I can see how that prayer would have appealed to my father, and indeed to any parent. The gospel reading from John for today's feast is often chosen for a funeral Mass, and it was the gospel reading for my father's funeral Mass. We can sympathise with Martha's gentle rebuke of Jesus, 'If you had been here, my brother would not have died.' There was a recognition there of Jesus' healing power, but also an expression of disappointment that he did not come sooner. We can all feel a little let down by the Lord when a loved one dies. The timing of death rarely seems right to us. Jesus' response to Mary's disappointment and grief has spoken to believers ever since as they struggle to let go of a loved one from this life. 'I am the resurrection and the life. If anyone believes in me, even though they die they will live, and whoever lives and believes in me will never die.' Jesus is declaring that our communion with him, which his love for us and our faith in him creates, will not be broken by death. In virtue of that communion, we already live with his risen life, over which death has no power. The question Jesus then addresses to Martha is addressed to us all, 'Do you believe this?' On this her feast day we are invited to make her response to Jesus' question our own.

30 July, Saturday, Seventeenth Week in Ordinary Time
Matthew 14:1–12
In today's first reading, the prophet Jeremiah is almost put to death because he spoke God's word to the people, a word they did not want to hear because it required them to change their ways. In today's gospel reading, John the Baptist, another prophet, is put to death because he spoke God's word to Herod Antipas, the tetrarch of Galilee, a word he didn't want to hear, because it would have required him to change his ways. Both readings show that God's ways are often in conflict with human ways. What God asks of us can sometimes be heard as too demanding from a human point of view. Jesus was understood as a prophet in his lifetime. Indeed, in today's gospel reading Herod thought that Jesus was the prophet John the Baptist come back to life. Like the prophets before him, Jesus' proclamation of God's word was often heard by others as too demanding, too disturbing, and, as a result, he suffered the same fate as many of the prophets before him. Like John the Baptist, Jesus too was executed. Yet Jesus was more than a prophet who proclaimed God's word. He was the word of God incarnate. He could speak God's word in a fuller way than any prophet before him, including John the Baptist. Sometimes we will hear Jesus'

word as demanding and disturbing; he can set the bar very high indeed. At other times, we will hear Jesus' word as reassuring and comforting; he reveals God to be merciful and patient with human weakness. Behind every word Jesus spoke, both the demanding and the consoling words, stands the love of God for the world. All of Jesus' words are words of love and life; they reveal God's loving desire that we would have life and have it to the full. We are called to welcome every word Jesus speaks with the same love with which they have been spoken.

1 August, Monday, Eighteenth Week in Ordinary Time
Matthew 14:13–21

At the beginning of today's gospel reading, we find the disciples in a boat on the Sea of Galilee, battling with a heavy sea and a strong headwind. We can all find ourselves in that situation from time to time. In the gospel reading, the Lord who had been at prayer came to his disciples in their struggle. He may have been praying for his disciples and became aware of them struggling. The Lord is always praying for us. As Saint Paul says in his letter to the Romans, he is at the right hand of God interceding for us. Out of his prayer for us, he comes to us in our struggles, as he came to his disciples, saying to us as he said to them, 'Courage! It is I! Do not be afraid.' Peter showed more courage than the other disciples as he started walking towards Jesus across the water. However, he soon took fright and, feeling himself sinking, cried out, 'Lord! Save me!' Even when we respond to the Lord's call and show some courage, like Peter, we can soon find ourselves losing our nerve and beginning to sink. We seem to be going forward and then find ourselves going backwards again. Yet, just as the Lord reassured his disciples, calling on them to have courage, he reassured Peter, putting out his hand and holding him. The Lord is always there doing that for us too. He puts out his hand and waits for us to grasp it. When life feels fragile and we feel vulnerable, the Lord is always there to hold us, to keep us steady, and to give us the courage to keep going until we come to land in a firmer place. This is how the Lord is always working in our lives, and in response to his working we can do no better than say with the disciples in the boat, 'Truly, you are the Son of God.'

2 August, Tuesday, Eighteenth Week in Ordinary Time
Matthew 14:22–36
In the gospel reading the Pharisees criticises the disciples of Jesus for their lack of reverence for the body of traditions that had grown up around the Jewish Law, in particular the various regulations relating to the washing of hands before eating food. Jesus defends his disciples, however, by declaring that these regulations are not decisive in God's scheme of things. What comes out of people's mouths, what comes from their hearts, is more important before God than the food that goes into people's mouths. What comes from a person's heart is what defines the person, not what they eat or how they eat. It is the heart that counts; we often say of people that their heart is in the right place. On one occasion in Matthew's Gospel, Jesus says, 'Learn from me, for I am gentle and humble of heart.' He calls on us to have something of his own heart within us. In the Beatitudes he declares blessed those who are pure in heart, those whose hearts are focused on what God wants, just as the heart of Jesus was. Jesus seems to suggest that if we get the heart right, if our heart is like his heart, then all else will follow. Getting the heart right is above all the work of the Holy Spirit. It is the Spirit who creates within us a heart that is truly Christ-like. One of the most beautiful prayers in the Church's tradition is, 'Come Holy Spirit, fill my heart, and kindle in me the fire of your love.'

3 August, Wednesday, Eighteenth Week in Ordinary Time
Matthew 15:21–28

The unnamed pagan woman in today's gospel reading has been described as one of the great heroes of the Gospel tradition. It is not easy for us as readers of the gospels today to appreciate the barrier between Jews and pagans in the time of Jesus. Jesus himself shows an awareness of that barrier when he says to the pagan woman who approaches him for healing for her daughter, 'I was sent only to the lost sheep of the House of Israel.' In Matthew's Gospel it is only after the resurrection that Jesus sends his disciples to proclaim the gospel to all nations, Jews and pagans. Up until then, the focus of Jesus would be the renewal of Israel. However, this pagan woman is not prepared to wait. In spite of Jesus' great reluctance to respond to her request, her persistent faith in Jesus and her great wit finally brings crashing down the barrier between Jesus, a Jew, and herself, a pagan. A woman of outstanding faith brings forward Jesus' timetable for proclaiming the Gospel to the pagans. The woman stands in for all of us; she is a wonderful example for all of us of persistent faith. She kept on believing, even in the face of the Lord's silence and resistance. As a result, her faith created a space for the Lord to work in a powerful and unexpected way. She teaches us that the Lord needs our persistent faith if God's purpose for our lives and for humanity is to come to pass.

4 August, Thursday, Eighteenth Week in Ordinary Time
Matthew 16:13–23

In today's gospel we see the two sides to Peter. Initially he shows great insight into Jesus, identifying him as the Son of the Living God, and in response Jesus addresses him as the rock on which he will build his Church. However, Peter then goes on to rebuke

Jesus for speaking about his passion and death, and in response Jesus addresses him as Satan and as a scandal, a stumbling stone, and obstacle in his path. From rock to stumbling stone! It is hard to conceive of a greater contrast. Something of that same contrast, even contradiction, is in all of us when it comes to our relationship with the Lord. We have moments when we are in harmony with the Lord's will for us, and other moments when we are in conflict with his will for our lives. Yet the Lord kept faith with Peter, in spite of his failings, and the Lord keeps faith with us too, even when we show ourselves unfaithful to him. According to today's gospel reading, Jesus built his church on a rather flawed rock, a rock that could quickly become a stumbling stone. When addressing Peter as the rock, Jesus refers to the Church as 'my Church'. Because it is his Church, it will endure, even when those with pastoral responsibility for his Church fail. Because the Church has the risen Lord present within it until the end of the age (Matthew 28:20), the gates of the underworld, the powers of evil and death, will never hold out against it; they will not ultimately triumph. Paul declares that Jesus is the ultimate foundation on which the church is built (1 Corinthians 3:11). Even when, in our weakness as disciples, we become stumbling stones, he at least remains our rock.

5 August, Friday, Eighteenth Week in Ordinary Time
Matthew 16:24–28

Jesus asks a thought-provoking question in today's gospel reading, 'What will anyone gain if they win the whole world and ruin their life?' Jesus is suggesting that we can gain a great deal of what the world has to offer and values, yet lose out at some more fundamental level of our being. We can gain the whole world and, at the same time, lose our life, lose that which makes us truly alive with the life of God. Jesus declares that the opposite is also true.

People can lose a great deal of what is highly valued in the world and yet preserve their life, be fully alive with the life of God. Jesus tells his disciples and all of us in today's gospel reading that it is in following him that we will find this fullness of life. Following the Lord will often mean having to renounce ourselves; in that sense it will mean losing out in the eyes of many. Yet when this is done for the Lord's sake, out of love for him, out of our desire to be faithful to his values, we will grow into our true selves, the self that is made in the image and likeness of our Creator. The call to renounce ourselves can sound very negative to modern ears, yet the Lord's call is fundamentally a call to fullness of life. Our self-denial is in the service of that fullness of life which he desires for us all.

6 August, Saturday, The Transfiguration of the Lord
Mark 9:2–10

There was both a heavenly and an earthly dimension to Jesus. He was both Son of God and Son of Man, Son of Humanity. In today's gospel reading, Peter and the other disciples had an experience of the heavenly dimension of Jesus while on a mountain in Galilee. The world of heaven shone through him in a very striking way, and, as a result, his face shone like the sun and his clothes became as white as light. The disciples had a brush with heaven. They soon had to come down the mountain and would have to set out with Jesus on the road to Jerusalem, where he would be crucified and his face would look very different, broken and pained. On the cross, on the hill of Calvary, he was truly Son of Man, sharing our human brokenness and vulnerability. Yet Jesus was just as much Son of God on the hill of Calvary as he was on the hill of the transfiguration, as the Roman centurion recognised. Peter and the other disciples experienced Jesus as Emmanuel, God with us, on the mount of transfiguration. Yet Jesus was just as much God with us on the hill of Calvary. Jesus is God with us both in those really happy moments of our lives when we easily say ,'It is wonderful for us to be here', and in those troubled moments of our lives when we might find ourselves praying, 'My God, my God, why have you forsaken me?' The Lord is always with us in all his heavenly and risen glory. In every situation of our lives, the bright and dark ones, God the Father is saying to us, 'This is my Son, the Beloved … Listen to him.'

8 August, Monday, Nineteenth Week in Ordinary Time
Matthew 17:22–27

The story in today's gospel reading about the half-shekel has been described as one of the more curious stories in the gospels. The half-shekel was a tax that every Jew paid for the upkeep of the Temple in Jerusalem. The collectors of this half-shekel tax came to Peter to know whether Jesus paid this tax or not. In other words, was Jesus a good Jew? Did he support the Temple like every committed Jew? In the conversation Jesus subsequently had with Peter about this tax, Jesus says, 'the sons are exempt'. Jesus was in the process of forming a new family of disciples, who would be his brothers and sisters, and, thereby, sons and daughters of God. We all belong to that family. On the principle that fathers do not tax their children, Jesus concludes that the members of his new family do not have to pay a tax to God, their Father. However, even though in principle Jesus' disciples are free from this tax, they should pay it, so as not to give unnecessary scandal to those for whom it is important. Jesus is talking here about a deeper freedom, the freedom to renounce one's legitimate freedom out of love for others. This is what Saint Paul would call the freedom of the Spirit. It is the freedom to love, even if that entails renouncing our legitimate entitlements. For Jesus and Paul, loving consideration for others is a higher value than freedom. For us, as followers of Jesus, it is love that shapes how we exercise our freedom. The fundamental question for us as Jesus' disciples is not so much 'What am I free to do or not do?' but 'How can I serve the other in love, especially the most vulnerable?' When we live out of that question, then we reflect something of the freedom of God.

9 August, Tuesday, Saint Teresa Benedicta of the Cross
Matthew 25:1–13

Edith Stein was born in 1891 in Poland, the youngest of seven children of a Jewish family. She was a brilliant student and gained a doctorate in philosophy at the age of twenty-five. She lost her Jewish faith as a teenager. At the age of thirty she came upon the autobiography of Saint Teresa of Avila. It captivated her and she became a Catholic a year later. In her forties, she felt a call to the religious life and she became a Carmelite in 1932 in the convent in Cologne. Both Jewish and Catholic, she fled to Holland when the Nazis came to power. When the Nazis invaded Holland, she was captured and sent to Auschwitz where she died in the gas chamber on 9 August 1942. There were key moments in her life when, in the words of today's gospel reading, she heard the call, 'The bridegroom is here! Go out and meet him', and, having heard that call, she was ready with her lamp lit to go and meet him. Her reading of the life of Saint Teresa of Avila was one such moment, her becoming a Catholic was another, as was her decision to become a Carmelite nun. At different moments in her life, she heard the call of the bridegroom and responded generously. Gradually, over time, she came to see where the Lord was calling her. From a declaration of atheism in her teens she became a martyr of the Church, a woman who lived and died for the heavenly bridegroom. Her life reminds us that if we keep seeking after truth, the Lord will respond to our search and will draw us to himself. Our journey to the Lord may have many twists and turns, as it did for Edith Stein, but if we are faithful to the deepest desires in our heart, we too will hear the call, 'The bridegroom is here! Go out and meet him', and we will be ready to respond.

10 August, Wednesday, Saint Lawrence, Deacon and Martyr
John 12:24–26
Lawrence was a deacon of the church of Rome and died in the persecution of the Roman Emperor Valerian, in the year 254, four days after Pope Saint Sixtus II and his four fellow-deacons had been put to death. He was buried on the Via Tiburtina, one of the major roads out of Rome. Emperor Constantine the Great later built a basilica over his tomb. With various modifications made over the centuries, it remains today as the Basilica of Saint Lawrence Outside-the-Walls and is just one of seven major churches in his honour in the city. Lawrence has been venerated throughout the Church from the fourth century. The tradition about Lawrence is that he was a deacon from Spain in the service of Pope Sixtus II. He was put in charge of the administration of Church goods and care for the poor. He is also regarded as one of the first archivists and treasurers of the Church. In the words of today's first reading, he was someone who gave of himself, not grudgingly, but generously and cheerfully, to the Lord and to the Church. In the words of Jesus in the gospel reading, he is the wheat grain that fell to the earth and died, and in dying yielded a rich harvest. In that gospel reading, Jesus is addressing his disciples, all of us. He is reminding us that we find life by giving our lives away, by dying to our tendency to live for ourselves alone. Jesus is the supreme expression of the wheat grain that fell to the earth

and died, and in dying yielded a rich harvest. In giving his life for his flock and for all humanity, Jesus rose to new life and that new life has been poured into our hearts through the Holy Spirit, who is the foretaste or first fruit of eternal life. That pattern of gaining life for ourselves and for others through the giving of our life is to be the pattern of all our lives as people baptised into Jesus. As Paul says in our first reading, when we give of ourselves generously and cheerfully, there is no limit to the blessings that God can send upon us.

11 August, Thursday, Nineteenth Week in Ordinary Time
Matthew 18:21–19:1

People ask lots of questions of Jesus in the gospels. In today's gospel reading, Peter asks a very concrete question, 'How often must I forgive my brother if he wrongs me?' He goes on to suggest an answer that he might have expected Jesus to agree with – 'seven times!' The number 'seven' was a symbol of perfection in that culture, so to forgive someone seven times would seem like perfect forgiveness. However, not for the first time, Jesus would have shocked his hearers with his answer to a question. 'Not seven … but seventy-seven times.' Jesus seems to set the bar so high as to be beyond us. The parable he goes on to tell seeks to justify his call for such forgiveness without limit. The first servant owed an astronomical debt to a pagan king. Ten thousand talents would be equivalent to the vast international debts under which some developing countries labour today. He asks the king for time, but the servant could never have paid this debt back, no matter how much time he was given. The king simply cancelled the whole debt. Mercy triumphed over justice. Yet when this servant met a fellow servant who owed him a very small and manageable debt, he acted on the basis of a very brutal justice and, in so doing, lost the abundant mercy he had received. Jesus is reminding us in this parable that God's forgiveness is limitless. God's forgiveness has been poured out on us through the life, death and resurrection of Jesus. The parable calls on us to allow this boundless forgiveness to so touch and shape our lives that some of it flows through us onto those who offend and hurt us. It doesn't mean that forgiving another will ever come easily to us. It has been said that everyone agrees that forgiveness is a wonderful value, until they have someone to forgive. Yet, the more aware we become of ourselves as forgiven sinners, the freer we will become to forgive those who sin against us.

12 August, Friday, Nineteenth Week in Ordinary Time
Matthew 19:3–12

Very often in the gospels Jesus is presented as taking a much more relaxed attitude to the Jewish Law than the religious leaders of the time. He is much less strict about the Sabbath law of rest than they are, for example. Jesus heals on the Sabbath, even though this would have been considered work and, therefore, a violation of the Sabbath Law. When it comes to marriage and divorce, however, Jesus seems to have taken a stricter line than the religious leaders of the day. They understood, from the Book of Deuteronomy, that a man could divorce his wife, although a woman could not divorce her husband. This was the interpretation of the Law that was in vogue in the time of Jesus; it left women very vulnerable. Jesus, however, goes back behind the Book of Deuteronomy to the Book of Genesis and declares that God's original will was that a man and a human who become one flesh in marriage should not then go their separate ways. His vision of marriage was of a faithful relationship which reflected God's faithful relationship with his people. Jesus must have been as aware as we are today that, in reality, many marriages do not last. When that happens, people have to manage their lives and find love as best they can. We can certainly never judge. Yet, in faithfulness to the teaching of Jesus, the Church has to keep on proclaiming his vision of two lives becoming one in marriage, in a self-giving love. At its best, such a love is a kind of 'incarnation'. It is God's love in human form. In that gospel reading Jesus also speaks of the single life, those who are single for the sake of kingdom. That is a different expression of God's love in human form. Single or married, we are all called to allow God's enduring love to take flesh in our lives.

13 August, Saturday, Nineteenth Week in Ordinary Time
Matthew 19:13–15

The little scene in this morning's gospel reading of parents bringing children to Jesus is very striking. It is a gospel reading I always use on the occasion of baptism. When parents bring their children for baptism they are doing what the parents in today's gospel reading are doing, they are bringing their children to Jesus. Most of us seek to be the Lord's disciples because our parents brought us to Jesus on the day of our baptism. It is strange that Jesus' own disciples should try to turn the children away from Jesus. They probably reflect the cultural attitude of the time which regarded children as without status or significance. This was very much at odds with Jesus' own attitude. He not only insisted that the children be allowed come to him, but he declared that children have a privileged place in God's kingdom. 'It is to such as these that the kingdom of God belongs.' By implication, they should have a central place in the life and worship of the community of his followers. Jesus' words and actions in today's gospel reading place an onus on all of us to do whatever we can to bring children and young people to Jesus, to open them up to the riches of the

Gospel and of the whole Christian tradition. As a sign of how central children are to God's kingdom and to the community of believers, Jesus went on to lay his hands on them in blessing. We are all called to be channels of the Lord's blessing to our children today.

15 August, Monday, The Assumption of the Blessed Virgin Mary
Luke 1:39–56

For billions of years, the sun has been giving out massive amounts of light and heat, and will continue to do so for billions of years to come. How does it continue to generate all that energy? I don't know enough about the science of the sun to answer that question with any clarity. In today's first reading, there is a vision of a woman adorned with the sun, standing on the moon, and with the twelve stars on her head as a crown. Statues of Our Lady often depict her standing on the moon, with a crown of stars on her head. The sun element of the vision, 'adorned with the sun', doesn't feature very often. For the author the woman in question was probably a symbol of the Church. The woman faced with a second sign, the huge red dragon, was a symbol of the Church faced with the oppressive power of the Roman Empire that stood ready to devour the Church's children. However, from the earliest years, believers also understood the woman as a symbol of Mary who, according to the reading, gave birth to a son who was to rule all the nations. It is a glorious image of Mary, which is very suited to today's feast of the Assumption.

The dogma of the Assumption of Our Lady was proclaimed by Pope Pius XII in 1950. In making this proclamation, the pope was making official what had been the belief of the Church for centuries. From earliest times, believers understood that because Mary had a unique relationship with Jesus, she must also have a unique share in his glorious life. As her body carried the Lord in her womb, now her body, her whole embodied self, reigns with the Lord in glory in a unique way. From earliest days believers understood that Mary's death was an extraordinary event, befitting an extraordinary person. Because she belonged to the Lord in a special way, she already enjoys the fullness of new life with him. In the words of Mary in today's gospel reading, 'The Almighty has done great things for me.'

Today's feast is not just about Mary. It is about all of us. The great things that God has done for Mary God desires to do for us all. The transformation that Mary now enjoys is the hope of us all. In the words of today's Preface, Mary is a 'sign of sure hope'. As Paul says in today's second reading, 'all will be brought to life in Christ'. Mary may have belonged to the Lord in a unique way, but we all belong to the Lord through our faith. Our belonging to the Lord does not cease with death. We will continue to belong to him in eternity, as we come to share in his risen life. That is the hope that our faith gives us, and Mary's glorious assumption nurtures that hope. As God has done great things for her, we look forward in hope to the great things that God will do for us.

Yet God is already doing great things for us here and now. At the beginning of his letter to the Philippians, Paul expresses his confidence that God, who 'began a good work among you will bring it to completion'. God's good work is ongoing, within us and among us. What is God working to do in our lives in the here and now? Just as Mary's glorious assumption shows us the completion of God's work, Mary's earthly life shows us what the good work God wants to do in our lives here and now looks like.

If the first reading gives us a glimpse of Mary's glorious life, the gospel reading gives us a glimpse of her earthly life. The scene comes just after Mary said 'yes' to God's choice of her. God chose her and, in response, she chose God, she opened herself up to God's purpose for her life. Through Jesus, God has chosen each one of us, and, like Mary, we are invited to choose God by choosing Jesus. Her 'yes' to God's choice of her created a space for Jesus to live within her. She invites us to make a safe space for Jesus to live within us. In so far as that happens, God's good work will be accomplished in our lives. Making space for Jesus in her life inspired Mary to visit her cousin Elizabeth in her need. When we create a space for the Lord in our lives, he will inspire us to visit our loved ones in their need, and even to visit total strangers in need. According to the gospel reading, Mary's making space for Jesus to live within her inspired her to pray, to acknowledge God as the source of all that was good in her life. Making space for Jesus in our lives will inspire us to pray in the same way Mary prayed, acknowledging our dependence on God for all that is good. Mary's earthly life and her glorious assumption reveals to us God's good work in our earthly lives and the completion of that work beyond this earthly life.

16 August, Tuesday, Twentieth Week in Ordinary Time
Matthew 19:23–30

Jesus is often depicted in the gospels as saying something that leaves his disciples astonished. What he said was often out of character with what the disciples would have heard from others. Today's gospel reading gives us an example of the astonishment of the disciples at something Jesus said. The disciples were astonished because Jesus had said that it was easier for a camel to pass through the eye of a needle than for a rich man to enter the kingdom of heaven. The disciple very likely assumed that riches were a sign of God's favour, which is how they were often understood in the Jewish Scriptures. However, Jesus was aware that too many possessions can come to possess us and become a kind of god. One of the sayings of Jesus in the gospels is, 'You cannot serve God and mammon.' What the disciples saw as a blessing Jesus saw as a temptation and a danger. This insight of Jesus led the disciples to ask a kind of despairing question, 'Who can be saved?' They seem to be saying, 'If those we thought blessed by God might not enter the kingdom of heaven, what about the rest of us?' In response to his disciples' despairing question, 'Who can be saved?' we have one of those sayings of Jesus that can give us great encouragement. 'For God everything is possible.' Jesus seems to be saying that God can find a way of touching the hearts even of those who, like the rich young man, are possessed by their possessions. Jesus is declaring that God's ability to draw us to himself cannot be underestimated. Even a small opening in our lives will be greatly exploited by God. In his letter to the Romans, Paul makes the striking statement that nothing 'in all creation will be able to separate us from the love of God in Christ Jesus our Lord'.

17 August, Wednesday, Twentieth Week in Ordinary Time
Matthew 20:1–16
This is one of the parables of Jesus to which people often react negatively. There is a feeling that the workers who worked all day were hard done by because those who worked for the last hour were given the same wage. However, in the world of the story, the employer did not treat those who worked all day unjustly; he gave them a day's wages for a day's work. The surprise in the story is that the employer was exceptionally generous with those who worked for an hour, giving them a day's wages as well. No injustice was done to anyone, but some of the workers were the recipients of a surprising and extravagant generosity. Jesus began this parable, with the phrase 'The kingdom of heaven is like

…'. The world of God is reflected in the world of the story; the character of the employer reflects God in some way. Jesus appears to be saying that God's generosity will always take us by surprise. God's way of dealing with us breaks the bounds of what humans would consider just and fair. What God does for us far exceeds what we might do for God. God does not relate to us on the basis of what we have earned or deserved. God's generous love is pure gift; it is not a reward for labour rendered. We serve the Lord from one end of the day to the other, not to gain or earn his love, but in grateful response for the love already given to us long before we could do anything.

18 August, Thursday, Twentieth Week in Ordinary Time
Matthew 22:1–14

The parable in today's gospel reading is the story of a king who was determined that there would be a full house for the wedding banquet of his son. When two lots of servants got nowhere with those who had already said 'yes' to their invitation, the king sends out his servants a third time to the crossroads of the town to bring total strangers to the banquet for his son's wedding. We can hear in the story an image of the persistence of God, who continues to call even when people seem deaf to his call. The Lord does not give up on us, even when we give him good reasons for doing so. He continues to call out to us. The first reading from the prophet Ezekiel suggests that God not only continues to call us but that God is always at work in our lives. God's call is not just something external but God works from within. In that reading God promises to cleanse us, to give us a new heart, to put a new spirit within us. God will certainly do his part. The conclusion of the parable in the gospel reading suggests that we also have to do our part. Some of the guests were asked to leave because they were not wearing a wedding garment. In other words, they were casual about the king's invitation. God is not casual in our regard. He invests heavily in us and he looks to us for an appropriate response. Our lives are to bear fruit worthy of God's investment. As followers of his Son, we are to keep clothing ourselves with Christ.

19 August, Friday, Twentieth Week in Ordinary Time
Matthew 22:34–40

The first reading from the prophet Ezekiel is full of drama. The Lord, through the prophet, is speaking to a people who keep saying, 'Our bones are dried up, our hope has gone; we are as good as dead.' Any one of us can feel a little like that at certain moments of our lives. We feel dried up; we seem to have lost hope; we sense that we are only half alive, as good as dead. In our first reading, the Lord promises his people that he will raise them from their graves; he will put his spirit within them and they will begin to live again. The Lord makes the same promise to all of us when we feel only half alive and drained of hope. At such moments, the Lord invites us to come before him and to open our hearts to his life-giving spirit, the Holy Spirit, who will enable us to live again. I like that prayer to the Holy Spirit that we pray on Pentecost Sunday, 'Holy Spirit, Lord of light … Heal our wounds, our strength renew; On our dryness pour they dew.' The people of Israel in the first reading were like dry bones scattered in a valley, but the Lord wanted to breathe life into those dry bones, pouring the dew of his Spirit upon them. The Lord always stands ready to breathe life into us, by pouring his Spirit afresh into our lives. His Spirit will always lead us out towards others in love, lifting us beyond our tendency to turn in on ourselves in despondency. The Spirit will move us towards that love of God with all our being and the love of neighbour as ourselves, which Jesus speaks about in the gospel reading and that shaped his own life. When we allow the Spirit to generate the Lord's own love within us, then we will begin to come alive again. We will discover the Lord's own joy, which is one of the fruits of the Holy Spirit, working within us.

20 August, Saturday, Twentieth Week in Ordinary Time
Matthew 23:1–12
The Church is truly catholic; it embraces all nations. There is great diversity there, yet we are united in our faith, our hope and our love. In the gospel reading, Jesus says that we have one Father, namely God, which means we are all sons and daughters of the one God. We belong to one family of faith, under God our Father. In recent times, I have heard the Church referred to as a family of families. In the gospel reading, Jesus also declares that we have only one teacher, namely, himself, the Christ. Within the family of the Church, we are not only sons and daughters of the one Father, but we are also all pupils or disciples of the one Teacher. The fact that as a church we acknowledge one Father, God, and one Teacher, Jesus, means that, whereas there is great diversity in the Church, there is a fundamental equality and unity among its members. There is no place within this spiritual family for the kind of honour-seeking that Jesus is so critical of in the gospel reading. We are all called to keep promoting Jesus' vision of church which he puts before us in that gospel reading, the Church as a family of brothers and sisters under one heavenly Father, striving to life the life of loving service that Jesus, our brother and teacher, models for us so fully.

22 August, Monday, Queenship of Mary
Luke 1:26–28
During the Middle Ages, Mary was venerated as queen of the angels and saints. Pope Pius XII prescribed this memorial of the

Queenship of Mary for the universal Church at the close of the Marian Year in 1955. It is placed on this date of 22 August, a week after the feast of the Assumption, to show its close association with that feast. It is a feast that celebrates Mary's exalted place in heaven. Mary's exaltation bears out the truth of Jesus' saying, 'those who humble themselves will be exalted'. In today's gospel reading, we find Mary humbling herself. In her conversation with the angel Gabriel, she shows an open, questioning, spirit. She asked herself what Gabriel's greeting could mean. In response to Gabriel's extraordinary news, Mary asked, 'How can this come about, since I am a virgin?' She didn't claim to know everything. The kind of questioning, searching spirit that Mary displays is a sign of humility. It stands over against the attitude of those who claim to know more than they actually do. Mary's humble spirit is finally and fully revealed in her surrender to God's purpose for her life, even though she doesn't understand it fully at this moment. 'Let what you have said be done to me.' These words reveal Mary's willingness to allow God to have his way in her life, rather than insisting on her own way. In the Beatitudes, Jesus would declare those with such an attitude to be blessed, 'Blessed are the meek, for they shall inherit the earth.' Indeed, Mary could be described as a woman of the Beatitudes. She shows us the path we are all to take. If we enter into her humble attitude, allowing God to have his way in our life, we too will be exalted by God. We recognise Mary's queenship most fully when, like her, we give ourselves over to God's gracious purpose for our lives.

23 August, Tuesday, Twenty-first Week in Ordinary Time
Matthew 23:23–26
There are many prayers in the letters of Saint Paul. As well as encouraging and directing his churches, Paul also prayed for them.

There was a real pastoral dimension to his prayer. The needs and struggles of the churches he established were central to his prayer. There is a good example of Saint Paul's prayer for his churches in today's first reading. On one occasion Paul prayed, 'May our Lord Jesus Christ himself, and God our Father ... comfort you and strengthen you in everything good you do or say.' It is a striking prayer and one worth reflecting upon. Paul acknowledges God the Father and the risen Lord as the ultimate source of all that is good in our words and actions. God alone is completely good, but, with the Lord's help, God's goodness can be reflected to some degree in everything we say and do. It is through the Lord's strengthening presence to us that something of his goodness can take flesh in our own lives. In the gospel reading, Jesus spells out this goodness in terms of three basic qualities, 'justice, mercy, faith'. He was criticising the religious leaders for becoming obsessed with what is not so important in our relationship with God, such as the tithing of herbs, and neglecting what is really important, such as justice, mercy and faith. To act justly is to give to others what is their due as human beings, as sons and daughters of God. To show mercy often means going beyond justice, attending to people's basic needs irrespective of who they are or what they have done. Faith or faithfulness refers to a loving, faithful relationship with God, finding expression in loving, faithful relationships with others. Jesus is saying that when it comes to our relationship with God, these are the qualities that really matter. This is the goodness that the Lord desires to find in our lives and that he can bring about in our lives, if we are truly open to his working, the working of his grace, within us and among us.

24 August, Wednesday, Feast of Saint Bartholomew
John 1:45–51
We know very little about Saint Bartholomew, but he has been traditionally identified with Nathanael who features in today's

gospel reading. According to the last chapter of John's Gospel, Nathanael was from Cana in Galilee, which was not very far from Nazareth and much the same kind of place. Yet when Philip announces to him that they identified Jesus of Nazareth as the long-awaited Jewish Messiah, Nathanael responds by asking, 'Can anything good come from that place?' An example perhaps of small-town rivalry! Nathanael started off dismissing Jesus on the basis of where he was from. However, once Nathanael met Jesus for himself, his view of him changed completely. He declared in Jesus' presence, 'You are the Son of God, you are the King of Israel.' The gospel reading suggests that there is no substitute for a personal encounter with Jesus. Without that personal encounter, Nathanael would have continued to dismiss Jesus outright. It was Philip who facilitated Nathanael's personal encounter with Jesus. Through Philip, the Lord called Nathanael to 'come and see'. It is because he came and saw, and met with Jesus for himself, that Nathanael ceased to be a sceptic and became a disciple. The Lord is constantly calling on us to 'come and see', to meet with him in a very personal way, one to one, rather than just knowing about him by hearsay. As we respond to that calling and allow the Lord to meet with us, we will be changed by the encounter.

25 August, Thursday, Twenty-first Week in Ordinary Time
Matthew 24:42–51

When we look at the prayers of Paul in his letters, the prayer of thanksgiving appears as frequently as the prayer of petition. When he is not praying for his churches, he is thanking God for them. In today's first reading, we find an example of such a prayer of thanksgiving. He says to the members of the church in Corinth, 'I never stop thanking God for all the graces you have received through Jesus Christ. I thank him that you have been enriched in so many ways.' Paul had the great gift of being able to recognise and name the way God was working in the lives of others, and then publicly to give thanks to God for it. In the words of Jesus in the gospel reading, he was 'awake' to the Lord's coming through others, the Lord's engagement in the lives of others. In the gospel reading, Jesus calls on us to be prepared for the unexpected coming of the Son of Man, and Paul in the first reading calls on us to wait for the Lord Jesus Christ to be revealed. Yet Paul reminds us that the Lord who is coming is also at work here and now in all our lives, in and through the Holy Spirit. As Paul says in that reading, 'You will not be without any of the gifts of the Spirit while you are waiting for our Lord.' Paul encourages us to be awake to, alert to, the workings of the Lord's Spirit in our own lives and in the lives of others, and to give thanks to God for all the ways we and others have been enriched by the Spirit. It is easy to get disheartened and discouraged about many things. Paul reminds us that, no matter how dark the times, the Lord is always at work in a creative, life-giving way within each of us and among us all. Regardless of the situation in which we find ourselves, there is always so much to give thanks for, because of all the graces we are always receiving through Jesus, our Lord.

26 August, Friday, Twenty-first Week in Ordinary Time
Matthew 25:1–13

I am often struck by that line in today's gospel reading, 'The bridegroom is here! Go out and meet him.' In the parable the bridegroom's coming had been delayed. Only some of the bridesmaids had enough oil to light their lamps and greet him, in spite of his unexpected delay. They alone were ready to escort him through the darkness with their lamps alight towards the bride's house. These wise bridesmaids, as they are called, were ready for a possible late arrival of the bridegroom; they had prepared themselves for the long haul. To each of us it could be said, 'The bridegroom is here! Go out and meet him.' The bridegroom is the Lord. In the gospels Jesus spoke of himself as the bridegroom; in and through him, God was renewing the marriage covenant with his people. Every day of our lives the Lord is here, and every day we are invited to go out and meet him. We are called each day of our lives to welcome the Lord's coming to us, even when his coming is late and unexpected, even though he may come to us in ways that seem strange or foolish from a human point of view. As Paul says in today's first reading, God's wisdom is often experienced as foolishness by humans. We are to welcome the Lord each day with our lamps burning, with the flame of faith and the fire of love alive in our hearts. The Lord's coming to us each day is assured and he looks to us for a faithful and reliable response to his coming. The Lord is here for us, and he asks us to be there for him, like the wise bridesmaids. Like them, we need to be there for him for the long haul. Even when the Lord seems absent, we need to keep the flame of our faith and the fire of our love brightly burning. We can be tempted to give up on the Lord, like the foolish bridesmaids, perhaps thinking he has given up on us. The Lord never gives up on us; he is faithful to us, to the end, and he looks for the same faithfulness in us.

27 August, Saturday, Twenty-first Week in Ordinary Time
Matthew 25:14–30

The wealthy property owner in today's gospel reading is evidently a generous and trusting person. Before departing on a journey abroad, he entrusts very large sums of money to three of his servants, to each in accordance with their ability to make good use of this generous gift. The property owner was not expecting these large sums of money back. He just wanted his servants to make good use of them. Two of the servants, recognising the generous and trusting nature of their master, felt free to use well what they had been given in the trading market of the day. As a result, they increased the value of the asset they had been given. The third servant did nothing with what he had been given. Rather than recognising the generous and trusting nature of his master, he was paralysed by his image of his master as demanding and hard-hearted. Fear of his master enslaved him and he did nothing with what he had been given, not even the minimal initiative of placing the investment in a bank to gain interest. What is Jesus saying to us through this parable drawn from daily life of the time? Perhaps he wants us to recognise how generous God has been with each one of us, how much he has entrusted to us. God has given us the greatest treasure of all, his Son. God has also given us abilities that allow us to share this gift of his Son with others, in how we think, speak, act and live. God wants us to respond to his generous and trusting investment in us by living fearlessly out of all that he has given us. We are to be courageous in our witness to his Son. We are to take risks in our efforts to ensure that the riches of the Gospel are received by as many as possible. God can deal with failure, even bringing great good out of it. However, there is little God can do with fearful inactivity.

29 August, Monday, The Passion of Saint John the Baptist
Mark 6:17–29

You may be familiar with the expression, 'speaking truth to power'. It can often be a dangerous business. John the Baptist spoke God's truth to the powerful Herod, telling him that it was against God's Law for him to marry his brother Philip's wife, as he had done. For speaking this truth, John incurred the anger of Herod's wife,

Herodias, and her resentment towards John was a factor in John's unjust persecution. However, the other factor in John's execution was Herod's own moral cowardice. The gospel reading says that Herod knew John to be a good and holy man, and that he liked to listen to him. Yet he ordered John's execution at the request of his wife because he had promised her daughter anything she wanted. He didn't want to lose his honour by refusing her unexpected request for the head of John the Baptist. Herod knew he was killing a good and holy man, but his honour and reputation meant more to him. When evil is done, such as the killing of the innocent, it is often due to a combination of factors, a coming together of the moral failings of several people. The opposite is also the case. The doing of some good is often due to a coming together of the moral virtues of several people. There is a coalition of evil in the gospel reading, Herod, Herodias and her daughter are a kind of unholy trinity. However, there is also a coalition of good there as well. There is John the Baptist, and his disciples who ensured he had a dignified burial even if he had an undignified death. When Jesus called people of all sorts to follow him, he was forming a coalition of good to work for the coming of God's kingdom on earth. It came to be called the Church. We all belong in that coalition of good. We are called by the Lord to work together to further God's good work in our world. Sometimes we will have to do that in the face of the kind of coalition of evil that is there in today's gospel reading.

30 August, Tuesday, Twenty-second Week in Ordinary Time
Luke 4:31–37

In our first reading today, Saint Paul says that the depths of a person can only be known by his own spirit. In other words, I know myself better than others know me; my own depths are more open to me than to someone else. That is not to say that I understand my own depths fully, but I am better placed to understand myself than to understand someone else. I may remain something of a mystery to myself, but I will be even more of a mystery to others. My own spirit is more likely to probe my own depths; someone else's spirit is less likely to probe my own personal depths. In a similar way, Saint Paul says in that reading that only the Spirit of God can probe the depths of God. Only God's Spirit knows God. Yet Paul reminds us in that reading that we have received God's Spirit, the Holy Spirit, and the Holy Spirit helps us to know God. Indeed, Paul says there that God and the things of God will be seen as nonsense by those who are not open to receiving the Spirit of God. We need the Holy Spirit to come to God, to relate to God, to be in communion with God. The Spirit enables us to be astonished by God and his Son Jesus. It is said of the people of Capernaum in today's gospel reading that they were astonished by what Jesus said and did, and that his teaching made a deep impression on them. That suggests that they were open to the Holy Spirit at work through Jesus, and at work in their own lives. We need to keep praying, 'Come Holy Spirit', because it is the Spirit who helps us to recognise and appreciate the ways that the Lord is present to us and at work among us.

31 August, Wednesday, Twenty-second Week in Ordinary Time
Luke 4:38–44

In the gospel reading the people of Capernaum were so impressed by the ministry of Jesus that they wanted to prevent him from leaving them. He had made such a positive impact on them that they wanted to hold on to him. Yet Jesus did not give in to what the people of Capernaum wanted, understandable as it was, because he knew that what God wanted of him was something different.

God wanted him to move on to the other towns of Galilee. 'I must proclaim the good news of the kingdom of God to the other towns too,' he said. Jesus seems to have been clear about what God wanted and when that clashed with what others wanted he always remained faithful to what God wanted. Sometimes in our own lives too we can find a conflict between what other people want of us and what we believe God is asking of us. The Gospel calls on us not to be at the mercy of what people want when it is at odds with what we experience as God's call in our lives. The Holy Spirit, the Spirit of the Lord, is given to us to help us to be faithful to God's call even when it means finding ourselves at odds with others, including the very good intentions of others. It was following a period of prayer in a lonely place that Jesus articulated clearly to the crowds what he believed God was asking of him: 'I must proclaim … .' Our own times of prayer will open us up to the guidance of the Holy Spirit as to what God desires for us. Through prayer, the Holy Spirit will also help us in our weakness, giving us the strength to follow through on what he has made known to us about God's desire for our lives.

1 September, Thursday, Twenty-second Week in Ordinary Time
Luke 5:1–11

In today's gospel reading, Simon and his companions had worked hard all night fishing, but had caught nothing. It is often the way that our hard work can appear to bear very little fruit. Then Jesus called on them to set out into the deep again, at the least promising time for catching fish. Peter set out in response to Jesus' word and, amazingly, without doing much work at all, he and his companions landed an astounding catch of fish, so much so that their nets began to tear. Their hard work had borne no fruit, and now Jesus seemed to have gifted them this extraordinary catch. For Simon Peter, this was pure gift, an experience of the Lord's abundant generosity. Sometimes, the Lord can grace us in similar ways. We work hard and nothing happens, and then, without our doing much, we are abundantly graced. It was this experience of the Lord's abundant love and generosity that brought home to Simon Peter his own unworthiness to be in the Lord's presence. 'Leave me, Lord, for I am a sinful man.' The more we come to experience the Lord's love for us, the more we realise how small our response to that love is. Peter experienced himself at that moment by the shore of the Sea of Galilee as a loved sinner, and that is what we all are. Pope Francis often speaks of himself as a loved sinner. Yet, in spite of Peter's sense of his unworthiness before Jesus and his desire to put space between Jesus and himself, Jesus had important work for Peter to do. 'From now on it is people you will catch.' The Lord wants to work through each of us, imperfect as we are. Even though we may be tainted by sin, the Lord can work powerfully through us, if, like Simon Peter, we set out in response to his word.

2 September, Friday, Twenty-second Week in Ordinary Time
Luke 5:33–39
In today's first reading, Saint Paul tells the members of the church in Corinth, 'There must be no passing of premature judgement. Leave that until the Lord comes.' In other words, only the Lord is in a position to judge someone because, as Paul puts it, only he 'can reveal the secret intentions of human hearts'. Only the Lord sees deeply enough to make a true judgement of others. Therefore, we need to be very slow to judge others, or even to judge ourselves. In that reading, Paul also says, 'I will not even pass judgement on myself.' In the gospel reading we find the Pharisees passing premature judgement on Jesus' disciples because they do not follow the Pharisees' regulations regarding fasting. Jesus defends

his disciples against this judgemental attitude, explaining that with his coming something very new has arrived. His ministry has the quality of a wedding feast, and who would think of fasting at a feast? His ministry is like new wine that calls for new wineskins, a new way of imagining how we relate to God. Jesus' disciples have been caught up in this celebratory good news. It is not fair to judge them because they don't want to drink the old wine. The risen Lord's ministry continues to have the quality of the joy of the wedding feast today. His presence continues to be like new wine which requires new wineskins. The Lord is always leading us into new territory that breaks with where we have been. His presence among us is dynamic. The Holy Spirit is always ahead of us and we have to keep catching up with his lead. It is not enough to say, 'The old is good', to quote the ending of the gospel reading. There is much good in the old, but the Spirit of the Lord is always breaking new ground, and that is something to rejoice in, not to complain about. What we need above all is the freedom to go where the Spirit is leading us.

3 September, Saturday, Twenty-second Week in Ordinary Time
Luke 6:1–5
I am struck by that question that Paul asks in today's gospel reading, 'What do you have that was not given to you?' Paul is reminding us that, ultimately, everything is gift. Because everything is gift, he says, we should not boast as if it was all down to us. I think we can agree with Paul that so much of what matters in life is gift. We receive much more than we achieve. Because so much is gift, we constantly need a spirit of gratitude. A restless spirit that drives us beyond where we live towards places unknown is something good, but so also is that receptive spirit that helps us to appreciate more fully where we already are and what we have

been given. In the gospel reading, we find the disciples going through a cornfield, picking ears of corn, rubbing them in their hands and eating them. They experienced the cornfield as God's gift to them, allowing them to satisfy their hunger. No doubt, after the disciples passed through there was plenty more corn for harvesting. There was another group, the Pharisees, who, looking at what the disciples were doing, did not see a group of people rejoicing in God's good gifts to us. Rather, they saw people who were breaking God's Law relating to the Sabbath. Jesus, however, strongly defends the actions of his disciples. Jesus knew what the Sabbath was about; he was, after all, Lord of the Sabbath. The Sabbath day was especially a time to acknowledge God's good gifts to us and to give thanks for them. Each day we are asked to be thankful, because we recognise that so much that is of value in life has come to us as gift.

5 September, Monday, Twenty-third Week in Ordinary Time
Luke 6:6–11
We can sometimes imagine that the Church at its very beginning was a kind of perfect community of faith and love and that only in the course of its history did things begin to go wrong. However, the letters of Paul, our earliest Christian documents, show us that there were as many problems in the Church at its very beginning as in the course of its subsequent history. In today's first reading Paul has to deal with a serious moral lapse within the community, what would have been regarded at the time as a case of incest. What happened is bad enough, but it is compounded by the response of others in the community to this situation. 'How can you be so proud of yourselves?' Paul asks. It is as if the members of the community are boasting of a new-found freedom. How could some in the early Church have interpreted the message of Jesus

so wrongly? In that reading, Paul calls on the church in Corinth to get rid of this yeast that threatens to corrupt the whole community, what he calls 'the old yeast of evil and wickedness'. Just as Paul is deeply disturbed by the behaviour of some in the church, so, in the gospel reading, Jesus is deeply disturbed by those who claim to be committed to the ways of God. The Pharisees interpret God's Law in a way that forbids the doing of good on the Sabbath, such as curing the man in the synagogue whose right hand was withered. Jesus has to ask them the question, 'Is it against the law on the Sabbath to do good, or to do evil?' The answer, of course, is that it is against the law to do evil. In God's eyes, good can be done any day of the week. We are all prone to drifting from what God desires for our lives and the lives of others. That is why we need to keep returning to the life and message of Jesus, so as to be reminded of God's ways. We also need to keep opening ourselves to the Spirit of Jesus, the Holy Spirit, for the strength to walk daily in those ways.

6 September, Tuesday, Twenty-third Week in Ordinary Time
Luke 6:12–19

When Jesus' disciples once asked him to teach them to pray, it was because they had often seen him pray. They sensed that there was a special quality to his prayer and they wanted to pray as he prayed. In response to their request on that occasion, Jesus taught his disciples the prayer that has come to be known as the Lord's Prayer, or the Our Father. Jesus' practice of prayer, which so impressed the disciples, is in evidence at the beginning of today's gospel reading. 'Jesus went out into the hills to pray; and he spent the whole night in prayer to God.' Very few of us could manage to pray the whole night long. There must have been something exceptional about Jesus' prayer. That is because there was something exceptional about his relationship with God; he was God's unique Son. Yet Saint Paul reminds us in one of his letters that God has poured the Holy Spirit into our hearts so as to draw us into a sharing in Jesus' own relationship with God. It is the Holy Spirit in our lives who moves us to prayer. Our prayer is no so much our activity as the activity of the Holy Spirit within us. In that sense, our prayer consists in surrendering to the activity of the Holy Spirit deep in our hearts, entering into the prayer of the Holy Spirit within us. Jesus' prayer flowed into his life. In today's gospel reading, it inspires his choice of the twelve from among the larger group of disciples. His prayer also moves him to come down from the mountain and minister to those who needed his presence. Our prayer too will shape our lives, even though we are not always aware of it. Our communion with the Lord in prayer creates a space for him to be in communion with others through us.

7 September, Wednesday, Twenty-third Week in Ordinary Time
Luke 6:20–26

The version of the Beatitudes we find in Luke's Gospel is very disconcerting in many ways. Jesus declares blessed those who are poor, who are hungry and who weep. He declares unfortunate those who are rich, who are full and who laugh. This is not the way we normally see things. Indeed, it is the very opposite to how most people in most cultures would think. There is something shocking in these beatitudes and woes. Jesus is not saying that poverty is a blessing in itself. Rather he is declaring that the poor are blessed because God will work to transform their situation. It is the situation of being vulnerable that creates a space for God to work. It is often our need that opens us up to God. It is often those who are afflicted in any way who are most likely to experience

God's nearness and God's help. In contrast, those who appear to have everything often have no sense of their need for God and are not open to God's transforming presence. The gospel reading assures us that our pain, our suffering, our affliction can be a blessing because it can open us up to experience the generosity of God towards us. It can create an opening for the Lord to work powerfully within us and through us.

8 September, Thursday, The Nativity of the Blessed Virgin Mary
Matthew 1:1–16, 18–23

On the feast of the Nativity of the Blessed Virgin Mary, we read one of the gospel accounts of the nativity or birth of Jesus. We remember the day of Mary's birth because of the role she would go on to play in the life of Jesus. Jesus had many disciples in the course of his public ministry, but he only ever had one mother. Mary's relationship with Jesus was truly unique. Yet, as well as being his mother, Mary was also his most faithful disciple. This aspect of her relationship to Jesus is one she shares with us all. Today's gospel reading speaks of Mary as having conceived Jesus 'by the Holy Spirit'. The gospels portray Mary as a woman of the Spirit, completely open to the Spirit's promptings. Not only was her son conceived by the Spirit, but her whole life was shaped by the Spirit. As a woman of the Spirit, she was not only the mother of Jesus but, in the words of Paul in today's second reading, she was a true image of God's Son. Paul declares in that reading that God intends all of us to become true images of God's Son. It is the Holy Spirit at work in our lives who will enable us to become true images of God's Son. We look to Mary to show us the person that God intends us to become, people of the Spirit who reflect God's Son to others by our whole way of life. In celebrating Mary's birthday, we are also celebrating our own baptismal calling. We will not be fully conformed to the image of God's Son in this earthly life, but each day of our lives we are called to grow into this image, in the power of the Spirit. As we do so, we can look to Mary as our inspiration and also as our help and support on this journey, calling on her to pray for us, sinners, now and at the hour of our death.

9 September, Friday, Twenty-third Week in Ordinary Time
Luke 6:39–42

Recent Covid times were difficult for the visually impaired. There were lots of signs around that we had to follow, some on the ground, others free-standing, others again on doors and windows, telling us where to stand, in which direction to walk, how far to place ourselves from others. Those who have serious sight impairment were not able to see all these signs and very often found themselves going the wrong way or standing in the wrong place. At such times, they needed people who are sighted to gently guide and direct them. In today's gospel reading, Jesus makes the obvious statement that a blind person cannot guide another blind person. A person whose sight is impaired needs someone who has good sight. Jesus applies this obvious principle to another area of human life, the moral area. Jesus declares that our own failings, which prevent us from seeing others clearly, should make us slow to become a moral guide for others. In the humorous image of Jesus, someone with a plank in their eye cannot go about trying to take the splinter out of someone else's eye. Jesus seems to be saying, 'Work on your own failings first, your own areas of blindness. Then you will be in a better position to be a guide to others.' A recognition of our own failings can make us more understanding of the failings of others. Jesus could see everyone clearly, because he saw them with the eyes of love. None of us are as loving as

Jesus and, so, we never see others with that clarity with which Jesus sees them. Jesus suggests in today's gospel reading that our inability to see others clearly should make us slow to put ourselves forward as their moral betters.

10 September, Saturday, Twenty-third Week in Ordinary Time
Luke 6:43–49

We occasionally have significant storms of wind and rain in Ireland, even in July and August. Rivers overflow and houses are inundated. We cannot but feel for the people who have to face into dealing with their flooded homes. Today's gospel reading shows that Jesus was familiar with the phenomenon of rivers in flood bearing down on people's homes. However, Jesus envisages a situation where some people's homes are not only flooded by rivers that overflow but actually collapse to the ground. In that scenario the fortunate houses are those that flood but remain standing nonetheless. Jesus explains that the difference between the houses that collapse and those that remain standing has to do with the quality of the foundation. Was the house built on rock or on soft soil? Jesus applies that phenomenon to our personal lives. How solid is the foundation on which our life is built? Is it solid enough to withstand the destructive forces that we sometimes encounter on our life journey? In the gospel reading, Jesus offers himself as the firm foundation, the rock, on which our lives can be safely built. Listening to his words and seeking to live out his words in the power of the Spirit will give a security to our lives that allows us to remain upright in bad times as well as good. Jesus suggests in the gospel reading that, just as builders need to build for the worst of times, we need to build our lives for the worst of times too. Jesus offers himself to us as the reliable resource and foundation for the ups and downs of life. Our seeking him out in response to his loving relationship with us will ensure that, in the words of the prophet Isaiah, when we pass through the rivers, they will not overwhelm us.

12 September, Monday, Twenty-fourth Week in Ordinary Time
Luke 7:1–10

Today's first reading is the earliest account of the Last Supper that we have in the New Testament. Paul wrote that letter to the Corinthians a good fifteen years before the first gospel was written, the Gospel of Mark. Paul never read a gospel, because none of them had been written by the time of his martyrdom, yet he gives us an account of the Last Supper in that reading which is very close to what we find in the gospels. What Jesus said and did at the Last Supper was part of the oral tradition at the time of Paul. It was passed on by word of mouth. Paul would have told the story of the last supper to the believers in Corinth when he first preached the Gospel to them. Writing this letter to them, five years later, he put that story in writing for the first time. Here we are, two thousand years later, hearing Paul's account of the Last Supper in his letter to the Corinthians. We are hearing it in the context of what Paul calls in that reading, the Lord's Supper, which was one of the terms for the Eucharist in the early Church. The Eucharist is the Lord's Supper and we are his guests. As the Lord's guests we have to live as the Lord, our host, would want us to live. That is the point Paul makes in that reading. He is putting it up to the church in Corinth to care for each other, especially for the weakest and most vulnerable. Otherwise, their celebration of the Lord's Supper is not authentic. Paul is saying that we cannot recognise the Lord in the breaking of bread, at the Eucharist, while failing to recognise him in each other. As we gather to receive the body of Christ in the Eucharist we recognise each other as the body of

Christ. It is striking that the words of a pagan centurion in today's gospel reading have made their way into our own Eucharist. He exemplifies the loving care of the weakest to which our celebration of the Eucharist commits us.

13 September, Tuesday, Twenty-fourth Week in Ordinary Time
Luke 7:11–17

When the people of Nain saw the extraordinary life-giving work that Jesus performed, they were filled with awe and praised God, saying, 'God has visited his people.' We too are drawn to Jesus because we recognise that in and through him God is visiting his people, all of humanity. The life, death and resurrection of Jesus was a visitation from God. The unknown and invisible God is made visible and knowable in the person of Jesus. In today's gospel reading, Jesus reveals God to be one who brings new life out of death and who restores the loving relationship that has been broken by death. Jesus brought the deceased son of a widow back to life and then immediately gave him back to his mother. There is an image here of how God, through Jesus, continues to work in our lives. God is always at work bringing new life out of our various experiences of death, whether it is the physical death of our loved ones, our own personal death or all those anticipations of death that we experience in the course of our lives. The gospel reading suggests that God's work of bringing new life out of death involves bringing together again loved ones who have become separated from each other. We can be confident that in bringing us to new life beyond this earthly life, the Lord will restore us to our loved ones, as he restored the young man to his mother. Jesus reveals God to be a God of life and love, who works to bring new life out of death and to restore and enhance all our loving relationships.

14 September, Wednesday, The Exaltation of the Holy Cross

John 3:13–17

When we had our parish pilgrimage to Rome and Assisi a few years ago, I bought a wooden cross. It is a replica of the cross that spoke to Saint Francis in the church of San Damiano in Assisi. On that occasion Francis heard the Lord call on him to rebuild his church. The cross is really a painting on wood of Jesus on the cross. The image is very unlike the image of Jesus on the large crucifix in the side chapel of our parish church. There it is very evidently the suffering Jesus that is depicted. On this cross from Assisi Jesus looks very serene. There is no trace of suffering in his face. It is almost like the glorious Christ on the cross with his arms outstretched to embrace all. That image is very appropriate for today's feast. This is not like Good Friday, where we dwell on the sufferings of Jesus. This feast proclaims the triumph of Jesus on the cross. What was the nature of that triumph? It was firstly the triumph of life over death. Those who put Jesus to death did not have the final say, because God the Father raised him high, in the words of Saint Paul in today's first reading. It was secondly the triumph of love over hatred. Human hatred for Jesus did not have the last word, because in and through Jesus crucified, the love of God for humanity was shining brightly. In the words of the gospel reading, God so loved the world that he gave his only Son. It was also the triumph of mercy over sin. In today's first reading, the people of Israel cried out, 'We have sinned by speaking against the Lord.' However, when they looked upon the bronze serpent they experienced the Lord's life-giving mercy. When we look upon the face of the Lord on the cross, we too find mercy; we experience the cross as the throne of grace. Today's feast celebrates the good news that God turned the tragedy of Calvary into a triumph for us all. Through the cross, God's life-giving love and mercy was embracing us all. Today's feast also reminds us that in our own personal experiences of Calvary, the Lord is present with us in a loving and merciful way, working on our behalf to bring new life out of our suffering and dying.

15 September, Thursday, Our Lady of Sorrows
Luke 2:33–35

There is a hymn associated with today's feast called in Latin, 'Stabat Mater', literally, 'The mother stood'. The title is taken from the opening verse of the hymn, 'At the cross her station keeping, / Stood the mournful Mother weeping, / Close to Jesus to the last'. This memorial of Mary is closely associated with the crucifixion of Jesus, which is why it is celebrated the day after the feast of the exaltation of the cross. There is no greater sorrow for parents than the sorrow brought on by the death of their child. Many of us will have grieved the death of a parent or both parents, and we accept such grief as part of life. However, the grief of a parent for a deceased son or daughter is of a different order. In today's gospel reading, Simeon closely associates the coming suffering of Mary's child and her own suffering. Jesus is destined to be a sign that is rejected and a sword will pierce her own soul too. Because of her unique relationship with Jesus as his mother, what was to happen to him would have a significant impact on her. The opening verse of the Stabat Mater concludes, 'Close to Jesus to the last'. Mary's sorrow was the inevitable consequence of her closeness to Jesus in love. Mary shows us our own calling, rooted in our baptism, to remain close to Jesus in love to the end, faithfully following him all the days of our life. We are called to be as faithful to him as she was. Our closeness to the Lord, our commitment in love to him, will sometimes take us to the foot of the cross, as it took Mary there. Yet, if we remain faithful to the Lord, we will experience his even greater faithfulness to us, as Mary did when Calvary soon gave way to Easter Sunday and the coming of the Holy Spirit at Pentecost.

16 September, Friday, Twenty-fourth Week in Ordinary Time
Luke 8:1–3

Today's gospel reading shows us that women played a very important role in Jesus' ministry. It mentions a large group of women, three of whom are named, who travelled with Jesus and who provided for him and his close associates out of their own resources. They were clearly women of some financial means, as demonstrated by Joanna who was the wife of Herod's steward, which was a very important position to hold in the royal court. They point ahead to the vital role women were to play in the Church and continue to play today. The gospel reading reminds us that Jesus was not only a giver but a receiver. He once spoke of himself as the Son of Man who came not to be served but to serve and to give his life as a ransom for many. Jesus gave everything, his very life, so that we might all come to share in his risen life, as Paul reminds us in today's first reading. Yet Jesus also knew how to receive from others. He may have come to serve rather than to be served, but he also needed the service of others, such as the service of the women in today's gospel reading, and he allowed himself to be served by others. The risen Lord continues to serve us today, in all sorts of ways, but he also continues to need our service. He needs our willingness to serve him and others, if his own service is to be effective in our world today. We too are called both to serve and to be served. We each have much to give to others and also much to receive from others. We can each bring the Lord into the world in a way that is unique to each of us, and we each need others to bring the Lord to us. Today, in the light of the gospel reading, we might thank God for all who have served us, particularly for all those women who in various ways have brought the Lord to us in the course of our lives.

17 September, Saturday, Twenty-fourth Week in Ordinary Time
Luke 8:4–15

Both of today's readings are linked by the image of the sowing of seed. In the first reading, Paul uses the image of the seed to speak of the transformation that awaits us beyond this earthly life. In the verses following our reading, he declares, 'Listen, I will tell you a mystery! We will not all die, but we will all be changed.' Paul recognises that human language is not capable of fully expressing the nature of this change. Earlier in this letter he wrote that 'no eye has seen, nor ear heard, nor the human heart conceived, what God has prepared for those who love him'. However, he sees in the famer sowing seed on his land an intimation of the change that awaits us beyond this earthly life. The seed has to die as seed, losing its physical body, before it can rise again with a new body as a stalk of wheat. The dying of the seed makes possible the rising of the wheat grain. In a similar way, for Paul, the dying of our physical body makes possible the raising of our spiritual body. In this earthly life, according to Paul, we are embodied souls, whereas in the next life we will be embodied spirits. We will retain our embodied identity, but our physical body will give way to a spiritual body. Our ultimate destiny is to be conformed to the image of the heavenly man, the risen Lord. If Paul relates the image of seed sowing to our ultimate destiny, Jesus relates it to our present response to God's active involvement in our lives. The parable of the sower and its interpretation recognises that the seed of God's word, powerful as it is, can be restricted in its impact by obstacles in our own lives. We may not take God's desire to be in communion with us through his Son seriously enough; our response to God's initiative towards us may not be sufficiently rooted to withstand the storms of life; we can allow our relationship with God to become choked by the pleasures and cares of life. Yet if there is any openness at all in our lives, any patch of good soil, God will be able to bring his good work in our lives to completion, and we will attain the glorious destiny that Paul portrays in the first reading.

19 September, Monday, Twenty-fifth Week in Ordinary Time
Luke 8:16–18

For the next two weeks, our first reading will be taken from books in the Jewish Scriptures that are known as the Wisdom Literature. Much of this literature is the fruit of long reflection on human experience; it can have a timeless quality to it. Today's first reading calls on us not to put off an act of kindness for someone until tomorrow, if we can do it today. There is a wisdom in that instruction that is valid for every age. In the gospel reading, Jesus speaks as a kind of wisdom teacher. He says that a lighted lamp is not meant to be covered by a bowl or put under a bed, but on a lamp stand so that people may see the light. This is a common-sense observation, but what is Jesus implying by it? Perhaps he is saying that our light, the light of our faith, is intended to shine brightly before all, rather than be hidden away. Our faith in the Lord, our relationship with him, is to shine through our whole way of life. One of the ways that the light of our faith can shine is by following the advice of our first reading, by taking the opportunities for acts of kindness towards others that come our way each day. Elsewhere in the gospels, Jesus calls on us to 'let your light shine before others, so that they may see your good works and give glory to your Father in heaven'. When we allow the light of our faith to shine through our ways of relating to others, that light gets brighter. That is the implication of what Jesus says at the end of today's gospel reading: 'Anyone who has will be given more.' As we try to give expression to the light of our faith in our lives, we create a space for the Lord to nurture and deepen our faith in him, our relationship with him.

20 September, Tuesday, Twenty-fifth Week in Ordinary Time
Luke 8:19–21

It is often the way in the gospels that people cannot reach Jesus because of the crowd around him. Zacchaeus had to climb a tree to see Jesus because of the crowd. The blind man tried to make contact with Jesus by shouting towards him but the crowd around Jesus told him to be quiet. Parents wanted to bring children to Jesus for him to bless them, but the crowd of disciples around Jesus tried to prevent them from doing so. In all of those cases, Jesus reached over the crowd to the person or group who wanted to make contact with him. He called Zacchaeus down from his tree and told him that he wanted to go to his home; he told the crowd to bring the blind man to him; he rebuked his disciples for trying to block parents from bringing their children to him and then proceeded to take the children in his arms and bless them. In today's gospel reading, it is the mother and brothers of Jesus, his own flesh and blood, who cannot get to Jesus because of the crowd gathered around him. However, on this occasion, Jesus does not reach over the crowd to his family to make contact with them. Rather, he declares that his real family are those who hear the word of God and keep it. Jesus withdraws from his blood family in a way that he didn't withdraw from others who tried to make contact with him. He wanted to show clearly that he was in the process of forming a new family. Membership of this family would be determined not by blood but by the willingness to hear the word of God as Jesus proclaims it and then to put that word into practice. We all belong in this new family by virtue of our baptism. We look to Jesus as our brother, to God as our Father, and to Jesus' mother as our mother. We show that we are faithful members of this family by listening carefully to the word of Jesus and seeking to live it every day of our lives.

21 September, Wednesday, Saint Matthew, Apostle and Evangelist
Matthew 9:9–13

During the time of the Covid-19 lockdown when our churches were closed for public worship, many people missed very much the freedom to come to the Lord present at Mass in his Word, in the Eucharist and in the gathered community. Yet, even when we cannot be present at Mass, the Lord can come to us, wherever we are. That is one of the messages of today's feast of Saint Matthew. Matthew did not come to the Lord. The Lord came to him. According to today's gospel reading, he was sitting at his customs post, going about his daily professional business, when the Lord came to him and said to him, 'Follow me.' That coming of the Lord had a transforming effect on Matthew. He left his lucrative tax-collecting business and become one of the Lord's closest associates, and he went on to give his name to one of the four gospels. The story of Matthew reminds us that the Lord comes to us where we are. He meets us at the heart of our daily lives. In the gospel reading, Jesus went on to share table with Matthew and his associates in the tax-collecting business; he had dinner with them, which scandalised the Pharisees. The Lord comes to our table too. Even when we cannot come to the table of the Eucharist, the Lord wants to share table with us, as he shared table with Matthew, and so many others in the gospels. Every time we sit at table in our homes, it is good to recall that the Lord is present with us. He is in communion with us. Any time that we allow ourselves to become aware of the Lord's presence to us is a moment of Holy Communion. Matthew's Gospel concludes with the promise of the risen Lord to his disciples, to all of us, 'I am with you always, to the end of the age.' We can keep drawing strength from the Lord's presence to us in every place we find ourselves.

22 September, Thursday, Twenty-fifth Week in Ordinary Time
Luke 9:7–9
The first reading today has a rather downbeat mood to it. The author wonders about the value of human work, asking, 'For all his toil, his toil under the sun, what does man gain by it?' He looks out on nature and, rather than being inspired by it, he just sees tiresome and repetitive motion: 'All things are wearisome.' He looks out on all of life and concludes that there is nothing new to be found there: 'What was, will be again.' For the author of this book, the Book of Ecclesiastes, life is a puzzle that doesn't make much sense to him. Some people think this is a strange book to have made its way into the Bible. Yet the outlook of this writer is true to the human condition. We may have all felt a little like this at some time in our lives. There is much in life to be puzzled over, many questions that seem to defy rational answers. In the gospel reading, Herod is also puzzled, but the focus of his puzzlement is Jesus. His puzzlement about Jesus made him anxious to see Jesus. However, his puzzlement did not bring him to faith in Jesus. Later in Luke's Gospel, the Pharisees come to Jesus and say, 'Herod wants to kill you', and in Luke's story of the passion of Jesus, Herod mocks Jesus before sending him back to Pilate, who will seal Jesus' fate. A questioning, puzzled spirit doesn't always lead us to God. However, neither are honest questioning

and puzzlement alien to deep faith. The author of the first reading, for all his scepticism, was a person of faith. He believed that God was at work in the world, even though he didn't understand what God was doing. Believers in every age, including Jesus himself, have hurled the question 'Why?' at God. If we can open up our questioning, puzzled spirit to the Lord in prayer, he will work through it to bring us closer to him.

23 September, Friday, Twenty-fifth Week in Ordinary Time
Luke 9:18–22

Timing is important in life. The value of something we do is often determined not just by what we do but when we do it. Some initiatives can be very worthwhile at the right time but very unhelpful if the time is wrong. If someone makes a simple request of us, we might normally take it in our stride. However, if the request comes just at the time we have heard bad news or experienced a significant loss, it can be like the straw that breaks the camel's back. In the first reading, the author declares that there is a time for all sorts of activities. He is really saying that there is a right time for all these activities, such as laughing and mourning. He was implying that there is a wrong time for such activities as well. Laughing in the presence of someone who is grieving would be very untimely. As one of the proverbs in the Book of Proverbs expresses it, 'Like vinegar on a wound is one who sings songs to a heavy heart'. We can all get our timing wrong. It can take a certain wisdom to get our timing right in relation to others. Jesus always seems to have got his timing right. In today's gospel reading, he asks his disciples the question, 'Who do you say I am?' He had to pick the right time to ask this question. There was no point asking it too early into his ministry or his disciples would not have had enough exposure to Jesus to answer it correctly. He couldn't leave it too late into his ministry to ask this question or there wouldn't be enough time for Jesus to give his disciples further instruction as to who he was. The gospel reading says that Jesus had been praying alone before he asked his disciples this question. He brought the question to God in prayer and that helped him to get his timing just right. Prayer can help all of us to get our timing right when it comes to others. In prayer, we open ourselves to that wisdom from on high, which enlightens us and helps us to be timely in all we say and do.

24 September, Saturday, Twenty-fifth Week in Ordinary Time
Luke 9:43–45

Today's gospel reading says that everyone was full of admiration for all that Jesus did. Just from our reading of the gospels we can understand why people would admire Jesus so much. On one occasion, after Jesus cured a deaf man, people said, 'He has done all things well.' Jesus did not allow such admiration to go to his head. According to the gospel reading, at the very time when people were full of admiration for him, he reminds his disciples that 'the Son of Man is going to be handed over into the hands of men'. Jesus knew that this admiration wouldn't last. He didn't want his disciples to get carried away by the admiration that surrounded him and them. Yet, when he tried to warn them about the darker days that were coming, the gospel reading says that his disciples 'did not understand him … and they were afraid to ask him about what he had said'. We can all sympathise with the disciples here. When things are going well, we don't like to be reminded that the situation might change for the worse. We all struggle to come to terms with bad news, especially when it is going to impact us personally. On a warm sunny day, we don't want to be reminded that winter is coming. When things are difficult, we don't like to hear the message that things might get worse before they get better. We all struggle to come to terms with the darker experiences of life. Yet the Lord does not ask us to face into those dark experiences alone. He journeys with us through them, helping us to keep going, just as he kept his disciples going, appearing to them after he had been put to death. In the words of today's psalm, the Lord is our refuge from one generation to the next. In difficult times, we need to keep turning to the risen Lord and drawing strength from the power of his presence to us. At the beginning of each day, we could pray in the words of today's psalm, 'In the morning, fill us with your love'.

26 September, Monday, Twenty-sixth Week in Ordinary Time
Luke 9:46–50
Today we begin to read from the Book of Job. In our reading, Job is portrayed as a man whose faith in God endures even when a whole succession of misfortunes befalls him. Having lost his property and, more significantly, his children, he remains a person who acknowledges God in prayer: 'Blessed be the name of the Lord.' Job's faith was put to the test but it didn't weaken. Many people's faith can be put to the test and they ask, 'Where is God in all this?' Yet the portrait of Job in today's reading encourages us to keep the faith, even in testing times. Job points ahead to Jesus who also kept faith in God even as he hung from the cross. The term 'keeping the faith' could imply that faith is something static to be safely preserved. However, faith is dynamic, because it is a relationship with God, and, like all relationships, it is always open to further growth. Today's gospel reading shows that the faith of the disciples was certainly in need of further growth. They were preoccupied with greatness, as the world understands it, the gaining of honour and renown for oneself. Jesus' response

to them shows us that a life of faith needs to have very different preoccupations. He identifies himself with a child, a symbol not of greatness but of weakness and vulnerability, and declares that the way to welcome himself and God his Father is through welcoming the frail and vulnerable among us, not trying to keep up with the highly regarded and influential. The disciples, even though people of faith, were a long way from having the mind of Christ. The life of faith is lived as a response to the Lord's call to grow more fully into his mind, his outlook, his values and attitudes. It is a lifelong journey into the mind of Christ. In our gospel reading, one of the disciples, John, was resentful of the good work that people who were not disciples of Jesus were doing. This was not the mind of Christ either. Jesus' response to John shows that the workings of God's grace beyond the community of the disciples is to be welcomed and celebrated. In so many ways, we can all have much growing up into Christ to do.

27 September, Tuesday, Twenty-sixth Week in Ordinary Time
Luke 9:51–56

Today's gospel reading marks a turning point in the story of Jesus as told by Luke. Up until this point in Luke's Gospel, Jesus' public ministry has been located in Galilee. Now Jesus leaves Galilee and begins his journey to Jerusalem. Because Jerusalem has a reputation as 'the city that kills the prophets and stones those who are sent to it' (Luke 13:33), Jesus has to steel himself for this journey. As Luke tells us in our gospel reading, 'Jesus resolutely took the road for Jerusalem.' He knew where this journey would lead, yet he also knew he had to take it. God's Messiah must head for the city of David. Having set out on this journey, Jesus immediately experiences a taste of the rejection that awaits him in Jerusalem, as he is rejected by the first Samaritan village he seeks to enter. In our own lives we often become aware of some difficult journey we have to make. We hesitate before this journey, yet we know it is right and good for us to make it. It might be a visit to someone we know who has been recently bereaved. We know it is going to be difficult, and, yet, we also know we must make this visit, so we steel ourselves for it. The path of being a disciple of the Lord, the path of dying to ourselves so that others may live more fully, is often a difficult one. Yet it is the path of life, for ourselves and for all who cross our path. The Lord has gone this way before us; he is with us as our strength in those moments when we struggle to take some path we know we must take. His Spirit within us empowers us resolutely to take the road that is true to our deepest selves, our baptismal identity.

28 September, Wednesday, Twenty-sixth Week in Ordinary Time
Luke 9:57–62

In today's gospel reading, Jesus meets with three people, one of whom he calls to follow him and two who offer to follow him. The two who offer to follow him seem to make very reasonable requests of Jesus before they set out with him. One wanted to bury his father, and the other wanted to say goodbye to his family. However, Jesus denies both requests and insists that they leave with him right away. There is an urgency to the work that Jesus is doing which overrides all other considerations, even the closest family duties and ties. We get a glimpse here of the urgent pace at which Jesus must have worked during his relatively short public ministry. Perhaps he sensed that his time was short and that there was much to be done if God's work in which he was engaged was to endure into the future. We can be grateful for Jesus' sense of urgency because God's good work through Jesus has touched the lives of us all, two thousand years after Jesus' death and resurrection. We all need something of Jesus' sense of urgency today when it comes to our relationship with him. The Lord needs us to answer his call today. We can be easily tempted to put off until tomorrow or at some time in the future what the Lord may be asking of us now. We sense a call to do something, which we know is in keeping with the Lord's good work, and we hesitate. We allow less important considerations to hold us back and deflect us. As one of the psalms expresses it, 'O that today you would listen to his voice.' Growing into the Lord's sense of urgency, with the help of the Holy Spirit, is an important dimension of our daily baptismal calling.

29 September, Thursday, Saints Michael, Gabriel and Raphael
John 1:47–51

There are many angels in the Bible but only three of them are named. Michael is portrayed as the defender and protector of believers from Satan and evil. Gabriel brought the good news of the forthcoming birth of John the Baptist and Jesus. Raphael was instrumental in healing the blindness of Tobit in the Book of Tobit. They were all God's messengers, revealing God's presence in different ways. They point ahead to God's greatest messenger, who is Jesus. In today's gospel reading, Jesus speaks of himself to Nathanael as the one on whom the angels of God are ascending and descending. The background to his image of ascending and descending angels is a dream that Jacob had in the Book of Genesis. In his dream he saw a ladder connecting heaven and earth with angels ascending and descending on it. When he woke up he concluded that the place where he had been sleeping must be the gate of heaven, the house of God, and he proceeded to build an altar there. He called the place Bethel, which in Hebrew means 'House of God'. In speaking the way he does, Jesus claims to be that gate of heaven, that house of God. He is the supreme connection between heaven and earth. In Jesus heaven comes to earth in a way that is not true of any angel. Jesus reveals God's presence to us as fully as any messenger from God could. When we look upon Jesus, we are looking upon the face of God. That is why there is always more to see in Jesus. As Jesus says to Nathanael, 'you will see greater things'. We can never exhaust the fullness of God that is to be found in Jesus. In our relationship with Jesus, there are always 'greater things' to see. Our relationship with the Lord is always an adventure that continues to open up new horizons, new vistas on God and on God's relationship with us.

30 September, Friday, Twenty-sixth Week in Ordinary Time
Luke 10:13–16
In the gospel reading, Jesus laments the fact that the people of the town of Chorazin and Bethsaida did not appreciate all that he had done among them. They were indifferent to the Lord's gracious works in their midst, and were not in any way moved by them to turn more fully towards God. We too can sometimes miss the ways that the Lord is moving among us. His presence among us will generally express itself in very ordinary, unspectacular ways. It might take the form of an unexpected kindness that someone shows to us, an invitation we receive that we had not expected, a word of appreciation or support at a time when it was needed, a positive and willing response to a call that we make on someone. We do not always reflect on such moments of grace as times when the Lord is touching our lives. We don't always notice the Lord passing by. At the end of our day, it can be good to look back over that day and to notice where the Lord has been gracing us with his presence, and, then to quietly give thanks for that. The responsorial psalm this morning reminds us that the Lord notices us, 'O Lord, you search me and you know me, you know my resting and my

rising ... '. In noticing us, he also calls on us to notice him, as he passes by in often unobtrusive ways.

1 October, Saturday, Twenty-sixth Week in Ordinary Time
Luke 10:17–24

There is a strong note of joy in today's gospel reading. The seventy-two disciples whom Jesus sent out on mission now return to Jesus, rejoicing at the success of their mission: 'Even the devils submit to us.' They are joyful because their work has borne such good fruit in the lives of others. Jesus is also joyful in our gospel reading. 'Filled with joy by the Holy Spirit, he said, "I bless you, Father, Lord of heaven and earth ... ".' The source of Jesus' joy was his deeply personal relationship with God his Father, in the power of the Holy Spirit. This is the joy that Jesus wants his disciples to experience. When they express their joy to him at the success of their mission, Jesus says to them, 'Rejoice, rather, that your names are written in heaven.' They are to rejoice in their relationship with God and the wonderful destiny towards which that relationship is leading. Jesus knew that the mission of his disciples would not always be successful. Indeed, his own mission appeared to have ended in abject failure as he hung from the cross. Yet, in good times and in bad, in times of success and failure, God's loving relationship with Jesus' disciples will endure, just as on the cross Jesus did not cease to address God as 'my God' or 'Father'. God's loving relationship with us, which is a constant, is to be the source of our joy. It endures even when so much else has been taken from us, whether it is our health or our work or our loved ones. Saint Paul was so aware of the Lord's loving presence to him as he sat in his prison cell that he could write to the church in Philippi, 'I have learned to be content with whatever I have'. His joy was the fruit of the Spirit, and was rooted in God's loving relationship with him through Christ. This same joy is open to us all, even in times of great struggle.

3 October, Monday, Twenty-seventh Week in Ordinary Time
Luke 10:25–37

In today's gospel reading, it is said of the traveller who was attacked by robbers that he was left 'half dead'. It is an unusual expression in English, 'half dead', but we all know what it means. The man was very likely close to death. We can be 'half dead' in other ways, apart from the physical and bodily sense. We can be 'half dead' in the sense that the spark has gone out in us. We feel only half alive and sense that we are dragging ourselves around, without much energy or enthusiasm for anything. In such times, we often need others to breathe new life into us, just as in the parable the Samaritan breathed new life into the broken Jewish traveller. He did so by doing the good he was capable of doing. He did what he could, and that turned out to be quite a lot, bandaging the man's wounds, easing them with oil and wine, bringing him to an inn, a place of safety and hospitality, paying his expenses and promising to check in on him on his way back. He gave a little of his time and a little of his money to this unfortunate man and it made all the difference. The half-dead man came back to life. What the Samaritan did for the broken Jewish traveller is an image of what Jesus wants to do for us all. He is the great healer of body, soul and spirit. He is always present to us in a healing, life-giving way. What the Samaritan did for the injured man is also an image of what Jesus wants us to do for one another, 'Go and do the same yourself.' There is always something we can do for one another. Giving others a little of our time, a little from our own human and material resources, can make a huge difference to them. It can bring new life to the half-dead.

4 October, Tuesday, Twenty-seventh Week in Ordinary Time

Luke 10:38–42

Today's gospel reading suggests that frenetic activity, even when done for the Lord, is not always what the Lord wants. When Jesus arrived in Martha's house, she started to worry and fret about so many things. Her over-activity left her feeling burdened and resentful of her sister Mary, judging her for not doing her share of the serving. However, Mary was serving Jesus in a different way, sitting at his feet and listening to him speaking. Jesus had something to say, and Mary was attentive to his teaching. This seems to have been the kind of hospitality that Jesus was looking for, not the anxious, frenetic, serving that Martha was engaged in. Jesus gently reminds Martha, who was judging Mary, that she has something to learn from her sister. We know from our own experience that if we have something important to say we want those closest to us to listen to us rather than to be anxiously providing for us. When it comes to our relationship with the Lord, there is a time to stop and listen to him, just as there is a time to be active on his behalf, like the Samaritan in yesterday's gospel reading. Both are ways of serving the Lord, and both are important in their time. In today's first reading, Paul acknowledges that he once persecuted the church of God. At the time, he believed he was doing God's good work. He was anxiously and frenetically serving God by ridding his Jewish faith of this new and dangerous movement. What Paul really needed to do was to sit and listen to God. Eventually, God forced him to listen by revealing his Son to him as he approached the city of Damascus. Only after that transforming experience could he actively serve God in the way God wanted. Both readings today remind us that attentive listening to the Lord is at the heart of our relationship with him because it helps to ensure that our activity is shaped by what the Lord wants and not just by what we want.

5 October, Wednesday, Twenty-seventh Week in Ordinary Time
Luke 11:1–4

Today's first reading gives us a unique insight into a serious disagreement between Peter and Paul, two of the most significant leaders in the early Church. Paul accused Peter of 'not respecting the true meaning of the Good News' or, in a more literal translation, 'not straightforward about the truth of the Gospel'. The issue of the relationship between Jews and pagans within the early Church was a complicated one and there were different views on it. No doubt Peter, in acting as he did, would have regarded himself as respecting the truth of the Gospel. Committed believers have always had different views as to what constitutes the truth of the Gospel in relation to a whole variety of issues. Peter and Paul may have disagreed strongly on this occasion, but for many years afterwards they each preached the Gospel in different areas and each of them was put to death for the truth of the Gospel in the persecution of the church in Rome under the Emperor Nero. Although they may have disagreed on the particular issue in the church of Antioch relating to Jewish and Gentile believers in Jesus, they went on to show themselves united on the fundamentals. What are the fundamentals of the faith? They are to be found in the Creed we recite every Sunday. They are also to be found in the prayer that Jesus gave his disciples in today's gospel reading. We are to be united in the fundamental task of creating a space for the coming of God's kingdom. We are to be united in praying for and working for daily bread, both physical and spiritual, for all God's people. We are to be united in our shared recognition of ourselves as sinners before God and in our shared willingness to pass on to others the forgiveness we have received from God. We are to be united in looking to God for the strength we need to remain faithful to the truth of the Gospel when our faith is put to the test by the forces of evil. On those essentials, Peter and Paul would have been united.

6 October, Thursday, Twenty-seventh Week in Ordinary Time
Luke 11:5–13

In his teaching, Jesus often takes what is best in human behaviour and then says that God is so much better again. In today's gospel reading, Jesus declares that any good father will give his children what is good. Likewise, a good neighbour will provide hospitality to a friend in need in the middle of the night, even if he moans about it initially because all his family are in bed. Jesus is declaring that God is so much more generous and more loving than the best of human fathers and neighbours. That is why Jesus calls on us to ask God for what we need in the expectation of getting a response: 'Ask, and it will be given to you; search, and you will find; knock and the door will be opened to you.' Yet we are all aware that our prayers of petition are not always answered in the way we would like. We ask and don't always receive. However, Jesus' teaching in today's gospel reading suggests that no prayer of petition goes completely unanswered. God will always respond to our asking, our searching, our knocking on his door, even if not in the way we expect or want. At the end of the gospel reading, Jesus says, 'How much more will the heavenly Father give the Holy Spirit to those who ask him?' This suggests that whenever we come before God in our need, asking, searching, knocking, we will always receive a fresh outpouring of the Holy Spirit, the Spirit of the risen Lord. We will come to know more fully the power of the risen Lord's presence in our lives. In today's first reading, Paul speaks of God who gives us the Spirit freely. Our prayer of petition opens us up to receive this free gift of the Spirit more fully. In the strength of the Spirit we can then make our own the words of Paul in his letter to the Philippians, 'I can do all things in him who strengthens me'.

7 October, Friday, Our Lady of the Rosary
Luke 1:26–38

This Memorial commemorates the battle of Lepanto (7 October 1571), when a Christian fleet defeated the Turks. The victory was attributed by Pope Saint Pius V to the recitation of the Holy Rosary. This great Marian prayer is sometimes traced back to Saint Dominic and his confrères who preached against the Albigensian heresy in the thirteenth century. However, it seems likely to have taken its present familiar form in the fifteenth century. Since then, it has become a much-loved prayer of believers in every generation. The Rosary has been described as the Gospel on its knees. The fifteen decades, or twenty decades if we include the Mysteries of Light introduced by Pope John Paul II, are an invitation to reflect on the great mysteries of the Lord's life, passion, death, resurrection and glorification, and on the role of Mary within those great mysteries. The third glorious mystery of the Rosary invites us to reflect on today's first reading and the first joyful mystery invites us to reflect on today's gospel reading. Mary's 'yes' to God's call to her through the angel Gabriel made possible the beginning of the mystery of Jesus' life. The coming of the Holy Spirit at Pentecost upon Mary and the disciples made possible the beginning of the life of the Church. Mary was there at the beginning of the story of Jesus and at the beginning of the story of the Church. She was there throughout the public ministry of Jesus, even if in the background, and she was present in the hour of Jesus' passion and death. Mary contemplated and pondered upon the mysteries of Jesus' life, death and resurrection in a way that was unique to her, as a mother. Present at the beginning of the

Church, she is present with the Church throughout time, inviting us also to ponder and reflect upon the mysteries of the life, death and resurrection of her Son. The Rosary is a wonderful way to enter upon this contemplative journey in the company of Mary.

8 October, Saturday, Twenty-seventh Week in Ordinary Time
Luke 11:27–28

Paul says something very striking in today's first reading. He declares that baptism into Christ has collapsed some of the distinctions that were so evident in the ancient world, the distinction between Jew and pagan, between slave and free, and between male and female. He declares that through baptism, we are all one in Christ Jesus. Regardless of our state in life, in virtue of our baptism and our faith, we are all equally sons and daughters of God and brothers and sisters of Christ and of one another in Christ. What Paul writes would have been revolutionary in certain quarters in its time, and it remains a powerful reminder of our fundamental equality and unity in Christ today. We find something similar at play in today's gospel reading. A woman in the crowd singles out Jesus' mother for praise, pronouncing a beatitude upon her: 'Happy the womb that bore you and the breasts you sucked!' The woman, who was probably a mother herself, considered Jesus' mother to be uniquely blessed because of the unique son that she bore. Of course, she was right in a sense. Mary is uniquely blessed; we honour her in a way we don't honour any other woman. Yet, in his reply to the woman in the crowd, Jesus moves the focus away from his mother to all his disciples, to all of us here today, 'Still happier those who hear the word of God and keep it'. Jesus gives us there the essence of what it is to be a disciple, hearing the word of God as Jesus proclaims it, and keeping that word in our lives. If we do that, Jesus declares, we will be as blessed as the physical mother of Jesus, whoever we are, whatever our distinctive nature, our background or our social status. Mary, of course, was not only the physical mother of Jesus. She was also the ideal disciple, who heard the word of God, surrendered to it, and lived it to the full. We can all be like Mary in that regard, and, in so far as we are, Jesus declares that we will be as blessed as she is.

10 October, Monday, Twenty-eighth Week in Ordinary Time
Luke 11:29–32

Many of Jesus' contemporaries were slow to respond to Jesus' presence and message; they were insisting on some dramatic sign. In contrast, Jesus reminds them, people from outside of Israel, pagans, responded to God's messengers in the past. The Ninevites responded to the preaching of the prophet Jonah, and the Queen of Sheba responded to the wisdom of Solomon. These pagans were more receptive to God's presence in Israel than Jesus' own contemporaries were, even though Jesus is greater than the prophet Jonah and greater than the wise man Solomon. He is the fulfilment of all the prophets and the wise men and women of Israel and, still, so many of his contemporaries are unmoved by him. Jesus has no inclination to perform some kind of overpowering sign for such people who have been so indifferent to all that God has already been doing through his ministry. When Jesus says that there is something greater than Solomon here and something greater than Jonah here, we can apply the word 'here' to wherever we happen to be today. By 'here' Jesus did not just mean his own place and time. 'Here' refers to the time and place of each one of us. The Lord is here, with us now, wherever we happen to find ourselves, and he is here as someone greater than all the prophets and wise people of Israel. The Lord remains 'here' with you in your own place, your own home, your own room. He is there in all his risen power, inviting you to draw strength from his presence, and to live from that strength. Today's gospel reading reminds us that we are always in the presence of someone greater.

11 October, Tuesday, Twenty-eighth Week in Ordinary Time
Luke 11:37–41

In the gospels we often find Jesus at table with people. A great deal happens in the setting of meals. This is especially true of the Gospel of Luke, where Jesus shares table with disciples, like Mary and Martha and the two disciples walking to Emmaus, with those regarded by others as 'sinners', such as Zacchaeus, and with those who regarded themselves as living lives faithful to God's Law, such as the Pharisees. In today's gospel reading, Jesus is invited as a guest to the table of one such Pharisee. Noticing his host's preoccupation with external, ritual cleanliness, Jesus reminds him that what matters in God's eyes is a clean heart and a pure spirit. It is the inner life of the person that is important to God, according to Jesus. If the heart and spirit are right, then a way of life pleasing to God will follow. Saint Paul reflects that teaching of Jesus in the first reading when he memorably declares that 'what matters is faith that makes its power felt through love' or 'faith working through love'. Faith is that personal response to the Lord who emptied himself for us on the cross and now lives as risen Lord interceding for us. Such a personal response to the Lord's love for us is to be rooted in the core of our being, shaping our deepest self. From that Christ-self will flow, as Paul suggests, a life of love, a life which reflects the self-emptying love of the Lord for us all. It is always worth asking, 'What matters in our relationship with God?' The Pharisee in today's gospel reading was overly concerned with what doesn't matter all that much to God. The life and teaching of both Jesus and Paul show us what really matters to God.

12 October, Wednesday, Twenty-eighth Week in Ordinary Time
Luke 11:42–46

The 'lawyers' whom Jesus critiques at the end of today's gospel reading are not 'lawyers' as we use the term, people with an expertise in various kinds of civil law. In Jesus' day, 'lawyers' were the experts in religious law, the Law of God as found in the Jewish Scriptures and in the oral tradition that was a commentary on that biblical law. They would be more akin to theologians today, those who seeks to interpret the Christian tradition for the present time. Jesus accuses these lawyers of interpreting God's Law, God's will for his people, in a way that places an unendurable and unnecessary burden on others. In contrast, Jesus came to invite people into a life-giving relationship with God that empowers them to carry life's burdens and, indeed, to help carry the burdens of others. As he announced in his opening homily in the synagogue of Nazareth, he came to 'bring good news to the poor … release to the captives and recovery of sight to the blind and to let the oppressed go free'. He can do all this because the Spirit of the Lord was upon him. Jesus wishes to breathe this Spirit into all our lives. The Holy Spirit is a life-giving force in our own lives and, through us, in the lives of others. In today's first reading, Paul reminds us that 'the Spirit is our life', and if we allow ourselves 'to be directed by the Spirit' it will bear rich fruit in our lives, which Paul identifies as 'love, joy, peace, patience, kindness, goodness, faithfulness, gentleness and self-control'. This is the life that the Spirit of Jesus, the Spirit of God, can create within us. Far from describing someone who is burdened, this is the portrait of the human person fully alive.

13 October, Thursday, Twenty-eighth Week in Ordinary Time
Luke 11:47–54

Today we begin reading from the letter to the Ephesians, and we will be reading from it on weekdays for the next two weeks. We heard the beginning of the letter today. It is a wonderful prayer of praise to God for all the ways that God has blessed us in Christ. It speaks of 'the richness of the grace which God has showered on us' through the coming of Christ. In what does this richness of God's grace consist? According to the reading, it includes our being adopted as sons and daughters of God, sharing in Christ's relationship with God, the forgiveness of our sins, and God's ultimate plan to bring everything together under Christ as head. There is much to ponder in this articulation of the Gospel. The Gospel, which is embodied in the person of Jesus, is a wonderfully rich reality that could never be fully explored or appreciated in a human lifetime. Yet, clearly, God wants us to keep growing in our appreciation of this pearl of great price throughout our lives and to share our appreciation of it with others. However, in the gospel reading today, Jesus is very critical of the experts in the ways of God, the lawyers, who were best placed to appreciate the richness of God's grace in Jesus and to bring others to an appreciation of him. Instead, Jesus says, they have taken away the key of knowledge, not going in themselves and preventing others who wanted to from going in. They refused to respond to God's wonderful gift to humanity through his Son and they also made it very difficult for others to respond. Our calling, in contrast, is to value the treasure of the Gospel, the pearl of great price, and to lead others to appreciate its worth too.

14 October, Friday, Twenty-eighth Week in Ordinary Time
Luke 12:1–7

In today's gospel reading, Jesus makes a distinction between two kinds of fear, false fear and true fear. His disciples are not to fear their opponents who can only kill the body. Rather, they are to fear God, who has power over both body and soul. However, this 'fear' of God is more akin to a sense of awe and reverence before God. Jesus goes on to speak of God as the loving Creator who is aware of and cares for the smallest of his creatures, such as the humble sparrow, five of which could be sold for two pence in the village market. Jesus goes on to declare that each one of us is worth more than hundreds of sparrows. God's loving care for us is so much greater than his care for one sparrow. Jesus declares that God knows each of us through and through, using that striking image of God counting the hairs on our head. It is a symbol of God's loving concern for and interest in the details of our lives. There is no question of fearing such a God in the ordinary sense of the word 'fear'. Jesus reveals a God to whom we can entrust ourselves with great confidence. We can let ourselves go to God in the assurance that God wants nothing but the best for us. This loving, confident, relationship with God makes us fearless in the face of those who are hostile to our faith and the values and attitudes our faith gives rise to. The Creator God's loving relationship with us does not make us arrogant in any way, because we are aware that we can and do sin against God's great love. Yet, it gives us a confidence to live our faith in God and in God's Son publicly. In the words of the gospel reading, God's providential care for us gives us the courage to live our faith not just 'in the dark' but 'in the daylight'.

15 October, Saturday, Twenty-eighth Week in Ordinary Time
Luke 12:8–12

It is clear from today's gospel reading that Jesus wants his disciples to declare themselves openly for him in the presence of others. He wants them to live their faith in him in broad daylight, and not to hide it away in some dark place. We can be slow to declare ourselves openly for the Lord today. We sense that such an open declaration of faith in the Lord will not always be well received by others. We live in an age that doesn't always understand or appreciate religious faith, and in our own Irish context, isn't always tolerant of our Catholic faith. We need support in living our faith publicly. It was the same for the first disciples, and in the gospel reading Jesus promises his disciples a very special form of support, the help of the Holy Spirit. He declares to them, 'When the time comes, the Holy Spirit will teach you what you must say.' That same Spirit is given to us all. We sometimes think of the Holy Spirit as given to us only at very particular, privileged, moments of our lives, such as the day of our baptism and the day of our confirmation. However, when Jesus says that when the time comes the Holy Spirit will help his disciples to witness publicly to him, he is suggesting that the gift of the Holy Spirit is always given to us at the time when we need it. There are times when, in the words of today's first reading, we need a 'spirit of wisdom and perception', such as when we have important decisions to make or when we need to have a significant conversation with someone. The Holy Spirit is given to us at such times, if we open our heart to receive him. There are other times when we need courage to live out of the values that are rooted in our faith, and again, the Holy Spirit is given to us at such times, if we open ourselves to his coming. We can trust that the Holy Spirit will always be there to help us, 'when the time comes', whenever that time is and whatever situation we find ourselves in.

17 October, Monday, Twenty-ninth Week in Ordinary Time
Luke 12:13–21
There is a wonderful statement towards the end of today's first reading from Paul's letter to the Ephesians: 'We are God's work of art, created in Christ Jesus to live the good life as from the beginning he had meant us to live it.' When we hear the expression

'work of art', we think of the work of some of the great painters or sculptors or musical composers. I suspect very few of us think of ourselves as a work of art. Yet each one of us is God's work of art, because we have been created by God in God's image and, according to our reading, God has also brought us to life with Christ out of his great love for us. Through faith we already share in the risen life of Christ, and we are destined to share that life fully. We will reach our full stature in eternity, but we are already God's work of art. God is the supreme artist who created us and then showered his goodness upon us through the life, death and resurrection of his Son. As God's work of art, we are called to live accordingly. In the words of the first reading, we are to live the good life, which is a life of love, kindness and generosity. We find the opposite of such a life in the gospel reading. In his parable, Jesus portrays a person who is totally preoccupied with himself and completely self-serving. He starts off very rich and as he gets richer his only concern is where to store his surplus. The thought of sharing his surplus with the needy never crosses his mind. When he died suddenly, his fundamental poverty is revealed. Jesus calls on us, in contrast, to be rich in the sight of God, by living as the work of art we are, revealing God's gracious love and goodness in our ways of relating to others.

18 October, Tuesday, Saint Luke, Evangelist

Luke 10:1–9

One of Saint Paul's co-workers was a man called Luke. In one of his letters, Paul refers to Luke as 'the beloved physician'. It is this co-worker of Paul who has traditionally been identified as the author of the two-volume work that we call the Gospel of Luke and the Acts of the Apostles. This was a very extensive literary work in two parts, consisting of the story of Jesus and the story of the early Church. Together they make up a quarter of the New Testament. We owe a great deal to this co-worker of Paul. In today's first reading, Paul is writing from prison, at a very vulnerable moment in his life. He mentions at the beginning of that reading that some of his companions have deserted him – Demas, Crescens and Titus. He declares, 'Only Luke is with me.' Luke is being portrayed as Paul's faithful companion and co-worker. Paul goes on in that reading to say that at his first defence, no one supported him, yet he could say, 'The Lord stood by me and gave me power.' Paul had no doubt about the Lord's faithful presence to him, and Luke's faithfulness to Paul was one expression of the Lord's faithfulness to him. We are all called to make present to others something of the Lord's faithful love. In the gospel reading from Luke, Jesus sends out seventy-two as his messengers and representatives. They are to proclaim the same message as Jesus, 'The kingdom of God is very near to you'; they are to cure the sick as Jesus did. The Lord wanted to be present to others through them. We can all think of ourselves as among that group whom the Lord sends out to make him present in a tangible way to others, just as Luke made the Lord's faithful presence present to Paul in a very tangible way. The Lord's harvest remains rich and we are all needed as his labourers. He looks to each of us to be channels of his faithful love to others.

19 October, Wednesday, Twenty-ninth Week in Ordinary Time
Luke 12:39–48

The theme of wisdom links today's two readings. In the first reading, Paul marvels at 'how comprehensive God's wisdom really is'. The marvellous wisdom of God was revealed in the person of Christ. This is why Paul in this reading can refer to 'the depths that I see in the mystery of Christ' and go on to declare that he has been entrusted with the grace of 'proclaiming to the pagans the infinite treasure of Christ'. For Paul, there was a depth to Christ that could not be fully explored in this life. The treasure of Christ was so immense that it could not be fully appreciated in this life. We could spend our lives exploring the depths of Christ and drawing forth from his immense treasure. God's wisdom revealed in Christ is a feast for the heart, mind and soul, which cannot be fully consumed this side of eternity. In that reading, Paul understands himself as a 'servant of this gospel'. He is called to make known something of the depths he sees in Christ, to share something of the infinite treasure of Christ, to communicate to others something of the comprehensive wisdom of God revealed in Christ. We are all called to be what Jesus in the gospel reading calls 'faithful and wise' servants. What the gospel reading calls 'our employment' is to share with others something of the feast of God's wisdom that Christ offers us, or, in the words of the gospel reading, 'to give them their allowance of food at the proper time'. Our baptismal calling is to keep growing in our appreciation of 'the mystery of Christ', and to keep growing in our freedom to share the wonders of this mystery with all who are longing to be fed at the table of life.

20 October, Thursday, Twenty-ninth Week in Ordinary Time
Luke 12:49–53
Today's first reading from the letter to the Ephesians is one my favourite passages in the New Testament. It is a prayer of Paul for the church in Ephesus. What Paul prays for is what we would all wish for, that our hidden self would grow strong through the Spirit, that Christ would live in our hearts through faith, that we would be planted and built on love, the love of Christ, that we would have the strength to grasp the breadth and length, the height

and the depth of the love of Christ, which is beyond knowledge, that we would be filled with the utter fullness of God whose power working in us can do infinitely more than all we ask or imagine. What a prayer! We could reflect long on any one of its elements. The content of Paul's prayer for us is reflected in the desire of Jesus for us in the gospel reading, when he says, 'I have come to bring fire to the earth, and how I wish it were blazing already.' Jesus seems to be referring there to the fire of the Holy Spirit which he wants to set alight in the hearts of all. It is the fire of God's love which Jesus ignites through his life and especially through what he calls in that reading his baptism, his death on the cross. It is through the fire of the Holy Spirit within us that Paul's prayer for us comes to pass, our hidden self grows strong, Christ lives in our hearts, we are planted and built on Christ's love, we come to grasp the dimensions of that love and we are filled with the utter fullness of God. When our inner self is built up in this way through the Holy Spirit, it overflows in a way of life that is pleasing to God. The Spirit bears rich fruit in our lives, thereby giving glory to God. There is a wonderfully exciting and consoling vision here of the Christian life.

21 October, Friday, Twenty-ninth Week in Ordinary Time
Luke 12:54–59
My father was very good at judging the weather. He would look at the sky and announce that it would be a good day or it would rain in half an hour. Generally, he wasn't too far off the mark. Many of us have weather apps on our phones these days. He was his own weather app. We talk a lot about the weather in Ireland, probably because we get such a variety of it. It has been said, 'we don't have a climate, we just have weather'. In the gospel reading, Jesus suggests that his own contemporaries were good

at reading the weather. They knew that clouds in the west meant rain, and that wind from the south meant heat. However, although they knew how to interpret the elements of earth and sky, they weren't so good at interpreting the significance of the times they lived in. Many of them could not recognise that God was working powerfully through the life and ministry of Jesus, and calling out to them through Jesus. They were impervious to God's unique visitation of them, through Jesus. It is not always easy to interpret the times in which we find ourselves. What is going on in all that is happening to us? Where is God to be found in it? What is God saying to us through it? We may not have easy answers to these questions, but it is good to be asking them. One thing we can be sure of is that God is present in all of our times and that he continues to speak to us through his Son in the midst of them. We need to be attentive to his presence and to what he may be saying to us. The Lord's word to us in our times will always be words of life, words that give us courage and hope, words that inspire us to be as generous and loving towards others as he is towards us.

22 October, Saturday, Twenty-ninth Week in Ordinary Time
Luke 13:1–9
When disasters strike out of the blue, it can be tempting to interpret them as God's punishment for sin. Jesus rejects such an interpretation at the beginning of today's gospel reading. One disaster brought about by human means is brought to Jesus' attention, the death of pilgrims due to Pilate's cruelty, and he goes on to speak of another disaster that doesn't appear to have had a human cause, the collapse of a wall killing eighteen people. In neither case, Jesus says, could it be said that those who died were greater sinners than anyone else. Jesus is acknowledging that perfectly innocent people die tragically and unexpectedly. That is

as true today as it was in Jesus' day. He declares that the frailty and vulnerability of our lives should lead us to turn to God every day of our lives, to repent, in the language of Jesus. The Covid-19 pandemic was a disaster on a world scale. Looking for sinners to blame for this tragedy is not a worthwhile exercise, Jesus suggests. Rather, this disaster has been an opportunity for us all to assess our relationship with God, and to deepen that relationship. The parable of the fig tree that Jesus goes on to speak in the gospel reading suggests that God waits patiently for us to turn more fully towards him. God is less like the vineyard owner who wanted to cut the fruitless tree down because it was taking up valuable space and more like the servant who looked after the vineyard and argued that the tree ought to be given more time. The Lord is always giving us time, but he looks to us to use the time to open our hearts more fully to his presence, his Spirit, so that our lives can be more fruitful, alive with the fruit of the Spirit. The Lord keeps giving us time, so that, over time, we can become, in the words of today's first reading, 'fully mature with the fullness of Christ himself' and 'grow in all ways into Christ'.

24 October, Monday, Thirtieth Week in Ordinary Time
Luke 13:10–17

We are all familiar with the emotion of anger. Sometimes, we can be angry for good reasons. Our anger often shows that there is something afoot that is not right or just. Our anger is saying something about a very unsatisfactory situation and we have to listen to it and, perhaps, act on it. At other times, our anger is saying something about ourselves more than about some external situation. Our anger is not really justified by anything that is unfair or unjust or plain wrong. We find this second kind of anger at work in today's gospel reading. A synagogue official is indignant because Jesus, on the Sabbath, healed a woman who had an eighteen-year-old infirmity. God was doing a good work through Jesus, yet this official was angry, because, in his view, the Sabbath Law was being broken. His anger was really saying something about his own restricted view of how God was to be honoured on the Sabbath day. As Jesus said, the official had no problem untying his donkey from the manger on the Sabbath, but he had a problem with Jesus untying a woman from a crippling condition on the Sabbath. It was the ordinary people who responded appropriately to what Jesus had just done. 'They were overjoyed at all the wonders he worked.' Joy, not anger, was what was called for. What Jesus did on the Sabbath was an act of love. He showed his love for the woman by freeing her from her bondage. An act of love is to be rejoiced over, whenever and wherever it happens. The gospel reading calls on us to recognise love when it is before us, even when it is in a form we do not expect, and then to rejoice in that manifestation of love. The gospel reading also calls on us to be as loving towards the oppressed as Jesus was. In the words of today's first reading, we are to 'follow Christ, loving as he loved you'.

25 October, Tuesday, Thirtieth Week in Ordinary Time
Luke 13:18–21

In the context of a funeral, I am often struck by references to the acts of kindness performed by the deceased over many years that were not evident to many, but know only to a few. It is often the way that small and hidden acts of love and kindness come to light only when a person's earthly life is complete. We live surrounded by small and hidden acts of goodness that may never become visible to us. They will never make headlines, because the people responsible for them do not publicly announce what they do. In today's gospel reading, Jesus says that the kingdom of God is like that. It is like the mustard seed that is sown in the ground. It is a tiny seed and, when placed in the ground, it is hidden, yet it produces a tree that provides shelter for the birds of the air. Jesus also says that the kingdom of God is like leaven that a woman puts in flour. Leaven is small and is hidden when placed in the flour, yet, because of its influence, bread is formed to feed the hungry. These parables immediately follow on from yesterday's gospel reading, which was the story of Jesus healing the crippled woman in the synagogue. This was a small act of loving kindness for one needy human being that went unnoticed by the bulk of humanity, indeed by the majority of people in Israel. Yet Jesus is saying that through such acts of loving kindness the kingdom of God gains a greater foothold on earth. We can all help to create an opening for the kingdom of God to come on earth through our own small and hidden acts of loving kindness towards others. We can remember one another in small and hidden ways. The visit, the card, the email, the phone call, can all make a difference to the quality of someone's life.

26 October, Wednesday, Thirtieth Week in Ordinary Time
Luke 13:22–30

It is clear from the first reading that this letter to the Ephesians accepts the institution of slavery as a given. Slavery was so endemic in that world that it would have been difficult to imagine a society without it. However, Paul seeks to humanise this institution, insisting that masters and slaves are to treat one another with deep respect and sincere loyalty. Furthermore, he reminds masters that both themselves and their slaves have the same Master in heaven who is not impressed by one person more than another. Those who are masters in this life are slaves of Christ, as are their slaves. There is a fundamental equality between master and slave in the eyes of Christ. In the gospel reading, Jesus calls on his hearers to strive to enter by the narrow door. This exhortation is addressed to all, regardless of their place on the social ladder. It is not a case of one door and one stairway for slaves and another, grander, door and a more splendid stairway for masters. All, slave and free, Jew and Greek, male and female, have to enter by the same narrow door. In the Gospel of John, Jesus identifies himself as the door to fullness of life. The door may be narrow but there is wonderful green pasture beyond it, or, in the imagery of the gospel reading, there is a wonderful banquet beyond it, at which people from the four corners of the earth are invited to gather. All can be guests, on an equal footing, at the feast in the kingdom of God. Yet, there is first the small matter of that narrow door. To enter by the narrow door is to walk in the way of Jesus, which is the way of loving respect for all, in particular those who were often denied respect in that culture, such as the vulnerable and dependent, the poor and the weak. All who walk through this narrow door of loving respect of others will experience the fullness of the Lord's love beyond it.

27 October, Thursday, Thirtieth Week in Ordinary Time
Luke 13:31–35
In one of the psalms we find the line, 'He (the Lord) will cover you with his pinions, and under his wings you will find refuge.' It is the image of a great bird protecting its young with its broad wings. It speaks of the Lord as a source of refuge and protection before what the psalm calls 'the terror of the night' and 'the arrow that flies by day'. In the gospel reading, Jesus picks up this imagery of the bird with its sheltering and protective wings. He says to the people of Jerusalem, 'How often have I longed to gather your children, as a hen gathers her brood under her wings.' It is a very motherly image, suggesting the mother's instinct to protect her

young. It speaks to us of the Lord's desire to have a very personal and intimate relationship with us all, which serves as a refuge and a source of strength in times of trial, enabling us to go forth and confront evil in its various forms with goodness, hatred with love. In the first reading, Paul uses a much more male and, indeed, martial, image, calling on us to put on the armour of God, so as to resist when the worst happens. Among other items, he identifies this armour as the shield of faith and the sword of God's word. Jesus' image of the hen gathering her brood under her wing presupposes a willingness on the part of her brood to be gathered. However, as Jesus says there, 'You refused'. The longing of Jesus to gather the people of Jerusalem to himself did not meet with a corresponding longing to be gathered on their part. The Lord who desires an intimate relationship with us that provides protection and strength can only do so much to make that relationship happen. He needs a corresponding desire on our part. He needs us to long for him as he longs for us. He needs us to put on some of that armour Paul mentions in the first reading.

28 October, Friday, Saints Simon and Jude, Apostles
Luke 6:12–19

Simon and Jude are mentioned among the twelve apostles in today's gospel reading. In our Catholic tradition, Saint Jude has been venerated as the patron saint of desperate cases. People have traditionally invoked his intercession when their need was at its greatest. He is known as the patron saint of the impossible. The origin of this belief lies in the fact that the name Jude and Judas are really the same, and people were reluctant to pray to Saint Jude in case they ended up praying to Judas the traitor, unless, of course, they were really desperate and all other options had failed. Simon is called the zealot in our gospel reading, to distinguish him from Simon Peter. This suggests that he had a zeal to do God's will as expressed in God's Law. According to tradition, Jude and Simon were martyred on the same day. In today's first reading, Paul tells us that we are all being built into a spiritual house where God lives, a holy temple in the Lord, the foundations of which are the apostles and the prophets. There is a striking image here of the Church as a spiritual building made up of living stones, resting on the apostles and prophets. Elsewhere, Paul says that the cornerstone of this spiritual building is Jesus Christ. The physical buildings we call churches are a symbol of that spiritual building in which we are all living stones. Just as our parish church has solid foundations, today's feast reminds us that we, as Church, have solid foundations as well. We rest on the apostles, like Simon and Jude, with the Lord as our cornerstone. Our calling is to allow our lives to be shaped by those foundations and that cornerstone. The Lord who, according to our gospel reading, prayed all night before calling the twelve, intercedes for us all so that we may true to our calling to become living stones in the holy temple of the Church. We become living stones by allowing the Lord to reveal his loving presence in the world in and through our lives.

29 October, Saturday, Thirtieth Week in Ordinary Time
Luke 14:1, 7–11

In today's first reading, we are given a wonderful insight into a deeply personal struggle within Paul. Writing from prison with the prospect of death before him, he finds himself pulled in two directions, each of which is very praiseworthy. He feels a desire, a pull, towards death because it means being with Christ. He feels another desire or pull to stay alive in order to continue serving the church in Philippi by helping them to progress in the faith. We often find ourselves in a situation where we have a choice to make, not so much between what is good and what is not good, but between one good and another good. Whichever path we take will be a good path, but we try to discern which path would be better. For Paul, death leading to a deeper communion with Christ would, in some respects, be a much better path. Yet he eventually expresses his wish for the other path, staying alive and serving the Church, continuing his work which is bearing such good results in the lives of others. In the end, the decisive question for Paul is, 'What would best serve the well-being of others, especially their spiritual well-being?' It is a good question to ponder when we are trying to discern between two paths, both of which are good. In the gospel reading, Jesus witnesses people for whom a very different question is important. They are asking, 'How can I receive the greatest honour?' There is a competitive spirit among them to choose the places of greatest honour at table. Jesus makes clear that this is not a valid question for his followers. Rather, we are called to humble ourselves, to empty ourselves, in the loving service of others, as Jesus himself did. If we do so, we will go on to receive the only honour that is worth having, the honour that comes from God. Beyond this earthly life, we will be exalted, as Jesus was.

31 October, Monday, Thirty-first Week in Ordinary Time
Luke 14:12–14

In the time of Jesus, people with resources used them to gain something for themselves, such as honour, renown and recognition. If they used their wealth to help build a public building, their name would appear in some prominent place on the building as one of its benefactors. Much the same happens today at times. Someone uses their wealth to build a library and it is called after them. There is nothing inherently wrong with being generous with a view to getting something in return. In today's gospel reading, Jesus is a guest of a wealthy host and he is aware of the practice of wealthy people inviting other wealthy people to a meal so that the favour can be returned in due course. A small circle of wealthy, privileged people give generously among themselves with a view to receiving back as much if not more than is given. Jesus, however, challenges his host to break out of that narrow circle of mutual giving and receiving by inviting to his table people who cannot return his invitation because they don't have the resources to do so, the poor, the crippled, the lame and the blind. Jesus is calling for a generosity of spirit that is not in any way calculating. He calls on all of us to be generous with what we have without any thought for a reward or a return. We are to find our joy in the giving itself, rather than in the return from the giving. One sure way of taking this path is to give to those who appear to have nothing to give us back. However, more often than not, in giving to those who seem to have nothing to give us in return, we actually end up receiving more from them than we give to them. Our giving opens us up to receiving from the Lord's generosity.

1 November, Tuesday, Feast of All Saints
Matthew 5:1–12

A teacher once asked her pupils what a saint was and one of them, thinking of the stained-glass windows in her church, said that a saint was someone who lets the light in. Out of the mouths of children wisdom often comes. Saints are indeed people who let the light of Christ's presence shine through their lives. Just as there are many colours in a stained-glass window, so there are many ways of reflecting the Lord's presence. Each of us reflects the light of his presence in a unique way. Today we remember all those through whom the light of the Lord's love streamed into our world.

They are the people whose lives have blessed and graced us. When we think of them, we thank God for them. When we have been in their company, we felt the better for it. They somehow brought out the best in us and helped us to become all that God was calling us to be. Some of them are with the Lord in heaven. Many are living with us now. They are often to be found in our families, among our friends, in our neighbourhood, in the places where we live and work.

The great majority of such people will not feature on the Church's official list of canonised saints. Today's feast includes all the saints on that list, but it commemorates a vastly greater number of saintly people. The first reading speaks of a 'huge number, impossible to count, of people from every nation, race, tribe and language'. The reference to 144,000 in that reading is not intended to be restrictive. In the Book of the Apocalypse, all numbers are symbolic. The number 144,000 is understood as 12 by 12 by 1,000, with the first twelve representing the twelve tribes of Israel and the second twelve representing the twelve apostles, the pillars on which the Church rests, the figure 1,000 indicating a very large number impossible to count. In other words, 144,000 symbolises all of God's faithful people both before the coming of Christ and since then, all who have responded to God's call by lives of loving faithfulness to God and to others. It could be said that the feast of all saints is the feast of goodness, wherever it is to be found. At the beginning of his letter to the Philippians Paul says, 'I am confident of this, that the one who began a good work among you will bring it to completion by the day of Jesus Christ.' God's good work in our lives began in our mother's womb. There was a new beginning of that good work on the day of our baptism. That good work has been ongoing ever since, and will only be brought to completion in eternity. According to our second reading, it is only in eternity that we will be like God, as loving as God is loving, as holy as God is holy, because it is only than that we will see God as God is. Today we celebrate the feast of all those people in whom God's good work has been clearly visible.

We are also celebrating the presence of God's goodness in each of our lives, the good work that God is already doing in us and through us. As Saint John reminds us in today's second reading, 'we are already the children of God'. The Holy Spirit has been poured into our lives, making us sons and daughters of God, giving us a share in Jesus' own relationship with God. That is the significant good work of God that has already begun in us and will continue in us for the rest of our earthly lives. Deep within each of us there is a Spirit-shaped identity, a core of divine goodness. Our calling is to keep growing into that identity, to allow that core of goodness to find expression in our lives. In the Beatitudes of today's gospel reading, Jesus gives us a portrait of that lived goodness. In many ways, Jesus' Beatitudes are his own self-portrait, but they are also the portrait of the person in whom God's good work is being brought to competition. Jesus is painting a portrait of the saint, or, at least, of a saint in the making. Such people are poor in spirit, recognising their dependence of God for everything. They are gentle, in the sense of not arrogantly insisting on their own way but allowing God's way to prevail in their lives. They are pure in heart, with a single-minded focus on what God desires. They mourn because the world is not as God intended it to be, so they hunger and thirst for God's justice to prevail in the world. They reveal God's loving mercy to others, making the peace of God's heavenly kingdom a reality on earth, even if that means being persecuted, having to take the way of the cross. Such people, Jesus declares, are truly blessed because they have chosen a path that will be life-giving for themselves and for others. Hopefully, on this feast of all saints, we can all recognise something of ourselves in that portrait of goodness that Jesus puts before us in the Beatitudes.

2 November, Wednesday, Commemoration of All the Faithful Departed

Mark 15:33–39; 16:1–6

Today we remember that the love we have for one another in this life is stronger than death. One of the ways we express our love for our loved ones in this life is by praying for them. We pray for our loved ones, we light candles for them, we get Masses offered for them. Such prayer of intercession is central to our faith. When our loved ones die, we continue our prayer of intercession for them. At every Mass, during the Eucharistic Prayer, we pray for our loved ones who have died. The tradition of having Mass said for those who have died on the anniversary of their death is still very strong in many parts of the world, including here in Ireland. We somehow sense that just as our loved ones can benefit from our prayers while living in this life, they can continue to benefit from our prayers when they have moved on from this earthly life to the next life. We may not be able to articulate clearly how our loved ones who have died can benefit from our prayers. When it comes to the afterlife, so much remains in the realm of mystery. Yet, we believe in what the Creed calls the communion of saints, that deep spiritual bond between those of us who are still on our earthly pilgrimage and those who have come to the end of that pilgrimage and are now with the Lord. One of the ways we give expression to that bond is through prayer. We pray for our loved ones who have died, and we believe they can pray for us. In Mark's Gospel, from which we have just been reading, a group of women followed Jesus in Galilee and then from Galilee to Jerusalem.

They were present when Jesus was dying on the cross, although at a distance. They saw where he was buried. On the first day of the week they came to anoint his body with spices. They wanted to preserve their communion with him in some way, even after his death. To their amazement, they discovered that Jesus would remain in communion with them in a way they could never have imagined. Having been raised from the dead, he would meet them in Galilee, and would be present to them for the rest of their lives. Death did not break the Lord's communion with his followers, and it does not break the communion between our loved ones and us. Today we give special expression to that communion by our prayerful remembrance.

3 November, Thursday, Thirty-first Week in Ordinary Time
Luke 15:1–10

A question we might sometimes ask ourselves in our more reflective moments is, 'What do I really value in life?' At the conclusion of today's first reading, Saint Paul gives his own answer to that question: 'I believe nothing can happen that will outweigh the supreme advantage of knowing Christ Jesus my Lord.' For Paul, his relationship with the Lord is the supreme value, before which even those religious credentials he boasted about in the past now seem of little value, such as keeping the Jewish Law faultlessly. We spend our lives growing in our appreciation of the Lord as our supreme value, as 'my Lord'. What did Jesus really value in life? Today's gospel reading suggests that we are all his supreme value, especially when we find ourselves lost in some way or other. The two parables Jesus speaks in response to the criticism of the Pharisees and the scribes reveal his real priorities. He is like the shepherd searching for his lost sheep or the woman searching for her lost coin, in that his whole ministry is driven by his search of those who feel lost in themselves or lost to God or to the faith community. Jesus valued those whom the religious leaders of the time dismissed as sinners. The Lord values us, even when others are tempted to give up on us, or we are tempted to give up on ourselves, because of what we have done or failed to do. To the extent that we grow in our appreciation of how much the Lord values us, we will be freed to keep valuing him above all else in life, recognising, with Saint Paul, 'the supreme advantage of knowing Christ Jesus my Lord'.

4 November, Friday, Thirty-first Week in Ordinary Time
Luke 16:1–8
Sometimes the principal characters in the stories that Jesus tells leave a lot to be desired. The younger son who left home in the parable of the prodigal son comes to mind. Very often those characters who leave a lot to be desired have some redeeming feature to them. That younger son did make the journey home again, even if it was out of desperation. Today's gospel reading gives us another example of a story in which the principal character is anything but a paragon of virtue. He is described as a dishonest steward who was wasteful with his master's property. Yet, he too had a redeeming feature. Perhaps Jesus is reminding us that everyone has some redeeming feature. The redeeming feature of the dishonest steward was his shrewd ability to take decisive action when his back was to the wall, so as to ensure that after he lost his job there would be people who would be well disposed towards him. Jesus' comments on the story suggest that we have something to learn, not from his dishonesty, but from his shrewdness, from his ability to take decisive action when required. Very often our following of the Lord requires us to take decisive action to ensure that we continue to take the path the Lord is

calling us to take. There can be something we need to do or to stop doing if, in the words of today's first reading, we are to remain faithful to the Lord.

5 November, Saturday, Thirty-first Week in Ordinary Time
Luke 16:9–15

The issue Jesus raises in today's gospel reading is the relationship of his followers to money. He presupposes that some of his followers will have money over and above what they need. He didn't call everyone to sell all their possessions in response to his call to follow him. At present, money is scarce for many who desire to follow Jesus. Some have lost their job or have seen their wages greatly reduced. Yet, the issue of how to use our financial and material resources remains an important one for all of us who seek to walk in the way of Jesus. What Jesus warns against above all in the gospel reading is becoming a slave of money. Rather than possessing money, we can allow money to possess us. Jesus uses the language of trust in relation to money in the gospel reading. 'If you cannot be trusted with money, that tainted thing, who will trust you with genuine riches?' God puts his trust in us to use our financial resources well, whether we have a lot or a little, and that means using them to serve the well-being of others. As Jesus says, we are to use money to win us friends who will go on to welcome us into the tents of eternity. According to Paul in our first reading, this was the attitude of the members of the church in Philippi to their financial resources. They used some of these resources to serve Paul in his need. As Paul says to them in that reading, 'When I left Macedonia, no other church helped me with gifts of money. You were the only one.' Paul assures them that in return for their generosity towards him, 'God will fulfil all our needs, in Christ Jesus, as lavishly as only God can'. Paul reflects the message of

Jesus here that when we are generous with what we have been given we open ourselves up more fully to experiencing God's generosity towards us, both in this life and the next.

7 November, Monday, Thirty-second Week in Ordinary Time
Luke 17:1–6

There is a certain realism about the opening words of Jesus in today's gospel reading, 'Obstacles are sure to come'. He is very aware that the world in which we live will present many an obstacle to living as his disciples. There will be temptations and pressures that will draw us in a different direction to the one that the Lord might want us to take. Given that obstacles to faith will come from the world in which we live, Jesus insists that such obstacles should not come from within the community of faith. Disciples are capable of leading other disciples astray. Believers can give scandal which makes the journey of faith more difficult for other believers. As members of Christ's body, our calling is to support one another as we try to live our faith in the Lord in today's world. Something of Paul's support for Titus comes through in today's first reading. Paul refers to Titus as 'true child of mine in the faith, that we share'. The rest of the gospel reading outlines two ways that we can support one another on the journey of faith. One way is by our willingness to forgive one another when we wrong each other: 'If he wrongs you … and says, "I am sorry", you must forgive him.' The other way we can support one another is by living the faith we have to the full, even if, at times, our faith seems very weak and small to us. Yes, we can all pray, as the apostles do in the gospel reading, 'Increase our faith', but in response to our prayer, the Lord will remind us, as he reminded them, that even our little faith, a faith the size of a mustard seed, if lived generously, creates a space for the Lord to work powerfully through us.

8 November, Tuesday, Thirty-second Week in Ordinary Time
Luke 17:7–10

The short parable Jesus speaks in today's gospel reading reminds us that we never have a claim on God. After we have done all that God asks of us, we cannot then say to God, 'I am due some recompense for all that I have done.' That would be usual in the world of human affairs. People expect to be recompensed in proportion to the work they have done. However, that is not how we are to relate to God. God is never in debt to us, no matter how generous we have been towards God. This is because our good work on God's behalf is itself due to God's good working within us. All the good we do is of God. Without God's loving initiative towards us, we could do nothing that is pleasing to God. Saint Paul speaks in today's first reading of how God's grace was revealed towards us in the life, death and resurrection of Jesus. We have been greatly graced by God and all that is good in our lives is the fruit of that gracious initiative of God towards us. In faithfully serving God we are giving back to God what God has already given to us. Yet, elsewhere, the gospel makes clear that our efforts to serve the Lord well will always be met by further loving initiatives of the Lord towards us. The Lord's love for us is a given; it doesn't have to be earned. Our lives of loving service in response to the Lord's love for us open us up more fully to the Lord's love for us. As Jesus says elsewhere, if we give to God, it will be given to us by God; a full measure, running over will be poured into our lap.

9 November, Wednesday, The Dedication of the Lateran Basilica
John 2:13–22

The Church of Saint John Lateran in Rome is one of the four great Basilicas of the city, the other three being Saint Peter's

Basilica, Saint Mary Major's Basilica and the Basilica of Saint
Paul outside the Walls. It is the cathedral church of the pope in
his role as bishop of the diocese of Rome. It is called 'Saint John'
after the two monasteries that were once attached and that were
dedicated to Saint John the apostle and Saint John the Baptist.
As the cathedral church of the pope it has the title 'Mother and
Head of all the Churches of the City and of the World'. There are
many wonderful churches in Rome and throughout the world, yet
we are all very aware that the Church is not primarily a building,
no matter how grand. The Church is the community of faith that
gathers in the building we call church. That is why ,at the beginning
of today's first reading, St Paul says to the community of faith in
Corinth, 'You are God's building.' The most impressive physical
building of worship among Jews in Paul's time was the Temple in
Jerusalem. Yet, in that same reading, Paul says to the community
of faith in Corinth, 'You are God's Temple.' Interestingly, in the
gospel reading, Jesus, while standing in the magnificent Temple in
Jerusalem, identifies himself as the Temple or sanctuary of God.
'Destroy this sanctuary and in three days I will raise it up.' Jesus
was claiming to be the place where God dwells among humanity,
not the physical Temple in Jerusalem. Paul reminds us that we,
the community of faith, are the place where God wishes to dwell
among humanity. As living stones in God's building, God's
Temple, each one of us is called to reveal God's loving presence
to others. One of the reasons we gather in a building like this, a
church, is to receive the grace and strength we need to be true
to our calling to be living stones in God's spiritual building. The
Lord needs us to make tangible his loving and merciful presence
in our world today.

10 November, Thursday, Thirty-second Week in Ordinary Time
Luke 17:20–25

In the time of Jesus, people thought of the kingdom of God as a future reality, as something that would come to earth at the end of time. The Pharisees in today's gospel reading ask Jesus when exactly this will happen. They had heard him say, 'the kingdom of God is at hand'. They wanted Jesus to be clearer about the timing of its arrival to earth. In reply, Jesus makes the striking statement, 'You must know, the kingdom of God is among you.' Jesus was saying to them that the kingdom of God had already arrived in and through his ministry. It hadn't arrived fully. As Jesus goes on to say to his disciples in the gospel reading, the day of the Son of Man has yet to come. It is only then that the kingdom of God will come fully. However, the kingdom of God is already present in all that Jesus was saying and doing. It would further break into our world through his death, resurrection and the sending of the Holy Spirit. The risen Lord would say to us today what he said to the Pharisees, 'the kingdom of God is among you'. It is among us when God's will is being done as it is in heaven, when believers' lives are shaped by the Holy Spirit, when people relate to God and to one another in the same loving way that Jesus did, when people live the values of the Beatitudes and put the Sermon on the Mount into practice, even at great cost to themselves. In the first reading, Paul called on Philemon to create an opening for the coming of the kingdom of God by welcoming back his runaway slave no longer as a slave but as a brother in Christ. The kingdom of God is among us. Each one of us in our day-to-day lives can make visible the presence of the kingdom of God by living the Gospel message in the power of the Spirit. Then we will put new heart into one another, in the words of today's first reading.

11 November, Friday, Thirty-second Week in Ordinary Time
Luke 17:26–37

In the gospel reading Jesus refers to the ordinary business of human living, namely, eating, drinking, buying, selling, planting, building, marrying and raising a family. We are all engaged in some or all of these activities. Along with other activities, they are all essential to human living. Yet Jesus is saying that there is something even more important, and that is our openness to receive the coming of the Son of Man, our welcoming of his presence to us. He is inviting us to look beyond all the many worthwhile activities we are engaged in and to notice his presence at the heart of it all. We are to pay attention to the Lord present in the midst of life. We could refer to this as a contemplative attitude towards living. We remain engaged in all the activities that make up our usual day but we recognise that there is a more at the core of it all, and that more is the Lord seeking us out, calling out to us. What is his call to us at the heart of all that we do? We find the answer to that question in today's first reading, where Saint John refers to the fundamental commandment, 'Let us love one another.' To say that the Lord is at the heart of all our living is to say that Love is at the heart of all our living, the Lord's loving presence to us and his call to us to reflect his love for us in the way we relate to one another, to love one another as he loves us. Whenever, in the midst of all our activities, we are seeking to open ourselves more fully to the Lord's loving presence to us and to pass on that love to those we meet, then we are contemplatives in action. All our activities will be shaped by the Lord's presence.

12 November, Saturday, Thirty-second Week in Ordinary Time
Luke 18:1–8

It can be tempting for many people to lose heart these days for all sorts of reasons. The parable in today's gospel reading speaks directly into that situation. The widow had many reasons to lose heart. Even though she had right on her side and was entitled to receive justice from the judge, she had the misfortune to come up against a judge who had no fear of God or respect for others. She could easily have given up but she didn't. She somehow found the energy to keep coming to the judge until, eventually, the judge, for reasons of self-interest, gave her the justice she was entitled to all along. The judge was a powerful figure in that culture and the woman, as a widow, had no power. She was among the vulnerable and weak. Yet, she proved stronger than the judge in the end. She never lost heart. Jesus spoke that parable to encourage all of us to keep the faith, to keep praying to God, never giving up hope, never losing heart. We have all the more reason than the widow never to lose heart because she was up against an unjust judge, whereas we are engaging with a loving God who cares for us in all the details of our lives. Yet, at the end of the gospel reading, Jesus wonders aloud if he will find the kind of persevering faith among his followers that was displayed by the woman. 'When the Son of Man comes, will he find any faith on earth?' Perhaps we could each answer that question of Jesus by saying, 'Yes, you will.' The gospel reading encourages us to resist the temptation to lose heart. It calls on us to keep praying, trusting that the Lord will not fail us in the end.

14 November, Monday, Thirty-third Week in Ordinary Time
Luke 18:35–43
In last Saturday's gospel reading from Luke Jesus told the parable of the judge and the widow in which the widow was a wonderful example of a faith that endures in the face of evil and that finds expression in persevering prayer. In Jesus' day the widow would have been someone who lived on the margins, without power or

influence or prestige. In today's gospel reading, also from Luke, we have an even more marginalised person, a blind beggar. Jesus approached this man as he drew near to the city of Jericho. This blind beggar showed something of the same gutsy faith and persevering prayer as the widow in the parable Jesus told. Unlike her, he wasn't up against an unjust judge. Rather, he was up against the crowd who were travelling with Jesus. When he cried out to Jesus for help, they told him to keep quiet. Like the widow, he wasn't put off by this rebuke; he simply shouted all the louder. Unlike the crowd, Jesus did not ignore him or rebuke him but addressed him in a very personal and respectful way. 'What do you want me to do for you?' He recognised the man's faith – 'Your faith has saved you' – and granted his request. The Lord does not ignore us when we approach him with the kind of persevering prayer the blind man displayed. The Lord responds to a faith that endures in the face of hostility and obstacles of various kinds. He may not respond in the precise way we had expected but he will respond; we will be graced in some way in response to our prayer for help. When the blind man realised his prayer had been answered, his prayer did not simply stop; it became a prayer of praise instead. There comes a time when our own prayer of petition needs to give way to the prayer of praise in response to the many ways that the Lord graces us.

15 November, Tuesday, Thirty-third Week in Ordinary Time
Luke 19:1–10

It is not often that the first reading and the gospel reading dovetail as well as they do today. In his message to the church in Laodicea, the risen Lord says, 'Look, I am standing at the door, knocking. If one of you hears me calling and opens the door, I will come in to share his meal, side by side with him.' According to the gospel reading, Zacchaeus, to his amazement, found the Lord standing at the door of his house knocking. When Zacchaeus opened the door, the Lord came in to share a meal, side by side with him. That day in Jericho was like any other day, yet it was an exceptional day. The Lord was knocking on the door of Zacchaeus' life and, after welcoming the Lord with joy, Zacchaeus was empowered to take a new direction, 'I am going to give half my property to the poor … '. Instead of exploiting others, he would share his resources with them. The Lord is always knocking on the door of our lives. He is always seeking us out. Zacchaeus, for all his ill-gotten wealth, was a seeker, even to the point of climbing a tree just to catch a glimpse of Jesus passing by. However, Jesus didn't want simply to catch a glimpse of Zacchaeus. He wanted to share table with him, to enter into communion with him. The Lord wants to enter into communion with each one of us. However, he needs to find in us something of the searching spirit of Zacchaeus. If we seek the Lord, we will soon discover that the Lord is seeking us with much greater urgency. If we welcome the Lord's searching love, then, like Zacchaeus, we too will find ourselves empowered to live in more loving ways.

16 November, Wednesday, Thirty-third Week in Ordinary Time
Luke 19:11–28
The parish book club met recently to discuss the book we had undertaken to read in the previous month. It was called *The First Ten Professed*. These were the first ten professed nuns of the new order of the Holy Rosary Sisters, based in Killeshandra in County Cavan in the 1920s. They went to Nigeria in response to the call of Bishop Shanahan, a Holy Ghost bishop who was based there. These were ordinary women from a variety of backgrounds, yet what they had in common was a desire to serve the Lord and the

Church where the need was great. I was struck by their courageous and generous spirit. They were all gifted in different ways and they wanted to place those gifts at the service of the Lord and his people in a place far from home and completely foreign to them. Their courageous spirit is the opposite of the attitude of the third servant in the parable in today's gospel reading. He had been gifted by his master but he did nothing with what he had been given out of fear of his master, fear of failure perhaps. Those ten women were not successful in everything they tried to do, but they were generous and courageous. The Lord looks to us to use courageously the gifts we have been given to serve the coming of his kingdom in the world. Fear of others should not disable us. If we are courageous and generous in our service of the Lord, then he will work powerfully through us for the good of others, as he worked powerfully through those ten women and the women who came after them.

17 November, Thursday, Thirty-third Week in Ordinary Time
Luke 19:41–44
We have all shed tears at some time. Very often, we weep over those we love. We weep at the sickness and death of our loved ones. When we give our heart to someone in love, we know our heart will inevitably break. We accept the suffering that loving someone brings. The alternative is not to love anyone, which is the poorest form of life. Jesus was God's love in human form. His love for others had a unique quality and the suffering that his love brought him also had a unique quality. Because he loved more than any human being could, he suffered more than any human being could, and that suffering often led him to weep bitter tears. In today's gospel reading, Jesus weeps over the city of Jerusalem. Jesus had earlier said that he had wanted to gather the people of

Jerusalem to himself, as a hen gathers her chicks under her wings, but they refused his loving outreach to them. The rejection of his loving visitation to them brought him great suffering, which led to his weeping bitter tears over the city. 'If you had only understood on this day the message of peace.' Their rejection of Jesus' love would have tragic consequences for the city. Jesus was often powerless before human rejection of his love. We may love others but we cannot force their love for us; we are powerless before the mystery of their freedom to accept or reject our love. The Lord's love for us is not in doubt. What is in doubt is our willingness to receive his love and to respond to it. One of the most important questions Jesus asks in all four gospels is his question to Peter in John's Gospel, 'Do you love me?' It is a question addressed to each one of us personally. We are all invited to make our own Peter's response to Jesus' question on that occasion, 'Lord, you know everything, you know that I love you.'

18 November, Friday, Thirty-third Week in Ordinary Time
Luke 19:45–48

In today's gospel reading, Jesus refers to the Temple of Jerusalem as a 'house of prayer'. He clearly felt that some of the other activities that were going on there were working against it being the house or place of prayer that God intended the Temple to be. Every parish church is a house of prayer. We gather in our own parish church to pray together as a community. People also come into the church during the day for their own personal prayer. There is no other building that could be described as a house of prayer, a place whose primary role it is to support people in prayer. We need such spaces in our busy world with all its many activities. It is said in today's gospel reading that 'the people hung on the words of Jesus' as he taught in the Temple. Our parish church is also a place where we hear the word of the Lord, whether listening with others as that word is proclaimed in the setting of the Eucharist and other liturgical settings, or whether we reflect on the Lord's word to us quietly and alone. I sometimes see people with the readings for the following Sunday praying quietly on the word of God. We come into a house of prayer like this to pray and to hang on the Lord's word, so that we can go out to witness to the Lord's love and presence with greater energy and courage. That pattern of coming in and going out is at the heart of our lives as the Lord's disciples, coming in to pray and going out to live what we have prayed. This parish church, this house of prayer, is at the service of this important pattern in our lives.

19 November, Saturday, Thirty-third Week in Ordinary Time
Luke 20:27–40

In today's gospel reading, Jesus' opponents, the Sadducees, who did not believe in life after death, present a scenario to Jesus which seeks to make belief in life after death look ridiculous. It is obvious they understand that Jesus himself teaches the reality of life after death. Their challenge to Jesus is based on the false assumption that if there is life after death it will simply be a kind of continuation of this earthly life. In his reply Jesus challenges this false assumption. He declares that those who belong to the 'other world' beyond this earthly life 'no longer die'. They live with a life that is eternal. Therefore, there is no need for procreation or for marriage, which is the basis of procreation. In other words, because the life that we enter after death is eternal life, the way we will relate to each other in the life to come will be fundamentally different from how we relate to each other now. Jesus does not elaborate on how we will relate to each other in the next life; he simply states that this new way of relating to each other will be qualitatively different from how we relate to each other in this earthly life. When Jesus does speak about the life beyond this life, however, he uses images that suggest some form of communal life, such as the image of the great banquet at which people gather. He invites us to imagine a life in which we are in a new relationship with himself, with God, and with each other. Jesus' earthly ministry was about gathering people together around himself, forming a new kind of community. He understood this community, which was soon called the Church, to be a sign of the life to come; it pointed ahead to the communal life in God's kingdom. Yet Jesus suggests that the life of heaven is so totally new that no earthly experience can compare with it.

21 November, Monday, Presentation of the Blessed Virgin Mary
Matthew 12:46–50

This feast originated in the East. It commemorates the presentation of Mary to God by her parents in the Temple of Jerusalem when she was a child. It reflected the Church's understanding of Mary's subsequent grace-filled life, wholly given over to God's purpose for her life. Today's gospel reading suggests that there were times when she struggled to understand God's purpose for her life, especially in relation to her son Jesus. She sets out from Nazareth with other members of Jesus' family to Capernaum, where Jesus was ministering. Perhaps they wanted him to come home and rest. However, Mary subsequently discovered that this was not God's purpose for Jesus or for her. Jesus sent word out to Mary and his relatives that they no longer had any claim on him because he was starting a new family of his disciples and from now on they would be his mother and brothers and sisters. There was much here for Mary to ponder. What she wanted for Jesus was not necessarily what God wanted for him. In that sense, Mary's experience can be very close to our own. Like her, we may want to give ourselves over to God's purpose, we may want to do God's will, but, like her, we can struggle to discern what God's purpose for our lives is. We sometimes have to come to the painful recognition that what we want for ourselves and others isn't always what God wants. We can't allow ourselves to become too sure of God's desire for our lives and the lives of others. Like Mary, we have to keep ourselves open to where the Lord is leading us. Like her, we need to keep prayerfully pondering on our life experience, trusting in the Lord's promise that those who seek will find.

22 November, Tuesday, Thirty-fourth Week in Ordinary Time
Luke 21:5–11

In the time of Jesus, the Temple in Jerusalem was considered to be one of the Seven Wonders of the World. It is not surprising to find Jesus' disciples at the beginning of the gospel reading remarking on how it was adorned with fine stonework. It must have seemed to them that the Temple would last forever. We can imagine their shock when Jesus said to them, 'The time will come when not a single stone will be left on another; everything will be destroyed.' People must have wondered how God could allow this holy place associated with his presence to be destroyed. How could God survive its destruction? Yet, when the Temple was destroyed forty years later, God continued to work powerfully in the world, through the Jewish community and through the emerging church that came from the Jewish community. We are being reminded that even when so much of what would be considered important to God is destroyed, God endures. God's work on behalf of humanity is never destroyed. Even as his Son was being crucified, God was working powerfully to touch the lives of all men and women with his love. God will always bring new life out of death, new growth out of loss. God is always doing a new thing. That is worth remembering in times when we seem to be losing so much that is important to the life of faith.

23 November, Wednesday, Thirty-fourth Week in Ordinary Time
Luke 21:12–19

Every year at this time Aid to the Church in Need hosts a week of witness for persecuted Christians. It is an opportunity to Christians in Ireland to stand in solidarity with, and bear witness to, the heroic example of our persecuted brothers and sisters in faith across the world. We are invited to pray not only for persecuted Christians but for the persecutors of Christians as well. In today's gospel reading, Jesus tells his disciples that people will seize them and persecute them and hand them over to religious and political authorities. That warning of Jesus is still coming to pass in our world today. The persecution of Christians is reaching a crisis point. In terms of the number of people involved, the gravity of the acts committed, and their impact, Christians are more persecuted than any other group. Christianity is the most persecuted religion in the world with at least 80 per cent of all religious persecution globally inflicted against Christians in any given year. Over 9,500 churches are attacked annually around the world. We are fortunate to live in a society where freedom of religion is guaranteed under the Constitution. We can best support our persecuted brothers and sisters in Christ by living our own faith courageously, relying on the promise of Jesus in today's gospel reading to give us the eloquence and the wisdom we will need when our faith is put to the test. What Jesus calls for above all at the end of that gospel reading is endurance. We need to keep witnessing to our faith in the Lord when times are difficult and our faith is put to the test.

24 November, Thursday, Thirty-fourth Week in Ordinary Time
Luke 21:20–28

In today's gospel reading, there is a clear reference to the destruction of the city of Jerusalem, which happened forty years after the death and resurrection of Jesus. Jerusalem fell to the armies of Rome, under the general Titus, who went on to become Emperor of Rome. In the time of Jesus and the early Church, the all-powerful Roman Empire must have been seen as eternal, as destined to last forever. Yet, in the first reading, written towards the end of the first century, the author declares, 'Babylon the Great has fallen', 'Babylon' being a code name for 'Rome'. The author recognises that even the great, invincible, Roman Empire would not last forever, and declares that it is God and his Son who will last for ever. 'Victory and glory and power to our God.' In the gospel reading, Jesus speaks of himself as the Son of Man who will come 'with power and great glory'. Nothing lasts for ever, not even the great and powerful empires of the world. Only God and his Son endure; they are the beginning and the end, yesterday, today and tomorrow. God's relationship with us endures; Jesus' love for us lasts for ever and every day he says to us what is said at the end of today's first reading, 'Happy are those who are invited to the wedding feast of the Lamb.' The Lord calls us to his feast, in the future kingdom of heaven, but also in the here and now of the Eucharist. You will recognise that beatitude from the text of the Mass. The Lord's call to us to be in communion with him is the constant in the midst of all that is changing. That awareness can inspire us to always 'stand erect', holding our heads high, in the words of the gospel reading.

25 November, Friday, Thirty-fourth Week in Ordinary Time
Luke 21:29–33

Today's gospel reading comes towards the end of a passage that began with Jesus announcing that a time will come when not a single stone of the wonderful Temple in Jerusalem will be left on another. It must have been impossible for people to conceive of that ever happening. Yet, in the history of the world, so much has passed away that people thought would have been around for ever. Even in recent times so much has fallen that once seemed immovable; we only have to think of the many of the regimes of the Middle East. The recent Covid-19 pandemic brought home to us how vulnerable we all are and how quickly so much that we take for granted can pass away almost overnight. We are left asking, 'Will anything endure?' In today's gospel reading Jesus declares, 'Heaven and earth will pass away, but my words will not pass away.' The words of Jesus and the values they express will endure, and the one who proclaims those words, the Word made flesh, will endure. As the risen Lord says in the Book of Revelation, 'I am the Alpha and the Omega, the first and the last, the beginning and the end' When all else fails, the Lord will be there. His relationship with us endures, even when our relationship with him grows weak. As Paul says in one of his letters, 'if we are faithless, he remains faithful'. Indeed his relationship with us and ours with him endure beyond this life. His endurance is the foundation of our endurance. In the words of today's responsorial psalm, 'They are happy whose strength is in you. They walk with ever growing strength.'

26 November, Saturday, Thirty-fourth Week in Ordinary Time
Luke 21:34–36

The season of Advent begins with the vigil Mass later on today. Today's readings already have a very Advent feel to them, with the response to the psalm being the Advent prayer, 'Come, Lord Jesus!' and the call of the gospel reading to 'Stay awake, praying at all times.' The mood of Advent is that of prayerful waiting. It must have been the mood of Mary as she waited for her son to be born. When she visited Elizabeth, having conceived Jesus in her womb, Elizabeth greeted her as 'the mother of my Lord'. Mary had welcomed the Lord Jesus into her life by her 'yes' to God's call to her through the angel Gabriel. Advent is a season when, like Mary, we welcome the Lord Jesus into our lives more fully. One way of giving expression to our desire to welcome Jesus into our lives more fully is by praying that Advent prayer, 'Marana tha! Come, Lord Jesus!' Even to spend a few minutes of each day of Advent quietly praying that prayer to ourselves would be a wonderful way to prepare for Christmas. According to Jesus in the gospel reading, whenever we pray we are given strength, which allows us to stand with confidence before the Son of Man. We all need inner, spiritual strength, especially in these uncertain times. The angel Gabriel promised Mary that the power of the Most High would overshadow her. As we wait prayerfully this Advent, we too will be overshadowed by the power and strength of the Most High. As we open ourselves to the coming of the Lord Jesus, our inner self will grow stronger, and we will be able to bring something of the Lord's strength to others this Advent, especially to those most in need of it.